Collins

AQA GCSE 9-1
Psychology

Revision Guide

Jonathan Firth, Marc Smith and Sally White

About this Revision & Practice book

Revise

These pages provide a recap of everything you need to know for each topic.

You should read through all the information before taking the Quick Test at the end. This will test whether you can recall the key facts.

Practise

These topic-based questions appear shortly after the revision pages for each topic and will test whether you have understood the topic. If you get any of the questions wrong, make sure you read the correct answer carefully.

Review

These topic-based questions appear later in the book, allowing you to revisit the topic and test how well you have remembered the information. If you get any of the questions wrong, make sure you read the correct answer carefully.

Mix it Up

These pages feature a mix of questions from the different topics. They will make sure you can recall the relevant information to answer a question without being told which topic it relates to.

Test Yourself on the Go

Visit our website at **collins.co.uk/collinsGCSErevision** and print off a set of flashcards. These pocket-sized cards feature questions and answers so that you can test yourself on all the key facts anytime and anywhere. You will also find lots more information about the advantages of spaced practice and how to plan for it.

Workbook

This section features even more topic-based questions as well as practice exam papers, providing two further practice opportunities for each topic to guarantee the best results.

ebook

To access the ebook revision guide visit

collins.co.uk/ebooks

and follow the step-by-step instructions.

QR Codes

Found throughout the book, the QR codes can be scanned on your smartphone for extra practice and explanations.

A QR code in the Revise section links to a Quick Recall Quiz on that topic. A QR code in the Workbook section links to a video working through the solution to one of the questions on that topic.

Contents

Processes of Memory

Quick Recall Quiz

You must be able to:

- Understand different types of memory: episodic, semantic and procedural
- Explain how memories are encoded and stored.

Types of Memory

- **Long-term memory (LTM)** itself is not a single store but has different structures that encode and store different types of information.

Type of Memory	What is Remembered	Example
Episodic memory	Memory for life events	Remembering a family holiday
Semantic memory	Memory for facts	Remembering that a penguin is a type of bird; do not necessarily relate to specific life events
Procedural memory	Memory for a skill or an action	Remembering how to insert a SIM card into a phone; often hard to explain in words

- LTM and **STM (short-term memory)** functions are processed by different areas of the brain. The frontal lobe of the cerebral cortex is essential for STM and for related cognitive processes.
- Several brain areas are important for LTM. Most notably, the **hippocampus** – an area of the limbic system in the brain – is involved in the formation of new semantic and episodic LTMs.
- Case studies of people with brain damage demonstrate that long- and short-term memory are separate. For example, Henry Molaison had his hippocampus removed during brain surgery. His STM was unaffected and he was still able to form new procedural memories but he was unable to form new semantic or episodic LTMs, showing that these are processed by different structures of the brain (Scoville & Milner, 1957).

Memory in Everyday Life

- Problems with memory, such as forgetting facts or appointments, demonstrate how important memory is for everyday life.
- To function, people rely on holding things in STM as they work on them; they must be able to put new information into LTM and later bring it back to mind.
- Memory is an **active process** – that it is not like a box in the head where things are stored, but a process that people engage in constantly.

Key Point

Memory involves encoding information, storing it for a period of time, and then retrieving it at a later date. Memory is used to complete tasks, solve problems and make sense of new information.

Three Key Processes

- An everyday example of using memory could involve a person reading a new fact on a website one morning (**encoding**), engaging in other activities for a period of time (**storage**), and later in the day telling somebody about what they had read (**retrieval**). These processes typically refer to LTM, but the same processes happen in STM over a much shorter timescale. Storage is very limited and information must be retrieved quickly.

- **Encoding** means taking new information into memory. It is an **input process**.
- **Storage** is the process of maintaining information in temporary or permanent memory. To maintain the memory in storage, it usually needs to be consolidated by regular revision. Sleep also helps information to be consolidated.
- **Retrieval** means accessing the stored information and bringing it back to mind. It is the **output process**.

There are various ways that information can be retrieved.

- **Recognition** – the information is repeated, and the person compares it to what is in their memory. A multiple-choice test makes use of recognition memory.
- **Cued recall** – the person gets a cue of some kind, e.g. seeing someone's initial and remembering their name.
- **Free recall** – the stimulus is not present and there is no cue – the information is retrieved directly from memory, e.g. writing a quotation in an English exam. This is the most difficult form of retrieval.

How Memories are Formed

- Repetition is important for memory, as it provides more chances for information to be encoded. However, simply repeating things does not always cause them to be encoded to LTM, particularly if the information is hard to understand.
- The best way to build a new memory is to link the new item to what is already understood, and then repeatedly retrieve it from memory, preferably in a way that is spaced out over time.

> **Quick Test**
>
> 1. What term is used to mean taking new information in by converting it into a form that can be stored?
> 2. A person is asked for their postcode. After a moment's thought, they give the correct answer. Which process does this describe?

> **Key Point**
>
> Retrieval can be difficult. It often involves effort, and there is no guarantee that information which is stored in a person's mind will be successfully retrieved when needed.

> **Key Point**
>
> Memory is an active process which involves making sense of new information and linking it to what we know.

> **Key Words**
>
> long-term memory (LTM)
> episodic memory
> semantic memory
> procedural memory
> short-term memory (STM)
> hippocampus
> active process
> encoding
> storage
> retrieval
> input process
> output process
> recognition
> cued recall
> free recall

Structures of Memory 1

You must be able to:

- Describe the multi-store model of memory
- Describe the features of each store: coding, capacity and duration.

The Multi-Store Model

- Memory is a psychological ability that everybody uses on a daily basis. It is used to store information such as the names of people and places, facts for exams, as well as to remember skills and life events. It is an active process, where a person is constantly trying to make sense of their surroundings and link them to prior memories.
- According to Atkinson and Shiffrin there are three memory **stores**: sensory, short-term and long-term.
- Each store has a different way of processing (encoding) information, can hold a different amount of information (**capacity**) and can hold it for a different length of time (**duration**).
- **Sensory memory** is a very brief store and information is only taken into this memory if a person pays **attention** to it. This information will then pass to the STM. This typically happens when people find things interesting or emotional in some way. Sensory memory allows sensations such as sounds and images to be retained for a moment even before we have time to think about or process them. There is a separate sensory store for each of the senses: visual, auditory, and so on.
  - The auditory store in sensory memory can hold spoken words for around two seconds, allowing people to focus their attention on something that has just been said to them.
  - Research by Sperling (1960) showed that the visual sensory store has a very brief duration – less than one second – but a large capacity. This suggests that most of the sensory information that is initially processed by the brain will fade without ever entering STM.
- Short-term memory (STM) is often called 'working memory' because it is used for active processing of information in everyday tasks. It is not simply used for storage. You have to **rehearse** the information for it to transfer from STM to LTM. This means that holding information in the short-term store by repeating it again and again allows it to be encoded to LTM. Rehearsal also allows a person to hold information in their STM for longer, to prevent it being forgotten, as the STM has a limited duration (up to 30 seconds). It also has a limited capacity (5–9 items), as it can only take in and process a small number of items.

Key Point

The **multi-store model** presents a simple overview of the architecture of memory.

Key Point

The three key stores of the multi-store model are viewed as being joined together via the processes of attention and rehearsal.

> I would forget my friends' phone numbers very quickly unless I saved them or wrote them down. This shows the limited duration of short-term memory.

> It can be hard to learn new information, but once you fully understand it, you can remember it for many years. This is because it needs to be encoded to long-term memory.

- Long-term memory (LTM) is sometimes compared to recording a video. However, this misleadingly suggests that it happens fairly automatically and is retrieved in the same form as it was remembered. LTM potentially lasts a lifetime – memories that have been well understood and practised are essentially permanent. It also stores an unlimited amount of information.

The multi-store model

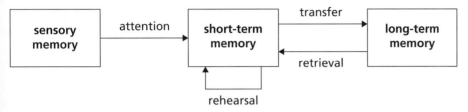

Encoding

- Encoding means taking information into memory. Each store encodes information in its own way, according to the model. This means that each store can only take in and process a particular type of information.
  - The sensory memory has a separate store for each sense, and therefore encodes information via all five senses – visually, acoustically and so on.
  - The STM encodes information based on its sound. This is called **acoustic encoding**.
  - The LTM encodes information based on its meaning. This is called **semantic encoding**.
- Information can be converted to the appropriate type of encoding for each store. For example, when someone reads a sentence (a visual task), the STM converts the words on the page into sounds. The fact that the long-term memory encodes things semantically has important implications. It suggests that when someone remembers something like a story or joke over a long period of time, they will remember the gist (i.e. the main meaningful ideas), but not the exact words used. The same applies to a concept learned at school. It also means that people will tend to forget things over the long term unless they understand them.

Key Point

The two main types of memory – short-term and long-term – have fundamentally different features.

Quick Test

1. What process is required for information to be transferred from sensory memory to STM?
2. Which type of encoding depends on understanding the meaning of new information?
3. Which memory store is involved if you walk into another room and then realise that you have forgotten why you came there?
4. Anna is trying to remember the names of the different types of cells that occur in plants. What type of long-term memory is she using?

Key Words

multi-store model
store
capacity
duration
sensory memory
attention
rehearsal
acoustic encoding
semantic encoding

Structures of Memory 2

You must be able to:

- Explain the primacy and recency effects in recall: the effects of serial position
- Describe and evaluate Murdock's serial position curve study.

Supporting Evidence for the Multi-Store Model of Memory

The Serial Position Curve

- An experiment that appears to support the multi-store model of memory was conducted by Murdock (1962).
- He gave participants lists of random words to remember, and compared the chance of each word being recalled with its position in the list.

Results of the Study

- The study found that words at the start of the list were better remembered than those in the middle. This is known as the **primacy effect**.
- Words at the end were better remembered too – this is called the **recency effect**.
- Overall, these effects can be shown on a U-shaped graph known as the **serial position curve**.

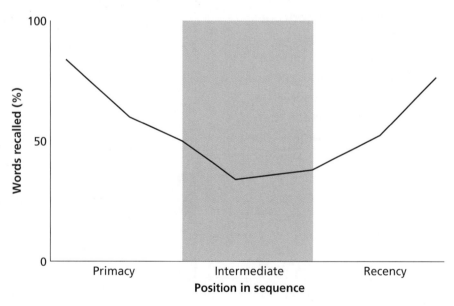

- According to the multi-store model, the primacy effect occurs because items at the start of a list are easier to rehearse, and therefore get encoded into long-term memory. By the middle of the list there are too many to rehearse.

- The recency effect occurs because the last few items are in short-term memory, but because of its limited capacity, the middle items are pushed out from short-term memory in a process known as **displacement**.
- This provides evidence that there is a distinction between STM and LTM.
- Murdock's study has good validity as it was carried out under controlled conditions. However, the task of recalling a list of words is artificial and doesn't reflect a real life task, which weakens the validity.
- Therefore, it might not reflect all other aspects of memory that we use daily, such as remembering which lessons we have on a particular day so that we have the right books.

Evaluation of the Multi-Store Model

- The multi-store model shows STM and LTM as separate stores, an idea which is supported by the serial position curve and by the fact that each store relies on different brain areas.
- A problem with the multi-store model is that it does not account for the use of **visual encoding** in either short-term or long-term memory. However, people are able to take in and store visual information such as faces and maps.
- The concept of rehearsal is also over-simplistic. People appear to be able to take in information without rehearsing it, and there are occasions when a lot of rehearsal fails to encode information to LTM.
- The multi-store model doesn't show the different types of LTM (see page 4) – another way in which the model is over-simplistic.
- The tasks used in research to support the multi-store model are usually very artificial. Word lists, for example, do not show us memory in real-life and this lowers the validity of the support.

Quick Test

1. Why couldn't the whole list of words from Murdock's experiment be held in short-term memory?
2. Explain one strength or one weakness of the multi-store model of memory.
3. If a friend tells you a list of their favourite films, which ones are you most likely to forget about later on – those at the start of the list, in the middle or towards the end?

Key Words

primacy effect
recency effect
serial position curve
displacement
visual encoding

Memory as an Active Process

Quick Recall Quiz

You must be able to:

- Describe the Theory of Reconstructive Memory, including the concept of 'effort after meaning'
- Describe Bartlett's War of the Ghosts study
- Identify and explain factors that affect the accuracy of memory, including interference, context and false memories.

Reconstructive Memory

- **Sir Frederic Bartlett** saw encoding and retrieval as an active process of building up a memory, motivated by the desire to understand. In other words, he saw remembering as being more like building something new rather than taking something out of storage.
- Following on from this research, he developed a theory of **reconstructive memory**. Bartlett realised that memories often have gaps in them, and that people use their existing schema knowledge to fill these gaps when they are retrieving a memory.
- He used the term '**effort after meaning**' to describe the way people try to make sense of new information, by using past information to make sense of it.

> ### Key Point
>
> Bartlett was the first professor of psychology in the UK. He was interested in how long-term memories can be forgotten and distorted, and how this process is affected by culture.

Bartlett's War of the Ghosts study

- In contrast to a lot of other memory research, Bartlett's research used realistic stimuli – he studied memory of stories and pictures.
- As discussed earlier, memory is an active process which involves people interpreting stimuli and linking it to prior memories. This concept connects to Bartlett's memory research.
- According to Bartlett, LTM is based around clusters of related meaningful information. These are called **schemas** (or schemata). A schema is a concept that people derive from life experience and which is influenced by their culture.
- When taking in new information to LTM, a person tries to make sense of it. This can be seen as making an effort to connect it to their existing schema for that concept. If the information is bizarre or unfamiliar, this process can cause it to be **distorted** by making it more similar to the existing schema.
- Bartlett's best-known study involved a native American folk story called War of the Ghosts. He wanted to find out if a person's memory for stories was affected by their schemas.
- He told this story to his research participants and then analysed their responses when they were later asked to remember it.
- The story was unfamiliar to their culture, so participants found it hard to remember. Bartlett noted four types of mistakes:

> ### Key Point
>
> The process of remembering doesn't involve passively taking in information but is an active process of making connections with existing schemas.

Additions	Participants added new material to help it make more sense to them.
Subtractions	Participants forgot sections that they hadn't understood.
Transformation to familiar	Participants changed things to make them more similar to what they were used to.
Preservation of detached detail	Certain unusual details that had caught people's attention were recalled, but not always in the right order, and unconnected to their original context.

- Bartlett concluded that the ideas from the story were forgotten or distorted because participants didn't have the cultural schemas in their LTM to connect the new information to.
- Additions demonstrated the use of the participants' own cultural schemas during the retrieval process.

Factors Affecting Memory

- As Bartlett showed, **culture** is a major factor that affects memory.
- Several other factors affect memory:
  - Some people suffer from amnesia which can result from a blow to the head or from brain damage. These individuals tend to forget episodic memories rather than procedural memories (skills) or facts.
  - Long-term memory is also subject to **interference** – mixing up two similar events or pieces of information.
  - The passage of time can make it hard to retrieve old LTMs, especially out of context.
  - Memories can be triggered by a **cue**, i.e. the presentation of related information, part of the memory or a question.
  - Reviewing and self-testing can help consolidate information in LTM.
  - It is easier to remember things in the **context** that we first learned them. Visiting the place where something was learned can act as a cue to retrieval.
- **False memories** are distorted or false recollection of an event that did not happen, but the person recalls it as if it were true.
- Researcher **Elizabeth Loftus** and her colleagues studied false memories. They told participants false stories that were supposedly about their own childhood. Many people later claimed that the events had actually happened.
- Loftus also found that false memories can be generated via **leading questions**. When people viewed a car crash and were asked how fast the cars 'smashed' into each other, they were later much more likely to say (incorrectly) that the video had shown broken glass (Loftus & Palmer, 1974).

> **Key Point**
>
> Interference and context can affect the success of memorisation, and certain situations can lead to false memories forming.

> **Key Words**
>
> Bartlett
> reconstructive memory
> effort after meaning
> schema
> distortion
> culture
> interference
> cue
> context
> false memory
> Loftus
> leading question

> **Quick Test**
>
> 1. Why was the War of the Ghosts story hard for Bartlett's research participants to understand?
> 2. Besides culture, name two factors that affect memory.

Where space is not provided, write your answers on a separate piece of paper.

Processes of Memory

1. Is memory best described as an active process or a passive process? [1]

2. Which of the following is true? Shade **one** box only. [1]

   A   Encoding new memories happens fairly automatically. ◯

   B   Memories are retrieved in exactly the same form as they were remembered. ◯

   C   Both encoding and retrieval often involve mental effort. ◯

   D   Items always enter long-term memory even if the person is not paying attention. ◯

3. Which of the following is an input process to memory? Shade **one** box only. [1]

   A Encoding ◯   B Storage ◯   C Retrieval ◯   D Forgetting ◯

4. Complete the following table. [3]

Example	Type of long-term memory
A Being able to ride a bike	
B Remembering your first day of school	
C Knowing that an MP is a type of politician	

Structures of Memory 1 and 2

1. Murdock (1962) conducted an important experiment into memory.

   a) What is the name for the graph showing the effects found in this study? [1]

   b) Explain how the experiment can be used to evaluate the multi-store model. [3]

2. Complete the sentences by choosing the best words from the selection below.
   You do not have to use all the words. [4]

   | encoding   meaning   words   semantic   visual |

   According to the multi-store model of memory, short-term memory takes in information using

   acoustic .... This means that it processes and stores the sounds of words or

   other items. In contrast, the long-term memory uses .... encoding – it stores information based on its meaning. This means that people tend to remember the gist of a story

over the long term, not the exact _____ .

3 Is rehearsal a sufficient process to encode new information to long-term memory? **[1]**

4 What is the name of the temporary memory store with which people can remember
a few items for several seconds? Shade **one** box only. **[1]**

A Encoding memory ◯ B Long-term memory ◯

C Short-term memory ◯ D Permanent memory ◯

5 State **two** ways in which short-term memory is limited. **[2]**

Memory as an Active Process

1 Complete the sentences by choosing the best words from the selection below.
You do not have to use all of the words. **[3]**

| interference | repression | short-term | harder | easier | distinctive |

Information can be forgotten because it gets confused with other information – a process

known as _____ . This happens less with unusual events because they are more

_____ , and therefore better remembered. It's also _____ to

remember things in the same physical location as where we first learned them.

2 Name **three** ways in which people may be in a different state when they try to
retrieve a memory. **[3]**

3 Which of the following describes a schema? Shade **one** box only. **[1]**

A A visual memory technique that can be used when revising. ◯

B A mental concept, influenced by life experience and culture. ◯

C The process of encoding things to long-term memory. ◯

D A belief that people have about other cultures. ◯

Perception and Sensation

You must be able to:

- Define sensation and give an example of a sensory process
- Explain the difference between sensation and perception
- Describe perceptual constancy, with examples.

The Difference Between Sensation and Perception

- In order for a person to respond to what is happening in the outside world, the senses process external cues such as light and sound. These are detected by specialist **receptor cells** in the body.
- This process is called **sensation**, and is the basis of how all animals experience the world around them.
- An example of receptor cells involved in sensation are the rods and cones found in the human retina, at the back of the eye. These are sensitive to light, although only cones can sense colour.
- For each sense, receptor cells send messages to **neurons** (nerve cells), which connect directly to the brain. For vision, these neurons form a pathway called the optic nerve.
- **Perception** occurs when the brain uses this information from the outside world to build up a mental image of what is happening. In other words, it must interpret the information that reaches the senses.
- A person's perception is not the same as the sensation received. For example, the process of visual perception must adjust images received by the eyes and make sense of them.
- The visual system has to allow for the fact that images hit the retina reversed and upside down.
- Perception is a rapid and largely effortless process, allowing people and other animals to react very quickly to external events such as threats.

> ### Key Point
>
> Sensation is the direct impact of the outside world on senses such as vision, while perception is the way this information is interpreted, allowing a coherent picture of the world to be built up by the brain's visual cortex.

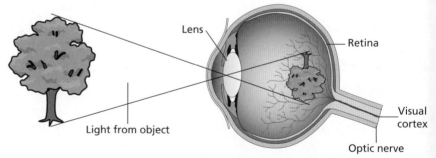

Perception involves adjusting sensory information.

The Role of the Brain in Perception

- Perception is possible because the brain builds up a picture of the world – using information from the senses and combining it with information from the memory.
- Many receptor cells must work together for perception to happen. A single rod cell can only detect how much light is hitting it. In order for an individual to see, a large network of these cells is required.

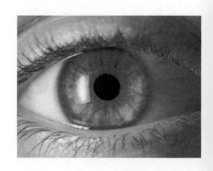

- If a stimulus in the world moves around, the **sensory cortex** of the brain can detect which way it is moving because of the changing pattern of light hitting the retinal cells. The shape of objects can be detected in a similar way.
- The perceptual systems of the brain therefore act like a computer, processing simple bits of information and building up a more complex picture that allows the individual to act – e.g. to pick up some food or to avoid something harmful.

Perceptual Constancy

- **Perceptual constancy** is the ability of the brain's perceptual system to make allowances for changes in the environment. Adjustments in visual perception are made to allow for the position and lighting conditions in four main ways.

Light constancy and colour constancy	An object is perceived as looking its normal (or expected) level of lightness/darkness even when lighting conditions change, as can be observed when reading a book in dim conditions – the paper still looks light, not dark grey. Similarly, people still perceive objects as having their usual colour, even when they are seen in darker or unusual lighting conditions. Grass still looks green after sunset, for example.
Size constancy and shape constancy	An object is perceived as having constant size even when it changes distance and therefore projects a different size of image onto the retina. For example, a train that pulls away in a station still looks the same size (it doesn't appear to shrink) as it gets further away and the image size changes on the retina. Likewise, an object which moves or rotates is perceived as being the same object, even though the image that is appearing to our retina may have changed radically.

- All of these constancies may seem obvious, but they require complex computation on the part of the brain. It is difficult to program a computer to recognise that objects remain the same through transformations of shape and light.

Key Point

The brain is able to make allowances for changes in colour and shape when we perceive an object under different conditions.

Stages in visual perception

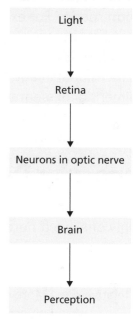

 Quick Test

1. What is the name of the process that occurs when receptor cells in the senses process external cues such as light and sound?
2. Perception depends on the brain interpreting the information that reaches the senses. Is this statement true or false?
3. Which perceptual constancy is involved when a blonde person's hair still looks blonde even when you see them at night?

Key Words

receptor cells
sensation
neurons
perception
sensory cortex
perceptual constancy
light constancy
colour constancy
size constancy
shape constancy

Visual Cues and Constancies

Perception

You must be able to:

- Describe monocular depth cues: relative size, occlusion, linear perspective, texture gradient and height in plane
- Describe binocular depth cues: retinal disparity and convergence.

Depth and Distance

- As the mind builds up a picture of the world by interpreting information from the senses, it needs to make sense of how close or far away objects are.
- This is known as **depth perception**, and is essential for survival in most species. For example, when a monkey or squirrel leaps for a tree branch, it must be able to calculate how close the branch is.
- **Depth cues** allow the brain to make sense of the two-dimensional image that hits the retina, converting it to a three-dimensional mental image of the world.
- In other words, depth cues are aspects of the visual scene that make it possible to work out how close or far away things are.

Monocular Depth Cues

- The simplest cues to depth and distance can be perceived using only one eye if necessary. These are therefore called **monocular** depth cues.
- Monocular depth cues include the following:

Relative size	More distant objects appear smaller than other similar objects. For example, the apparent size of a car on the road ahead allows a driver to perceive how close it is, given that most cars are roughly the same size.
Occlusion	If one object partially obscures another from where someone observes them, this shows that it must be the closer of the two.
Linear perspective	As things move further away, they appear closer together to the observer. This results in the perspective skills used by artists, where lines on a painting are drawn towards an imagined '**vanishing point**', making the painting look much more realistic.
Texture gradient	When objects are more distant, the eye takes in less detail of their surface texture. This results in objects that are further away appearing to have a smoother and simpler blurry texture.
Height in plane	Compared to a horizon line, people or objects that are closer will appear lower down, while more distant objects appear higher up (although the opposite is true for objects in the sky, e.g. the clouds in a painting). This cue is similar in principle to linear perspective.

Example of texture gradient.

Binocular Depth Cues

- The mind can build on these basic depth cues by comparing the different visual sensations from the two eyes. This results in further cues known as **binocular** depth cues.
- Most predators have two forward-facing eyes, indicating that these cues play an important role in precise judgements of distance.
- The eyes are at two different positions on the head. Differences between the images from the two eyes (at least for people who have the use of both eyes) give a cue to distance known as **retinal disparity**:
  - If an object is closer, the discrepancy between the two eyes will be quite large.
  - If an object is further away, there will be a smaller difference between the two eyes.
- A further binocular cue is **convergence** (or 'eye convergence'). This cue comes primarily from the muscles that move the eyes rather than from the image itself. When an object is closer, both eyes have to rotate inwards slightly in order to bring it into focus in the centre of the retina. For a more distant object, less rotation is required.

Line up two fingers, one in front of the other close to your face. Look at them with your right eye, keeping your left eye closed. Now close your right eye, and look at them with the left. Do the images that you see with each eye look the same? You should notice quite a large difference between how your fingers appear to each eye.

Now try moving your fingers further away from your face by stretching your arm out. Again, close one eye, and then the other. What can you see now? The difference between what is seen by each eye should be less. This is because the things that they are seeing (your two fingers) are now further away, reducing the amount of retinal disparity.

Retinal disparity

Key Point

A range of monocular cues and a smaller number of binocular cues allow an individual to perceive distance.

Binocular cues rely on differences between images processed by the two eyes.

Quick Test

1. A hill that is closer to you partially blocks your view of another hill which is further away. Which monocular cue to distance does this demonstrate?
2. A tree looks closer if you are able to see the patterns of its leaves and bark. Which monocular cue is being used in this situation?
3. Which binocular cue relies on detecting how much the two eyes have to rotate in order to see an object?

Key Words

depth perception
depth cues
monocular
relative size
occlusion
linear perspective
vanishing point
texture gradient
height in plane
binocular
retinal disparity
convergence

Visual Illusions

You must be able to:

- Identify and describe: the Müller-Lyer, Rubin's vase, Ames Room, Kanizsa triangle, Necker cube and Ponzo illusions
- Explain visual illusions: ambiguity, fiction, misinterpreted depth cues and size constancy.

What are Illusions?

- Taking in information from the senses is not always simple or accurate. Sometimes, two people may experience the same stimulus via their senses but perceive it differently.
- An **illusion** is a stimulus that causes a person to see something different from what is actually there, or where there are two or more possible interpretations of the same image.
- There are several famous examples of illusions, all of which have been studied and debated by psychologists.

The **Müller-Lyer** illusion appears like a pair of arrowheads either pointing inwards towards a line, or outwards. Although the lines are the same length, most people perceive the line with the inward-pointing arrows as being longer.	
Rubin's vase is an illusion which can be interpreted as either two faces looking towards each other, or (using the space in between the faces) a vase.	
The **Ames Room** is a specially constructed room that appears ordinary when viewed from the front but is actually distorted, with one corner much further away than the other. If two people stand at the opposite corners, there is an illusion that one is much larger than the other.	
The **Kanizsa triangle** shows three circles with wedge-shaped sections removed like the corners of a triangle. People tend to see the sides of the triangle appearing faintly, especially towards the corner areas.	
The **Necker cube** is a two-dimensional shape that tends to be interpreted as a cube – but there are two possible ways that it could be facing, making it possible for a person to 'flip' the way they perceive the shape.	

Explanations for Visual Illusions

- Illusions show that some aspects of perception are fairly automatic. Even when you know about them, it is hard to avoid seeing the effect of the illusion.
- Illusions do not have a single explanation. Instead, they rely on several different factors that affect perception. All of them in some way cause us to perceive something inaccurately or lead to more than one possible interpretation that we struggle to reconcile.
- Two particular causes of illusion are ambiguity and fiction:

Ambiguity	There are two or more ways that a two-dimensional shape on the page or screen can be perceived. The Necker cube and Rubin's vase are examples of ambiguous figures.
Fiction	The person perceives something that is not actually there. The Kanizsa triangle is an example of a fiction – there is actually no triangle, yet people perceive one. According to the **Gestalt approach** to psychology, this is because of a tendency to perceive objects as wholes rather than many small parts, and to mentally connect objects that appear to belong together.

- Misinterpreted depth cues are another cause of illusions. Some illusions occur because the cues that guide us to depth and distance can also mislead the processes of perception.
- A key example of this is the **Ponzo illusion**. Here, the cue of linear perspective tricks the mind into thinking that the images closer to the vanishing point are larger.
- Depth cues are used in art with the aim of being misinterpreted, so that people perceive a flat, two-dimensional picture as a scene with depth and distance.
- Size constancy (see page 17) is another cause of illusions. When the context makes an object look closer or further away than it is, the process of size constancy causes it to appear larger or smaller than it really is. This occurs in the Ames Room illusion.

Key Point

Illusions are a much-studied group of stimuli that are either ambiguous or cause people to perceive things that are not actually there.

Ponzo illusion

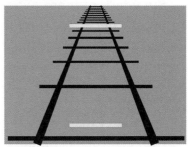

This shows two identical lines on top of a pair of lines which are drawn towards a vanishing point.

Key Point

Illusions can be caused by errors in the processing of depth cues and size constancy.

Key Words

illusion
Müller-Lyer
Rubin's vase
Ames Room
Kanizsa triangle
Necker cube
ambiguity
fiction
Gestalt approach
Ponzo illusion

Quick Test

1. In which illusion do people tend to see a triangle that is not actually there?
2. What term is used to describe illusions where an image has more than one possible interpretation?
3. Why do people experience the Ponzo illusion?

Theories of Perception

Quick Recall Quiz

You must be able to:

- Explain Gibson's direct theory and Gregory's constructivist theory
- Describe how the real world presents sufficient information for direct perception without inference
- Describe the role of motion parallax in everyday perception
- Describe how perception uses inferences from visual cues and past experience to construct a model of reality.

Explanations of Perception

- Perception involves building up a coherent mental representation of the world that is accurate and makes sense, and allows us to function in the world.
- The previous sections have highlighted the potential role of both a person's sensations and their expectations in this process. But which of these two things plays the more important role?
- Researchers have tried to explain how perception works. Their ideas are known as theories of perception. There are two main theories, which both focus especially on visual perception.

Gibson's Direct Theory

- The **direct theory** of perception takes the opposite view from the constructivist theory, assuming that perception is a matter of piecing sensory information together. It is based on the work of researcher **James Gibson**.
- The direct theory assumes two main things:

1. Expectations and knowledge do not play a major role in how perception operates.
2. The environment provides **affordances** to the perceiver. This means the information that it provides, helping its meaning to be understood, e.g. depth cues.

- **Bottom-up processing** is the term given to perceptual processes that are initiated by sensations from the world – in other words, processing based on affordances in the environment rather than cognitive processes.
- According to the direct theory, illusions are exceptions to normal perception. For the most part, people are able to perceive the world without distortions or ambiguity.
- Gibson thought that perception was largely innate. This means that people are born with the ability to do it – it's in their nature and they don't need to learn through experience how to make sense of sensory information.

The two perception theories

1.	Expectations and knowledge play a critical role in how people perceive the world.
2.	Perception mainly relies on information directly from the senses.

> **Key Point**
>
> Gibson believed that sensation is perception and if we can see something we don't need to perceive it. We can decide the depth, distance and movement of any object. Therefore Gibson's theory is that the real world presents us with enough information for us to make sense of it without us having to make inferences, based on past experiences.

Evidence for Gibson's Theory

- Gibson's view was that environmental affordances such as cues to depth are good evidence for direct processing. He believed that there is a single correct interpretation of sensations coming from the environment – it doesn't depend on who is looking at it.

- Gibson thought that all animals are able to perceive the world in similar ways. This view goes against the idea that perception depends strongly on memories and thought processes, because animals have simpler thought processes than humans.
- **Motion parallax** is the way that the visual world changes when a person or animal moves. Closer objects appear to move more, and more distant ones move less. According to Gibson, this usually allows illusions and ambiguities to be resolved.
- Gibson's colleagues supported the view that perception is innate by testing very young animals and babies on a perception test called the **visual cliff**, which involves a sheet of glass that is safe to walk on but looks like a cliff edge that they could fall over.
- The visual cliff experiment found that newborn animals and human babies are able to perceive depth, supporting the bottom-up theory.

Visual cliff

Gregory's Constructivist Theory

- A person's schemas can influence and distort what they remember and what they perceive. This is the focus of the **constructivist theory** by **Richard Gregory**.
- The theory states that while perceptions are based partly on the information that comes into our senses, to a larger degree they depend on our expectations and experience, and therefore on nurture and our upbringing.
- This view states that perception depends on making **inferences** based on past experiences. In other words, the information hitting the senses is limited, so some degree of problem solving is necessary in order to work out what the world is like.
- **Top-down processing** is a term for perceptual processing that begins with thoughts and memories, rather than with sensation.

Evidence for Gregory's theory

- Illusions provide an important piece of evidence for Gregory's theory. In general, they suggest that the mind is trying to make sense of partial or ambiguous information, and using schema knowledge and expectations to do so.
- Gregory studied the Müller-Lyer illusion, finding that it was not perceived by people who had lived in round houses for most of their lives, such as the San hunter-gatherer people of the Kalahari. This suggests that illusions can occur because of our cultural experience.
- The **hollow face illusion** also supports top-down processing. When people view an image of the back of a mask, they tend to perceive it as a face – the image 'pops out' and is not perceived as being hollow. Experience and expectations cause this to happen – people are used to seeing faces the correct way round and therefore (incorrectly) interpret the hollow mask as an outward-pointing face.

Hollow face illusion

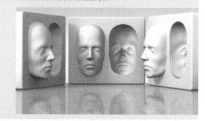

Quick Test

1. Which theory is supported by the role of depth cues in perception?
2. Which theory would predict that people in different cultures perceive the world differently because of their different experiences and beliefs?

Factors Affecting Perception

Quick Recall Quiz

You must be able to:

- Explain how perceptual set can be affected by motivation, emotion and expectations
- Describe the Gilchrist and Nesberg study of motivation, and the Bruner and Minturn study of perceptual set
- Describe some of the ways that culture can affect perception.

Errors in Perception

- The processes involved in perception do not always produce an accurate impression of the world. Illusions demonstrate how information from the world can be ambiguous.
- The way that people perceive the world is affected by **individual differences**. These are affected by life experience as people are more likely to perceive things the way they have in the past.
- Sometimes a person can see or hear things that aren't there at all, or feel tactile sensations such as pain without anything touching the skin. Things that we perceive in the absence of real sensations are called **hallucinations**.
- A dream is an everyday example of a hallucination – while people are asleep, they perceive things that are not actually there. Hallucinations can also occur as a reaction to drugs, or when a person is stressed or has a mental illness.

Perceptual Set and Research Evidence

- A person's **perceptual set** is a group of assumptions and emotions that affect perception. Having a perceptual set means that people are biased in how they perceive the world.
- The perceptual set is affected by several factors, in particular **motivation**, **emotion** and a person's **expectations**.

> **Key Point**
>
> Perception varies between individuals and is affected by a number of factors including motivation, emotion, expectations and cultural experience. Together, these factors are called the perceptual set.

- **Gilchrist and Nesberg (1952)** conducted a study where people were asked to judge the brightness of food colours. In one condition the research participants were hungry, and in another they had recently eaten.
- The researchers found that the colours of the foods were judged as being brighter and more vivid when people were hungry.

- **Bruner and Minturn (1955)** conducted a study that showed the role of expectations. Two groups of participants were shown the same ambiguous figure, which could either be perceived as a letter 'B' or the number '13'. One group were shown it alongside other letters such as 'A' or 'C', while the other group were shown it beside other numbers such as '12' and '14'.
- Participants' expectations led them to perceive the ambiguous figure in a way that fit with the other items. Even when the ambiguity was pointed out to them, the participants were still affected by their expectation – the letter condition, for example, stating that it looked more like a 'B' than a '13'.

- Bruner and Minturn's findings have real-life application as they help to explain why we sometimes make mistakes even when the stimulus is right in front of us. This shows the theory is a valid one as it can explain mistakes in real life.
- The study does not account for individual differences as it used an independent group design that may affect the study's validity as people in one group may have had key differences to people in the other group. Also, in real life we wouldn't usually look at ambiguous figures and therefore these findings may not be applied to a real-life setting so could be low in validity.

Factors in Perceptual Set

- Several different factors affect the perceptual set. Whether these are present or absent can determine what a person perceives. These factors can operate in combination for an even stronger effect.

Factor	Explanation	Example
Motivation	To an extent, people are more likely to perceive what they want to perceive.	A football supporter is more likely to perceive their favourite team's play as skilful, while someone who is a fan of a band is more likely to listen to one of their new songs and enjoy it.
Emotion	Fears and worries can affect perception, such as a fearful child thinking that a shadow looks like a monster.	Hunger is an example of an emotional feeling that can affect perception. Gilchrist & Nesberg's study demonstrated how it can affect the way a person sees objects.
Expectations	Perception can be affected by expectations, with people more likely to see what they expect to see.	Ambiguous figure illusions are a good example of this factor, as is Bruner & Minturn's study into the role of context.

- A person's perceptual set is not fixed. Factors such as hunger and motivation can change, meaning that the same scene or object could be perceived differently by the same person on different occasions.
- Expectations can also change, as they are based on past experience. New and more recent experiences can have an effect on what a person expects to see.

Culture

- Culture can also be considered a factor in a person's perceptual set. The culture that a person has grown up in or lives in affects their expectations because of their cultural knowledge and beliefs.
- Culture affects how people choose to represent the world in art. The assumptions that have formed the basis of Western art for centuries are not shared by certain other cultures around the world.
  - In a study of villagers in Zambia by Hudson (1960), it was found that they couldn't easily perceive occlusion, suggesting that depth perception may depend on culture.
  - However, the way people interpret pictures can't easily be generalised to perception in everyday life.

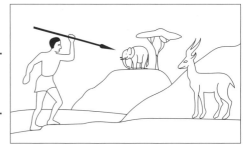

Cultures perceive depth cues in pictures in different ways, as shown by this image test of the relative distance of the animals.

Quick Test

1. What effect did hunger have on perception in the Gilchrist and Nesberg study?
2. Which concept can be defined as a group of assumptions and emotions that affect perception?

Key Words

individual differences
hallucinations
perceptual set
motivation
emotion
expectations

Where space is not provided, write your answers on a separate piece of paper.

Processes of Memory

1 Draw lines to match the terms. **[3]**

A Encoding   **i)** Output process

B Retrieval   **ii)** Loss of information

C Forgetting   **iii)** Input process

2 Explain the different types of retrieval that are involved in the following example: **[4]**

> Jana is sitting a psychology exam that has a set of multiple choice questions at the start. She then tries a section of questions where a diagram of the brain is labelled and the first letter of brain areas (e.g. 'C' for cerebellum) are given. Finally, she writes an essay describing what she knows about theories of perception.

3 Label the **two** brain areas shown below, and indicate whether they are essential for short-term or for long-term memory. **[4]**

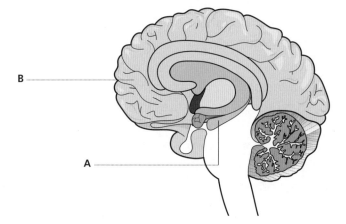

Structures of Memory 1 and 2

1 How long can items be held in short-term memory without making an effort to rehearse them? **[1]**

2 Is the short-term memory best described as a permanent store or a temporary store? **[1]**

3 How much information can long-term memory hold? **[1]**

4 What is most important for encoding semantic long-term memories – understanding the
meaning, or seeing a visual image? **[1]**

5 Draw a diagram of the multi-store model of memory. **[2]**

6 Complete the table, which summarises the multi-store model. **[5]**

Researchers who devised the model	
Names of the three stores	
Process by which information enters STM	
Process by which information is kept in STM for longer	
Process by which information is encoded to LTM	

7 Briefly describe a possible experiment that could be run to demonstrate the primacy
and recency effect. **[3]**

8 Read the following example. Then explain how the **three** stores of the multi-store
model are being used by the student. **[3]**

A teacher reads out a question and then immediately calls the name of a student who
was not paying attention. On hearing their name called out, the student takes a moment
to recall the question and then gives a correct answer.

9 How long does sensory memory last, and what is its capacity? **[3]**

10 Complete the sentences by choosing the best words from the selection below.
You do not have to use all the words. **[4]**

| curve | list | STM | first | encoding | LTM |

The serial position _____ can be used as supporting evidence for the multi-store

model. According to the model, the _____ few items from a list are repeatedly

rehearsed and therefore enter LTM. By the middle of the _____, there are too

many to rehearse and these items are therefore forgotten. The last few items can be retained

because they are still held in the _____.

11 Draw lines to match the definitions with the terms they relate to.   **[4]**

A Research study into the primary and recency effects	**i)** Displacement
B Forgetting due to new information entering STM	**ii)** Rehearsal
C Process essential for maintaining information in STM	**iii)** Murdock (1962)
D The type of encoding used in LTM	**iv)** Semantic

12 Which of the following is another term for short-term memory and emphasises that it is an active process? Shade **one** box only.   **[1]**

A LTM   ◯   **B** Working memory   ◯

C Free recall   ◯   **D** Hard drive   ◯

13 Which of the following is **not** true of short-term memory? Shade **one** box only.   **[1]**

A It is used for active processing of information in everyday tasks.   ◯

B People can use it to follow a series of instructions.   ◯

C It can rehearse items to store them for longer.   ◯

D It is simply used for storage.   ◯

14 Complete the sentences by choosing the best words from the selection below. You do not have to use all the words.   **[4]**

spaced	encode	repeating	understand	link	blocked

Repetition is important for memory, but simply _____ things does not always

lead to them being encoded to long-term memory, particularly if the information is hard to

_____ . The best way to build a new memory is to _____ the new

item to what is already understood, and then repeatedly retrieve it from memory, preferably in a

way that is _____ out over time.

15 Explain the role of attention in taking in new memories.   **[2]**

16 Explain the role of repetition in the process of encoding things to long-term memory.   **[4]**

Memory as an Active Process

1 An early British researcher studied distortions in memory using folk stories as materials.

    a) What was he called? [1]

    b) What **four** types of distortions did he find? [4]

2 Which of the following could result in a false memory? Shade **one** box only. [1]

    A Being asked a leading question ◯   **B** Forgetting something ◯

    C A blow to the head ◯   **D** Consuming caffeine or drugs ◯

3 Why was the story used in Bartlett's War of the Ghosts study hard for the research participants to understand and remember? [2]

4 Complete the table with the names of several factors that affect memory. [4]

	Familiar concepts and stories are easier to remember than unfamiliar ones.
	Information is gradually forgotten – although this can make a delayed revision session more effective.
	Information can be forgotten because it gets confused with other information.
	It's easier to remember things in the same surroundings as where they were learned.

5 Name **two** things that can act as a cue to retrieving a memory. [2]

Where space is not provided, write your answers on a separate piece of paper.

Perception and Sensation

1.   What is the technical name for a nerve cell?   **[1]**

2.   Why can we perceive objects accurately even when it gets darker?   **[2]**

3.   What part of the brain processes visual information?   **[1]**

Visual Cues and Constancies

1.   Explain why depth perception is important to humans and other animals.   **[3]**

2.   Explain **two** depth cues that the artist has used when painting the picture below.   **[4]**

3.   Do textures that are further away look sharper and more detailed?   **[1]**

Visual Illusions

1.   Is the process of perception always accurate? Explain your answer.   **[2]**

2.   Which illusion is shown in the following example?   **[1]**

3   Tick (✓) or cross (✗) the statements about the perception of illusions to indicate whether
they are true or false.   **[4]**

Statements about the perception of illusions	True (✓) or false (✗)?
Some illusions occur because the stimulus is ambiguous.	
There is one basic explanation for all illusions.	
The Ponzo illusion is based on ambiguity.	
Illusions stop working when you know about them.	

Theories of Perception

1   What is the name of the researcher who is known for his work on the direct theory
of perception?   **[1]**

2   Complete the sentences by choosing the best words from the selection below.
You do not have to use all the words.   **[3]**

illusions	perspective	affordances	visual	inferences	direct

The _____ theory of perception states that the world provides enough

information to the senses for perception to happen. This view states that organisms are able

to piece sensory information together without using memories or _____.

The theory also states that the environment provides _____, i.e. information

that helps the person or animal make sense of the world, such as depth cues.

3   a)   Which theory of perception states that inferences are a key aspect of perception?   **[1]**

     b)   Define inference and give an example.   **[2]**

Factors Affecting Perception

1   What term means the group of emotions and other factors that lead to a tendency
to perceive things in a particular way due to assumptions and emotions?   **[1]**

2   Give **two** examples of how people can sometimes fail to perceive the world accurately.   **[2]**

3   The same person can perceive a scene differently on two different occasions.
Explain why this is, mentioning at least **one** supporting research study.   **[4]**

Early Brain Development

You must be able to:

- Demonstrate a basic knowledge of brain development, from simple neural structures in the womb, of brain stem, thalamus, cerebellum and cortex
- Match brain areas to their psychological functions
- Describe the brain development of autonomic functions, sensory processing, movement and cognition.

- Developmental psychologists study how the mind and brain change across the lifespan, and particularly during childhood. They are interested in what causes an individual's personality and abilities to develop, and in the factors that can harm this process.

The Brain

- The human brain is part of the nervous system, i.e. the network of nerve cells throughout the body.
- The brain is composed of over 80 billion nerve cells (neurons) as well as other cells that support these neurons (the receptor cells of the retina are a specialist type of neuron that respond to light).
- Neurons are connected in a way that allows them to communicate and process information. This is what allows people to think, act and respond to the world.
- Each neuron is composed of a **cell body** with a nucleus, and has a fibre called an **axon** which connects it to other cells. The axon can carry an electrical signal to another area of the brain – sometimes a considerable distance.
- The axons of neurons also carry messages from the brain to the muscles, and from all parts of the body back to the brain as part of the senses.
- At the end of the axon is an axon terminal, which releases chemicals called **neurotransmitters**. These are picked up by other neurons, which can cause them to react and send out their own electrical signals.

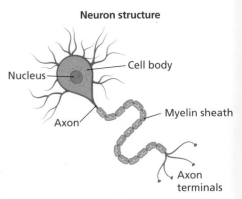

Neuron structure

Nucleus
Cell body
Myelin sheath
Axon
Axon terminals

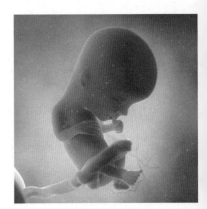

Brain Development in the Womb

- The human brain begins to develop around the third week after a baby is conceived, early in the embryonic stage of pregnancy (the first 10 weeks).
- During the earliest development of the nervous system its cells are **stem cells**, which can later transform into any type of neuron. True neurons begin to form on day 42 of a pregnancy, and all of the main structures of the central nervous system have taken shape by day 56.
- The child's entire brain is largely complete by half-way through pregnancy. By this stage, the unborn child is able to move around and respond to sounds.
- The fully developed brain has several main areas, as the table on the next page shows.

> **Key Point**
>
> Development is a gradual process of change that is largely outside of our control and begins before we are born. The brain's key structures are complete by birth.

Area	Function
Brain stem	Autonomic functions such as breathing and heartbeat
Thalamus	Completes some basic sensory processing and then relays signals to the cerebral cortex
Cerebellum	Controls precise physical movement and helps to coordinate actions
Cerebral cortex	Cognition – thinking, perception and most memory processes; the visual cortex is part of the cerebral cortex

Brain Development After Birth

- A newborn baby has a much more complex level of interconnections in their brain than an adult, with more axons connecting its neurons together.
- As the child ages, most neural development occurs not by producing new cells or axons but by pruning unnecessary connections. This allows the brain to become more attuned to its environment.
- Other connections are strengthened, as the child learns rapidly.
- A child's environment plays a major role in how it develops after birth. Children require a stimulating environment, with opportunities to play in creative and challenging ways.
- Children who are in a **deprived** environment will be at a disadvantage, and this is likely to harm their intellectual development. However, the child's brain is very adaptable, and most early periods of deprivation can be overcome.
- Psychologists have studied Eastern European orphans who were kept in very poor quality orphanages in the 1980s, and later adopted by British families. They found:
  - There was generally a huge improvement in the physical and mental health of the infants after adoption.
  - Physical development caught up rapidly compared with that of other children, but brain development was slower to catch up.
- Important structural changes in brain development continue until a person's late adolescence, and a few changes are still occurring into a person's mid-20s. The human brain therefore develops for longer than that of any other species.
- Even once it is no longer changing its structure, the brain still shows **plasticity** throughout life. This means that new connections can be formed and unnecessary ones can wither away.

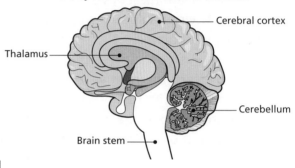

Anatomy and functional areas of the brain

Cerebral cortex

Thalamus

Cerebellum

Brain stem

Key Point

Unnecessary neural connections are pruned after birth as the baby attunes to its environment, and brain development continues until at least adolescence.

Key Words

cell body
axon
neurotransmitters
stem cell
brain stem
autonomic
thalamus
cerebellum
cerebral cortex
deprivation
plasticity

Quick Test

1. What is the function of the thalamus?
2. Which brain areas are essential for the following functions?
   a) breathing   b) perception   c) precise physical movement
3. What are autonomic functions?

Quick Recall Quiz

Nature and Nurture

You must be able to:

- Understand how the nature versus nurture debate relates to development
- Give arguments for the nature side of the debate
- Give arguments for the nurture side of the debate.

The 'Nature versus Nurture' Debate

- Human psychological development depends on both input from a child's environment, which includes their parenting, and the expression of genes.
- Although everyone agrees that both of these factors can have an effect, the relative importance of genes and of the environment in human psychological development is a matter of debate. Are personality, preferences, skills and flaws mainly due to genes or to life experiences?
- Some psychologists believe that genes are much more important than the environment, and that they largely determine what kind of personality and skills someone will develop. This is the **nature** side of the debate.
- Other psychologists think that upbringing and life experiences are more important. From this point of view, people are the way they are mainly because of what happens to them during their life. This is the **nurture** side of the debate.
- This debate impacts on a great many topics in psychology, such as:

  - Why are some people more intelligent than others? The nature side states that certain people are born with superior 'smart genes' while the nurture side focuses on upbringing and education.
  - Why are some people more friendly and outgoing than others? The nature side sees personality as innate, while the nurture side looks at life experiences.

Twin Studies

- The similarity of children to their parents is not useful evidence for the debate, because most children share both genes and an environment with their parents.
- One method used to get around this problem is the **twin study**.
  - Some of these studies compare the psychology of identical and non-identical twins within the same families.
  - Other twin studies look at the rare cases where identical twins have been adopted and raised by different families, allowing researchers to investigate how alike the twins are despite having different parenting and environmental conditions.
  - A limitation of adoption studies is that the adoptive families are often quite alike in terms of their culture and socio-economic status.

> **Key Point**
>
> The nature–nurture debate is the broad and ongoing argument over whether upbringing/environment or genetics play the main role in human psychology.

The 'Nature' Side

- A strong emphasis on the role of **genes**. A gene is a sequence of DNA and is held within every cell in the body. The **expression** of a gene is a term meaning that it causes the body to produce a protein. This production of proteins in the body (including the brain) is essential for all aspects of development.
- As genes affect the development of the body, they control the growth of the brain.
- Twin studies have found that identical twins tend to be more similar in intelligence and mental health than non-identical (or 'fraternal') twins.
- However, it's not simple to link a psychological factor such as a mental illness or someone's personality to a single gene. Abilities generally link to a mixture of genes, and can change over time.

The 'Nurture' Side

- Although genes are important, what truly makes human beings unique is their life experiences. This includes the people we spend time with.
- One of a person's most important sets of experiences, according to this view, is their **upbringing**, including the way their parents or guardians looked after them.
- Parenting seems to play a key role in a child's educational success. Some researchers have found that what parents do makes a bigger difference to education than what the child's teachers do!
- Culture is important in how people develop. Evidence comes from the fact that people in different cultures behave in different ways, e.g. they use different gestures and body language.

Combining the Sides

- It is important to realise that the two sides of the debate may both be correct on different occasions. Some psychological attributes such as personality might be largely genetic, while others such as criminal behaviour may be more to do with upbringing and culture.
- Any genetic influences on skills and personality could have an effect on later life experiences. For example, someone who was born with a more relaxed and outgoing personality might make friends more easily, and this would affect their life experiences. So genes and life experiences do not have separate effects on an individual, but work in combination.
- In addition, genes and the environment interact biologically. Genes can be switched off or on depending on life experiences. The study of this process is known as **epigenetics**.
- Epigenetics is one of the reasons why a gene might be expressed or not, along with other aspects such as developmental age.

Key Point

It is increasingly being understood how genes and the environment work together. Epigenetics is the study of how the environment impacts on whether genes are or are not expressed.

Quick Test

1. Name one psychological topic that the nature–nurture debate has impacted.
2. According to the nurture side of the debate, what major factors affect a person's personality and skills? Pick two of the following: parenting, biology, culture.
3. What term describes the situation where a gene is not switched on due to a lack of environmental stimulation?

Key Words

nature
nurture
twin study
genes
gene expression
upbringing
epigenetics

Piaget's Theories 1

You must be able to:

- Describe Piaget's stage theory and the development of intelligence
- Describe how Piaget's stage theory of cognitive development can be applied in education.

The Work of Jean Piaget

Jean Piaget

- **Jean Piaget** (1896–1980) was a developmental psychologist, and one of the most influential psychology researchers of all time.
- Piaget believed that children develop schemas (see Memory as an Active Process, pages 12–14), which change and develop as they grow up. For example, a young child may have a schema for 'dog', but as they get older they learn about different breeds of dog.
- Piaget thought that schemas develop through two key processes:
  - **Assimilation** means fitting new information into an existing schema.
  - **Accommodation** means changing a schema, or developing a new one.
  - For example, a young child may at first think that a zebra is a 'stripy horse', but then realise that it is a different animal. This results in two separate schemas.

Logical Operations

- Piaget was interested in how children think and reason. He noticed that this differs with age – younger children are not just worse at thinking than adults, but they solve problems in different ways.
- One example that Piaget studied was **centration**, the tendency of young children to focus on one element of a problem and ignore others.

> **Key Point**
>
> Piaget thought that children's understanding of the world was based on schemas, which can change through assimilation and accommodation.

- A demonstration of centration involves showing a child two glasses, one short and wide and the other tall and thin. Water is poured from the short glass into the taller one.
- Younger children say that there is now more water. Because they centre on the height of the water and think 'bigger means more', they fail to judge its volume accurately.
- Children who are around seven years old or above get the answer correct. They have developed the ability to make a **logical operation** in their mind. The logical operation here is to mentally reverse the process of pouring the water.

- The ability to complete logical operations allows older children to show **conservation** of volume, mass and other properties – realising that the appearance of an object can transform without it fundamentally changing.

Theory of Cognitive Development

- Cognitive development means the way that a person's thinking and understanding changes over time.
- Based on his experiments into children's logical operations, Piaget developed a **theory of cognitive development**, which stated that children's thinking goes through four main stages from birth to the age of 11 (see table).

Stage and Age	Features
Sensorimotor 0–2 years	Children's schemas are based on movements and they focus on learning how to interact with physical objects. By six months of age they develop object constancy – they understand that objects continue to exist even when out of sight.
Pre-operational 2–7 years	Children's thinking is highly **egocentric** – they can't understand how things look from another person's point of view. They also exhibit centration, leading to logical errors. They become able to use one object to represent another, e.g. in games.
Concrete operational 8–11 years	Children can make logical operations, no longer showing centration. They can mentally reverse operations, e.g. the pouring of liquid into different-sized containers, allowing conservation of volume. Their thinking is limited to concrete operations as they cannot yet solve abstract problems.
Formal operational 11+ years	A child cannot just solve concrete logical problems but can also think in the abstract, e.g. speculating logically about an object without it being present. They learn to process abstract mathematical symbols.

Piaget's Theory Applied to Education

- Piaget suggested that a child will learn to do things when they are biologically ready, so if they're not ready, they will fail. As children learn through discovery, schools should facilitate this learning with support.
- In the sensorimotor stage, sensory information is important. For example, a nursery environment could provide toys that light up.
- During the pre-operational stage, making models can aid discovery.
- In the concrete operational stage, sequencing of information becomes a skill they are discovering. For example, using counters to add up.
- Finally, the formal operational stage could involve discussing how things work in science.

Key Point

Piaget created a hugely influential theory of how children's cognitive processes develop through a series of stages.

Key Words

Piaget
assimilation
accommodation
centration
logical operation
conservation
theory of cognitive development
sensorimotor stage
pre-operational stage
egocentric
concrete operational stage
formal operational stage

Quick Test

1. What two processes can happen when people link information to a schema?
2. What term did Piaget use to mean focusing only on one aspect of a problem?
3. In which stage of Piaget's theory do children first learn to use one object to represent another?

Piaget's Theories 2

You must be able to:

- Evaluate Piaget's theory of cognitive development
- Explain the reduction of egocentricity and the development of conservation
- Explain and evaluate Hughes' policeman doll study
- Explain and evaluate McGarrigle and Donaldson's naughty teddy study.

Quick Recall Quiz

Evaluation of Piaget's Stage Theory

- Piaget's stage theory implies that children will struggle to learn new concepts if they are not developmentally ready.

Strengths

- Piaget's work can be applied in education. Piaget's stages closely match the way the school system is divided into different age groups, and is reflected in the methods of teaching and types of subjects covered. For example, subjects based on abstract reasoning such as algebra tend to be taught to children in the formal operational stage.
- Piaget's theory was one of the first to show that children's thinking is different from that of adults, and worth studying in its own right. It paved the way for future research.

Weaknesses

- Children develop at different rates. Stages can overlap and some people never reach the stage of abstract reasoning.
- The theory implies that children's thinking changes rapidly as they reach a new stage, when in fact cognitive development takes place slowly and gradually.
- Piaget's research focused on a small number of European children with professional parents, including his own children, and may therefore be culturally biased. The age at which the stages are reached can vary between cultures.

Research Evidence for Piaget's Theories

Three mountains problem

Three Mountains Problem

- Important evidence for Piaget's theory of cognitive development came from an experiment called the **three mountains problem**.

  – In this experiment, a child was shown a model with three mountains, each with something different at the top. Once the child had looked at the model, a doll was placed on it.
  – The child was then shown several photographs and asked to identify what the doll would be able to see. Older children tended to succeed, but those in the pre-operational stage chose a picture that was similar to what they themselves could see.

- The findings of the three mountains study supported the idea that younger children are egocentric – they can't picture the world from another person's point of view.

- However, critics of the study suggested that younger children only failed the three mountains problem because it was too difficult.
- Hughes (1975) created a simpler version of the experiment called the **policeman doll study**.

  – Procedure: 30 children between the ages of three and a half and five years were shown intersecting walls, a boy doll and a policeman doll. The policeman doll was put in various positions and the children were asked to hide the boy doll from the policeman. A second policeman doll was then introduced, and both dolls were placed at the end of the walls. The child was asked to hide the boy from both policemen; the children now had to take account of two different points of view.
  – Findings: 90% of the children were successful in putting the boy doll where the two policemen could not see it. This study showed that by age four, children have lost their egocentrism because they are able to take the view of another.
  – Evaluation: This study does not support Piaget's theory of conservation as it shows children can do things earlier than Piaget suggested. This study used a lab experiment and so validity was potentially low. The task did not reflect what the children would do in real life. This means we cannot generalise findings to a real-life situation.

Conservation of Number

- Piaget's concept of conservation includes thinking about number and quantity. He found that if a line of tokens are placed close together and then spread further apart, young children see that the line is longer and therefore assume that there are now more tokens.

- However, this experiment has also been criticised for being too complicated for young children to understand. Some children at the pre-operational stage could conserve, therefore showing a weakness of Piaget's stages as being too rigid. Some children will do things at a different pace.
- McGarrigle and Donaldson's (1974) **naughty teddy study** simplified the experiment by using a toy to mess up the tokens.

  – This time, the majority of children under the age of six correctly said that the number of tokens was unchanged, suggesting that children can conserve number earlier than previously thought.
  – The study could lack validity as the children who took part were all from the same school. This may mean the findings do not represent a broader range of children. Their educational background may be too similar and this is a weakness.
  – This study led to criticisms of Piaget's work and the way he might have confused children in his research when he asked them questions. Therefore, as an important part of constantly refining research, this study is a critical part of the scientific process in evaluating an established theory.

> ### Quick Test
>
> 1. One strength of Piaget's stage theory is that it has been widely applied in a particular area of society. Which area?
> 2. Which research study suggested that Piaget had underestimated young children's ability to conserve number?

> ### Key Words
>
> three mountains problem
> policeman doll study
> naughty teddy study

The Effects of Learning on Development

You must be able to:

- Describe learning styles including verbalisers and visualisers
- Describe Willingham's Learning Theory and his criticism of learning styles
- Describe and evaluate Dweck's Mindset Theory of Learning
- Explain the role of praise and self-efficacy in development
- Describe the difference between fixed mindset and growth mindset.

Learning Styles

- The theory of **learning styles** is a popular but controversial idea which suggests that everyone has a way of learning that suits them best – visual, auditory or kinaesthetic (i.e. movement-based).
- It suggests that educational activities are more effective if they match the person's learning style.

Evaluation of Learning Styles

- Although it has its supporters and is widely taught, several research reviews have concluded that there is no reliable scientific evidence for the learning styles theory.
- There is some evidence that having a preference for visual or verbal information is connected to biological differences, as described on the right.
- Learners with these preferences are sometimes called **verbalisers** and **visualisers**.

 Key Point

The concept of learning styles is not supported by scientific evidence.

- People who prefer to learn via words showed increased activity in verbal areas of their brain. Those who prefer learning via images showed increased activity in visual areas (Kraemer *et al.*, 2009).
- However, neither group learned better when they used their preferred style. So different ways of learning may be just a matter of personal preference.

Willingham's Theory

- Psychologist **Daniel Willingham** has argued strongly that the entire concept of learning styles is inaccurate and harmful. He states that the best way to learn something depends on the type of information. For example, it makes no sense to learn a map verbally.
- It is helpful for all learners to use their senses together where possible. Combining both verbal and visual information improves the rate at which people later remember information – a concept called **dual coding**.
- Willingham also argues that factual knowledge is essential. If people have good knowledge, they are better able to understand new information. Therefore, learning should involve learning facts, not just skills.

Dweck's Mindset Theory of Learning

- Some genetic factors appear to affect intelligence and abilities, but many psychologists think that beliefs and attitude also play a key role in the development of abilities, and therefore in success at school and beyond.
- Psychologist **Carol Dweck** has studied learners' beliefs and developed a theory which states that there are two main mindsets that people can have: fixed or growth.
- A mindset is not the same as a self-efficacy belief – it is an explanation of why people tend to develop positive or

negative self-efficacy. Some people believe that they are bad at something and there is nothing that can be done to improve. Others believe that they can improve with practice.

- Mindsets influence people's views on a range of their own abilities, e.g. intelligence, sports proficiency and art ability.
- Praise can also affect mindset:
  - If a child is rewarded and praised for being clever and producing perfect work, they are less likely to try new challenges. This encourages a fixed mindset.
  - If a child is rewarded and praised for making their best effort and for trying challenging new tasks, this encourages a growth mindset. They are also more likely to learn new things.
- An important implication of mindset theory is that people with a fixed mindset tend to fear mistakes, as they see a mistake as reflecting low ability. In contrast, people with a growth mindset may see a mistake as helpful feedback.

Evaluation of Mindset Theory

- In support of Dweck's theory, Blackwell *et al.* (2007) studied maths attainment in students. They found that students with a growth mindset continually improved their grades, whereas those with a fixed mindset stayed at the same level.
- The theory has been accused of being over-simplistic, with students sometimes given the message that success is about working harder and that failure is due to having the wrong attitude.
- It is difficult to measure which mindset people have. Some people seem to have a mixture of the two mindsets, or show different mindsets on different occasions.

Praise and Self-Efficacy

- A person's beliefs about themselves are not always accurate, and can be affected by a number of factors.
- One such belief is **self-efficacy** – a person's sense of whether they are good or bad at something.
- Getting negative messages from parents and teachers (e.g. parents saying, "She's not very clever") can affect self-efficacy. The message is **internalised** and becomes part of the person's self-efficacy beliefs. On the other hand, praise can have a positive effect.
- Praise and other feedback from teachers and parents can motivate learners and affect how they think about themselves, including their self-efficacy.

Fixed mindset	People think that ability levels are fixed, and that how well someone does at a task is largely due to factors outside of their control, e.g. genetics.
Growth mindset	People think that ability levels can be changed, and that how well someone does at a task is largely due to effort and learned skill.

> **Key Point**
>
> Praise can affect mindset and therefore learning.

> **Key Words**
>
> learning styles
> verbaliser
> visualiser
> **Willingham**
> dual coding
> **Dweck**
>
> fixed mindset
> growth mindset
> self-efficacy
> internalise

> **Quick Test**
>
> 1. Is there any sound scientific evidence for learning styles?
> 2. Isaac says, "I'm not bad at tennis – I just haven't got the hang of it yet." Which type of mindset is shown in this example?

Where space is not provided, write your answers on a separate piece of paper.

Perception and Sensation

1 What general name is given to the cells that our senses use to gain information about the world, for example the rods and cones found in the retina? **[1]**

2 Label the diagram to show the processes and body areas involved in visual perception. **[4]**

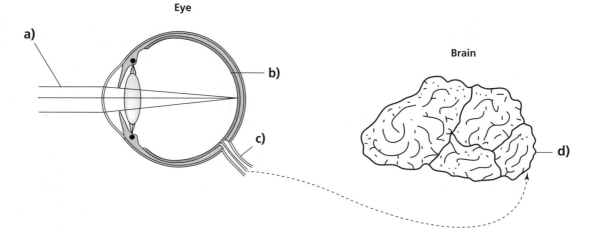

a) ....

b) ....

c) ....

d) ....

3 Briefly explain the difference between sensation and perception. **[2]**

4 Name **two** types of constancy which are features of visual perception. **[2]**

5 Is it easy to program a computer to perceive objects? Explain why / why not. **[3]**

Visual Cues and Constancies

1 Briefly explain what is meant by occlusion. [2]

2 The table shows **four** effects that people perceive as distance increases. Complete the relevant depth cues. [4]

Effect	Depth Cue
Lines appear to get closer together.	
Textures become less detailed.	
The difference between the images seen by the two eyes reduces.	
Objects appear closer to a horizon line.	

3 Sometimes predators such as cheetahs have to perceive the distance of one of their prey species such as a gazelle.

a) Why do many predators have two forward-facing eyes? [1]

b) What would happen if a cheetah failed to judge the distance of a gazelle that it was trying to catch? [1]

4 Complete the sentences by choosing the best words from the selection below. You do not have to use all the words. [4]

monocular	binocular	occlusion	relative	disparity	convergence

The simplest cues to depth and distance are the _____ depth cues, which

can be perceived using just one eye. These include _____ size, which means

that more distant objects appear smaller than other objects of the same type. Another cue

is _____, meaning that if one object partially obscures another from where

someone observes them, it must be the closer of the two.

5 In the renaissance, artists learned to portray depth and distance in their paintings.

a) What term is given for the point that lines converge on as they get further away, helping to demonstrate the cue of linear perspective? [1]

b) Why is it helpful to be able to use cues such as linear perspective in art? [1]

Visual Illusions

1 Are illusions mainly linked to perception or to sensation? **[1]**

2 Describe the Necker cube illusion. **[2]**

3 Which illusion is shown in the following image? **[1]**

4 Draw lines to match the illusions with their causes. **[3]**

A Necker cube   i) Fiction

B Ponzo illusion   ii) Ambiguity

C Kanizsa triangle   iii) Misinterpreted depth cue

5 Explain the role of misinterpreted depth cues in illusions. **[4]**

Theories of Perception

1 Name **two** researchers who have developed theories of perception, and name the theories with which they are associated. **[2]**

2 Explain which theory of perception is supported by the idea that animals and humans perceive the world in very similar ways. **[2]**

3 What term does the constructivist theory of perception give to the way that people try to make sense of incomplete sensory information? Shade **one** box only. **[1]**

A Motion parallax   ◯   B Inference   ◯

C Bottom-up processing   ◯   D A schema   ◯

4 What term does the direct theory of perception give to the effect that movement has on perception? Shade **one** box only. **[1]**

A The visual cliff   ◯   B Top-down processing ◯

C An illusion   ◯   D Motion parallax   ◯

5 Complete the following two sentences. [2]

A demonstration of how babies are able to perceive depth involved an experiment called the

_____. An illusion that showed the importance of expectations when trying to

perceive faces is called the _____ illusion.

6 Explain what is meant by an affordance and which theory it supports. [3]

Factors Affecting Perception

1 What general term do psychologists use to describe differences between people, including their age and culture? [1]

2 Which researchers conducted a study into expectations in perception, showing that the context (other letters or other numbers) affected how an ambiguous figure was perceived? Shade **one** box only. [1]

A Gilchrist and Nesberg ⭕   B Atkinson and Shiffrin ⭕

C Gibson and Walk ⭕   D Bruner and Minturn ⭕

3 What term is used to describe the group of assumptions and emotions that affect and bias perception? Shade **one** box only. [1]

A Light constancy ⭕   B Perceptual set ⭕

C Bottom-up processing ⭕   D Motion parallax ⭕

4 Explain what this picture can tell us about the role of culture in perception. [4]

5 Briefly explain **two** classic research studies that demonstrated factors in the perceptual set. [4]

Where space is not provided, write your answers on a separate piece of paper.

Early Brain Development

1. Name **two** parts of a neuron. [2]

2. An unborn baby's brain areas have developed by halfway through pregnancy.
True or false? [1]

3. Define plasticity. [2]

4. What is the difference between the brain stem and a stem cell? [2]

Nature and Nurture

1. Which side of the nature versus nurture debate states that genes play a more important role in human development than the environment? [1]

2. Name a type of research study that can be done to help provide evidence about the role of genes in development. [1]

3. Tick (✓) or cross (✗) the statements to indicate whether they are true or false. [4]

Statements	True (✓) or false (✗)?
Identical twins tend to be more similar in intelligence than non-identical twins.	
If one identical twin has a mental illness, then the other twin will definitely get it too.	
If a gene is expressed, this means that it causes a protein to be produced, affecting development.	
Cases where twins are raised by different families are rare and difficult to study.	

4. Explain the nurture side of the nature versus nurture debate. [4]

Piaget's Theories 1 and 2

1. Complete the following sentence: [1]

Piaget believed children develop _____, which change and develop as they grow

up through the processes of assimilation and accommodation.

2 What term means that children can't picture the world from another person's point of view? [1]

3 Explain the features of the concrete operation stage of development. [3]

4 Read the following scenario. State what cognitive process is taking place, and why. [2]

> A young boy is visiting the zoo. He looks at an antelope – a type of animal that he has never seen before. It has long legs and is brown, so he decides it must be a strange kind of horse.

The Effects of Learning on Development

1 What terms are sometimes used for learners who prefer to process new information verbally or visually? [2]

2 Complete the sentences by choosing the best words from the selection below. You do not have to use all the words. [4]

coding	influencing	visual	shapes	styles	harming	tactile

Education involves supporting and _____ people as they learn and develop, and is fundamentally connected to developmental psychology. The theory of learning _____ is a popular but controversial idea, which suggests that everyone has a way of learning that suits them: auditory, _____, or kinaesthetic. Reviews have shown that this theory is not supported by reliable scientific evidence – educational activities are not any more effective if they match the person's supposed learning style. However, people do learn better if they use a combination of modalities to take in information; a concept known as dual _____.

3 State **one** thing that can affect self-efficacy. [1]

4 Does Willingham think it is important to learn facts? Why, or why not? [2]

Sampling Methods

You must be able to:

- Explain what target populations are
- Explain what is meant by sampling from the target population
- Describe and evaluate the following sampling methods: random, opportunity, systematic and stratified and how to select samples using these methods.

Populations and Samples

- Most psychology research involves a process where researchers formulate a hypothesis, then gather and analyse data to test their hypothesis.
- To conduct their study, the researcher(s) will need to select or recruit an appropriate group of research participants to test.
- The term **target population** refers to the group of people who the researcher is interested in studying. It is not necessarily the whole population of the country, but could be a more specific group such as school students.
- A **sample** is a group of people who take part in an experiment or other research study. The sample is selected from among the people in a target population.
- There are various ways of selecting a sample, and these are called sampling methods.

Generalising

- The way a sample has been selected is important when it comes to evaluating research.
- Ideally, the researcher wants to be able to **generalise** from the sample to the target population. This means concluding that the findings from the sample will also be true of the wider population.
- Generalising is only valid when a sample is **representative** of the target population as a whole – in other words, it has similar characteristics. For example, a representative sample would have the same percentage of people from each ethnic group and age group as the target population does.
- A good sample is also large – this reduces the impact of random variations among the members of the sample.

Sampling Methods

Opportunity Sampling

- The most commonly used sampling method is **opportunity sampling**. This means selecting a group of research participants on the basis of who is easily available, e.g. a lecturer selecting their own students.
- Many opportunity samples are **biased** – the people who are easily available may not be representative of the target population.

> **Key Point**
>
> There are many different ways to select a sample from the target population. Opportunity sampling is the most commonly used.

Opportunity Sampling Example 1: A researcher is interested in studying all adults, and she obtains an opportunity sample that consists of her own university students. This sample would not have the same variety of ages and backgrounds as all of the adults in the target population, and is therefore biased.

- To select an opportunity sample, the researcher approaches members of the target population who are conveniently available without taking any other characteristics into account. These people are then asked for their consent to participate in the study.

Random Sampling

- A **random sample** is one where every member of the target population has the same chance of being selected.
- It is often considered the best sampling method as it generally results in a representative and unbiased sample. However, it is more difficult and time-consuming than opportunity sampling.
- The best way to be sure that everyone has the same chance of being selected is to number every member of the population using a complete list, and then use a **random number** table or computer program to select the participants.

Systematic Sampling

- A **systematic sample** uses a procedure that avoids groups of people being selected together, e.g. by picking every tenth name on a school register or every fifth house on a street.
  - Systematic samples tend to be representative, but it's not possible to guarantee that they are unbiased – this depends on the characteristics of the target population. It may be that every fifth house on a street is more expensive than the others, with wealthier occupants, meaning that selecting these ones will not result in a representative sample.
  - The starting point has to be random. After that, the selection of participants at set intervals reduces bias by avoiding the selection of pre-existing groups (which is a major problem with opportunity sampling).

Stratified Sampling

- A **stratified sample** involves selecting people in order to maintain the overall proportions of the target population in categories that the researcher considers to be important.
  - A true stratified sample has exactly the same proportions as the population. So if 30 per cent of the target population are elderly, then 30 per cent of the sample must be elderly.
  - A researcher may ensure a 50–50 proportion of males and females, or find people from every major career type so that the frequencies match those of society as a whole.
  - A stratified sample is representative, but only in the characteristics that have been stratified. It may be biased in other ways.

Opportunity Sampling Example 2: A student researcher approaches a group of people from his year in a school corridor and asks them to take part in his experiment; they agree. This sample is also biased – he is more likely to choose people who are approachable and/ or similar to himself.

 Key Point

All sampling methods have their flaws, but random sampling is the least likely to obtain a biased sample.

 Key Words

target population
sample
generalise
representative
opportunity sampling
bias
random sample
random number
systematic sampling
stratified sampling

Quick Test

1. Which type of sampling involves ensuring that every member of the target population has the same chance of being selected?
2. Opportunity sampling suffers from what flaw?

Variables and Hypotheses

You must be able to:

- Explain the role of the independent variable and the dependent variable in an experiment
- Explain what extraneous variables are and give examples
- Give examples of alternative and null hypotheses.

Experiments and Variables

- An experiment is one of the most important **research methods** used in psychology. It allows researchers to study human behaviour in a controlled and systematic way, by changing one variable and measuring the effect this has on another variable.
- A **variable** is any characteristic, attribute or environmental condition that can vary – in other words, it can have different values.
- Some example variables include:

how much you like your teacher	score on an IQ test	number of Facebook friends	how many hours someone revised for a maths exam	how many goals scored in one season

- A **normal distribution** is one in which the middle values are common while more extreme ones are progressively rarer, resulting in a graph that shows the frequency of values of the variable as a bell-shaped curve.
  - The normal distribution curve is symmetrical, and the frequency of scores declines the further they are from the area around the mean – rapidly at first, and then more slowly.
  - The mean, mode and median are all equal.
- Variables are often assumed to be normally distributed, unless researchers know otherwise.

A bell–shaped curve

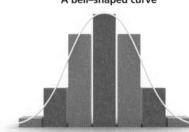

The IV and DV

- In psychology experiments, a researcher manipulates or changes the value of one variable and measures the level of another.
- An experiment therefore looks for a **cause-and-effect relationship** between two variables – if one variable is changed, does the other variable also change?
  - The variable that is manipulated is called the **independent variable**, or **IV** for short.
  - The variable that is measured is called the **dependent variable**, or **DV**. The level of this variable forms the data that a researcher analyses.
- An experiment has two or more **conditions** which are compared. These relate to different values of the IV. For example, a research study into the effect of caffeine on sleep quality might have a caffeine condition and a no caffeine condition.

Extraneous Variables

- To determine whether the IV has an effect on the DV, the level of every other relevant variable needs to be kept constant. This is known as experimental **control**, i.e. it has to be a fair test.
- Any variable other than the IV which could potentially affect the DV is called an **extraneous variable**, or **EV**. For example, the *amount of time available* is a variable that may affect scores on a DV, and must be kept constant.

Writing a Hypothesis

- Every research study expresses a hypothesis. This is a scientific prediction of what is expected to happen.
- Usually, the hypothesis predicts that the IV will have an effect on the DV, and also gives a rationale for this prediction based on past research.

> A hypothesis is typically phrased as follows: If (the IV) has an effect on (the DV), then there will be higher scores on (condition 1) than (condition 2).
>
> For example: *If having a nap boosts long-term memory, then students who take a short nap after revising for 30 minutes will remember more information than students who do not.*

- In experiments, the prediction that the IV will affect the DV is called the **alternative hypothesis** (or 'experimental hypothesis').
- Researchers must also have a clear idea of how their results will look if the IV does not affect the DV. This is known as a **null hypothesis**. In other words, this is a prediction of what will be found if the alternative hypothesis is not supported by the data. For the research study on caffeine, this would be stating that caffeine will not have an effect on sleep quality.

Non-experimental Research

- In non-experimental studies, there may not always be control over the key variables of the research study.
- Variables are just as important in non-experimental studies, but it may not be obvious which variable is having an effect on which.
- Many non-experimental studies lack control over EVs too – only experiments control the IV and keep EVs constant. This is a major strength of the experimental method.

Revise

Key Point

In order to test the effect of the IV on the DV, any extraneous variables must be kept constant.

Key Point

An experimental hypothesis is typically expressed in terms of two variables: the independent variable (IV) and the dependent variable (DV).

Key Words

research methods
variable
normal distribution
cause-and-effect
    relationship
independent variable (IV)
dependent variable (DV)
conditions
control
extraneous variable (EV)
alternative hypothesis
null hypothesis

> **Quick Test**
>
> 1. What term is used for the variable the researcher measures?
> 2. Write a suitable experimental hypothesis for the following variables: IV = quantity of caffeine consumed (500 mg versus 0 mg); DV is time taken to get to sleep.

Design of Experiments 1

You must be able to:

- Explain the use of laboratory, field and natural experiments
- Explain and evaluate independent groups design, repeated measures design and matched pairs design.

Location of Experiments

- As described in the previous section, it is necessary to control extraneous variables (EVs) in psychology experiments.

Laboratory Experiments

- One of the best ways to do this involves running the study in a controlled environment called a laboratory (or 'lab').
- An experiment based in a lab is called a **laboratory experiment**:
  - The lab can be any environment that allows the effects of distractions such as background noise to be reduced or preferably eliminated, such as an empty school room.
  - Usually participants are tested one at a time.
  - Lab experiments are very controlled but the setting is artificial, meaning that participants might not behave in the same ways that they would in everyday life.
  - In lab experiments people know they are being tested in some capacity and may not show their real behaviour. Although they may think they are helping the researcher in doing so, it means the findings can lack validity.
  - As lab experiments are highly controlled, cause and effect can be established as we can be sure that the manipulation of the IV has brought about change in the DV.

Field Experiments

- To study behaviour in a more authentic setting, a researcher may use a **field experiment**:
  - A field experiment is any experiment that is conducted in a participant's natural environment, such as their workplace or somewhere that they typically study or socialise. This leads to more realistic behaviour, but extraneous variables such as distractions and background noise can affect results.
  - To keep the setting as realistic as possible, it may be necessary to test several participants simultaneously, resulting in more extraneous variables.
  - High in validity as it is carried out in a natural setting. As participants are usually unaware they are being studied, they behave naturally. However, because they don't always know they are being studied, there may be ethical issues of consent, thus not giving their permission to take part.

Field experiments can be done in group settings

Natural Experiments

- A third type of experiment is the **natural experiment**.
  - The key difference between this and other types of experiments is that it is not set up – it occurs spontaneously in the real world, and the researcher records the outcome. For example, if some students used flash cards for revision and others did not, their exam results could be compared to see if those who used flash cards got better grades.
  - Ethically, the experimenter is not responsible for the outcome of the study, making natural experiments ideal for studying situations that could not be tested in other types of experiments, e.g. the effects of drug use.
  - It is impossible to control extraneous variables in natural experiments and there is no random allocation to conditions, making it hard to be sure whether the IV has affected the DV. For instance, using the example above, it could be that students who used flash cards were more hard working and better at the subject, the flash cards may not be why they did better.
  - Natural experiments are high in validity as they involve something naturally occurring, rather than setting up a situation in a lab. They tend to study one-off events so there are few opportunities to study these kinds of situations.

Experimental Design

- Experiments have two or more conditions that are compared, where the researcher allocates the participants to the various conditions. There are three main options, depending on the specific details of the study:
  - Sometimes, all participants complete both/all conditions of the experiment. This is a **repeated measures** design.
  - Sometimes, the participants are randomly divided into groups, and each group takes part in a single condition. This is an **independent groups** design.
  - Two separate groups of participants could be created by matching participants up on important characteristics such as age or ability levels. This is a **matched pairs** design.
- A condition that is used simply for comparison is known as a **control condition**. This is used as a baseline.

> **Key Point**
>
> Experimental design means the way that participants are allocated to the conditions of the study.

> **Key Words**
>
> laboratory experiment
> field experiment
> natural experiment
> repeated measures
> independent groups
> matched pairs
> control condition

> **Quick Test**
>
> 1. Which experimental design is being used if a participant only completes one condition of an experiment?
> 2. State one extraneous variable which can affect results in a field experiment.

Design of Experiments 2

You must be able to:

- Describe how a laboratory experiment or field experiment could be set up using standardised procedures
- Explain the ethical issues that apply to psychological research.

Research Procedures

- An experimenter must avoid any source of bias in their methodology. One important feature of a well-controlled experiment is the use of **standardised instructions**. These ensure that every participant is given exactly the same information at the start of the study (this also applies to non-experimental methods).
- Other aspects of the research procedure are also standardised, so that every participant experiences the same overall procedure.

Repeated Measures Design

- With a repeated measures design, **order effects** could bias the results. This is when participants improve or get worse at a task as they complete two or more conditions.
- To avoid order effects, the order of conditions is balanced so participants do not all complete the conditions in the same order as each other. This is known as **counterbalancing**.
- When counterbalancing, an equal proportion of the participants is divided among the conditions, each doing the conditions in a particular assigned order.

Independent Groups Design

- An independent groups design does not suffer from order effects because participants complete only one condition. However, they do suffer from participant variables – a type of EV. This is where differences between the participants, such as different ability levels, can affect the outcome.
- An important way to minimise the effect of participant variables and thereby avoid bias is to **randomly allocate** participants to the different conditions of the experiment.

Matched Pairs Design

- An advantage of matched pairs designs is that specific participant variables are controlled for by matching them up between participants. A limitation is that this does not control for all EVs, and it is more time-consuming to do than the other designs.

> ### Key Point
>
> In a repeated measures design, counterbalancing must be used.

Ethics

- Research must meet **ethical standards** and follow a range of procedures to ensure that people are treated fairly. Overall, the participants must be treated with respect and should come to no **harm**. This can include psychological harm such as stress and embarrassment. In the UK, researchers follow the ethical guidelines set out by the British Psychological Society.

Ethical Procedures

- Key ethical procedures include:
  - Seeking **informed consent** from participants. People must know what they are consenting to, including the type of task and how long it will take. For research on children, parental consent is necessary.
  - Ensuring that participants are aware that they have a **right to withdraw** at any point during a study.
  - **Debriefing** participants at the end of the study, thanking them for their participation and giving them any information that it was not possible to give them at the beginning, such as the aim/hypothesis of the study.
- Researchers must seek ethical approval from their university or employer before proceeding.
- For the most part, research that involves **deception** is seen as unethical, because participants have not given their informed consent to take part.
- It is also essential for researchers to treat data **confidentially**, and not to release or publish the names of research participants.

> **Key Words**
>
> standardised instructions
> order effects
> counterbalancing
> random allocation
> ethical standards
> harm
> informed consent
> right to withdraw
> debriefing
> deception
> confidentiality

> **Quick Test**
>
> 1. What problem could occur if every participant completed condition 1 of an experiment first, and then moved on to condition 2?
> 2. Why can't researchers publish the names of research participants in their studies?
> 3. What term means balancing the order in which participants compete experimental conditions?

Non-experimental Methods

Quick Recall Quiz

You must be able to:

- Explain the main types of data gathered in psychology research
- Describe non-experimental research methods – observation studies, interviews, questionnaires and case studies
- Evaluate non-experimental research methods.

Non-experimental Research

- Experiments are an essential part of psychology research, but sometimes other research methods are more appropriate.
- One advantage of certain non-experimental methods is that they get more in-depth results. There are two key types of data that psychology research obtains:
  - **Quantitative data**: data in the form of numbers
  - **Qualitative data**: data in the form of spoken/written words or some other non-numerical form.
- Ethical standards apply to non-experimental research. Additional considerations are explained below.

> **Key Point**
>
> There are several non-experimental methods, each with their own strengths and weaknesses. The best choice of method depends on the aims of the research.

Observation

- **Observation** involves studying behaviour as it happens and recording data in the form of notes or videos. Often this involves a **naturalistic observation** – observing a participant in an everyday context such as their workplace.
- There are key design considerations in observation studies:

  - An observation study will typically set out **categories of behaviour** in advance. A checklist can then be used to record how often each behaviour occurs.
  - A single observer may make errors, reducing the reliability of their data, especially if they are untrained. For this reason, some studies use two or more observers. **Inter-observer reliability** means the extent to which different observers record the same data from the same observation.

- An additional ethical standard which must be upheld is avoiding any **invasion of privacy**. Participants should not be secretly recorded or their private conversations listened to, for example.
- Disclosing the observation will impact on the behaviour of participants, and this weakness should be considered when analysing the results of an observation study.
- A strength of observation studies is the ability to gather data on behaviour as it happens, but they lack the control of experimental research.

An observation schedule

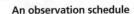

Participant number	Stands up	Scratches head	Eats a snack
P1			
P2			
P3			
P4			

Interviews and Questionnaires

- **Interviews** and **questionnaires** are widely used research methods in psychology. Both involve asking people questions about their behaviour or thoughts.
- The main difference between these two methods is that interview questions are asked face-to-face, and questionnaires are completed on paper or via a computer.

- There are two main types of question.

Open questions	Allow the participant to answer in any way they want, e.g.: "What do you think of your teacher?". They provide qualitative data that is detailed but hard to analyse.
Closed questions	Give participants a pre-determined choice of possible answers, such as a multiple choice, e.g. "Are you going to take this subject next year? Yes/no." They provide quantitative data, e.g. the percentage of people who chose each answer. Responses are quick to analyse but less in-depth, as people do not have the opportunity to express their thoughts in full.

- Interviews generally use a lot of open questions and therefore obtain qualitative data. Questionnaires usually focus on closed questions, but a mixture of both types of question can be used.
- An interviewer can explain questions where necessary and can also follow up on questions if the answer is interesting or unclear. This is an advantage of the interview method.
- The main strength of questionnaires is that they can easily be distributed to a lot of people via email/the internet.
- An advantage of both methods is that they allow an insight into people's thoughts that is not possible by simply observing them. However, people may not tell the truth or may be unaware of the reasons behind their own behaviour.

Case Studies

- A **case study** is an in-depth study of one individual or a small group. It is not a single way of gathering data. It typically involves several techniques such as brain scans and ability tests.
- Observations and interviews can be used as part of a case study.

Examples of types of data

	Primary Data	Secondary Data
Qualitative (verbal)	Open questions; descriptions taken during observations	Diaries; school reports
Quantitative (numerical)	Scores in experiments; numerical data from questionnaires, checklists and observations	Scores on school tests and exams; IQ tests taken for other purposes; government statistics

- Some of these techniques/methods involve gathering **primary data**, which is where the researcher obtains and uses new data directly from the participant(s), e.g. using an interview.
- Others involve obtaining **secondary data**, which has been generated before for a different purpose, e.g. government statistics or school tests, and the researcher obtains it and analyses it.

- Case studies are not an efficient way of studying a lot of people as they are time-consuming, but they are invaluable for studying unusual or unique cases, e.g. people with rare psychological disorders or brain damage. They gain in-depth findings.

Key Words

quantitative data
qualitative data
observation
naturalistic observation
categories of behaviour
inter-observer reliability
invasion of privacy
interview
questionnaire
open questions
closed questions
case study
primary data
secondary data

> **Quick Test**
>
> 1. "On a scale of 1–10, how much did you like primary school?" What type of data would be obtained from answers to this question?
> 2. Which research method is most suitable for studying an individual with an accidental brain injury?

Correlation and Data Handling

You must be able to:

- Explain and calculate descriptive statistics, using standard form and decimals
- Describe and evaluate the use of correlation studies
- Explain and interpret scatter graphs.

Average and Range Calculations

- An experiment or other research study generates data, e.g. a set of scores out of 20 on a memory test.
- **Statistics** are used to interpret and make sense of this data, as well as summarising it in a simplified form.
- It is important to be able to express an average score from a set of data, as well as how spread out the scores are.
  - The **range** shows the difference between the lowest and highest score, therefore giving an idea of how widely distributed scores are overall.
  - The **mean**, **median** and **mode** all express an average, central figure in different ways.

Mean: add up the sum of all scores in a set of data, and divide by the number of scores.

Median: place scores in order from low to high, and select the middle score. With even numbers of scores, the mean of the two middle scores is calculated.

Mode: the most common score in the distribution.

Calculations and Display of Data

- Researchers must not round any numbers until after the calculations are complete, at which point 3–4 significant figures will be shown.
- Standard form can also be used where appropriate to represent very large or small numbers, as can ratios, fractions and percentages.
- Frequency tables are used to count items in categories, such as the number of times behaviours occur during an observation study.
- One of the most common types of graph used for psychology experiments is the **bar chart**. They are helpful for displaying the results of two or more experimental conditions in a way that makes any difference between the mean scores clear to see.
- Another useful graph is the **histogram**. Rather than comparing two conditions, a histogram is used to display findings from a series of groups. For example, it could be constructed by using age categories (16–24; 25–34, etc.) along the x-axis, and percentage scores up the y-axis.

> **Key Point**
>
> An essential part of the research process is the analysis and display of results. The mean, median, mode and range provide a useful descriptive summary of results, and various types of graph are used to display the main findings visually.

Frequency table

Class interval	Tally	Frequency
0–39	|	1
40–79	卌 |	6
80–119	卌 卌 |||	13
120–159	卌 |||	8
160–199	||	2
200–239	|||	3
	Total =	33

Bar chart

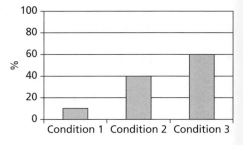

Histogram

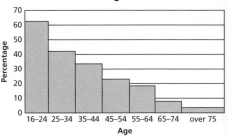

Source: Department of Health

Correlation

- **Correlation** studies could obtain data from any source, but it has to be quantitative data which shows a variable on a scale from high to low.
- Secondary data is often used, meaning that correlation can be used to study issues that would be impractical or unethical to study via an experiment. This is a strength of correlation.
- Two variables are studied; these are called **co-variables** (rather than IV and DV) because correlation studies do not demonstrate which variable is having an effect on which. In some cases, there will be no causal relationship at all.
- For this reason, researchers say that *correlation does not demonstrate causation*. This is the main weakness of correlation studies.
- Instead, correlation studies show whether two variables are related and, if so, how strong the relationship between the two co-variables is.
- Correlation studies typically display findings on a **scatter graph**.

> **Key Point**
>
> Correlation is used to analyse primary data gathered from a questionnaire study, or secondary data. It shows the direction and strength of a relationship between two co-variables.

- The scatter graph shows the **correlation strength** of the relationship between the two co-variables. The stronger the relationship, the closer the points are to forming a line on the graph, while weak correlations appear spread out.
- If there is no relationship at all, the dots will be scattered randomly. This is usually called a zero correlation.
- It also shows the direction of a relationship – as one variable increases, does the other increase or does it decrease? If the co-variables increase together, this is called a **positive correlation**. If one increases as the other decreases, this is called a **negative correlation**.
- A positive correlation will appear as a pattern on the graph which moves upwards from left to right, as in the example below.

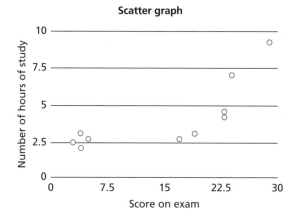

Scatter graph

> **Key Words**
>
> statistics
> range
> mean
> median
> mode
> bar chart
> histogram
> correlation
> co-variables
> scatter graph
> correlation strength
> positive correlation
> negative correlation

Quick Test

1. What type of graph is most suitable for comparing the mean scores on two experimental conditions?
2. What type of correlation is shown if, on a scatter graph, the points rise upwards from left to right and are bunched close together, almost forming a line?

Where space is not provided, write your answers on a separate piece of paper.

Early Brain Development

1 For what type of functions is the brain stem responsible? Give an example. **[2]**

2 Label the figure with A, B and C using the statements below to show the key areas of a neuron. **[3]**

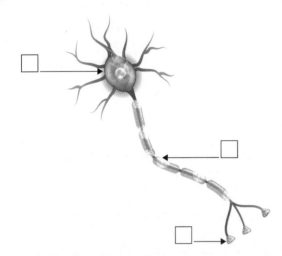

A Axon terminal, which can release neurotransmitters

B Axon, which can send a message elsewhere in the brain or body

C Cell body with nucleus

3 True neurons begin to form on day 42 of a pregnancy. Why is it unlikely that the unborn child can think and remember before this point? **[1]**

4 The visual cortex is part of the cerebral cortex. Which part of the brain acts as a relay between the senses and the visual cortex? **[1]**

5 How many neurons are there in the human brain? Shade **one** box only. **[1]**

A Fewer than 1 billion ⭕   **B** Between 1–20 billion ⭕

C Between 20–80 billion ⭕   **D** Over 80 billion ⭕

6 Which area of the brain controls precise physical movement and helps to coordinate actions? Shade **one** box only. **[1]**

A The cerebral cortex ⭕   **B** The cerebellum ⭕

C The brain stem ⭕   **D** The thalamus ⭕

7 Complete the sentences by choosing the best words from the selection below. You do not have to use all the words. **[4]**

| brain | pruning | nervous | newborn | neurotransmitters | axons |

The human _____ begins to develop soon after conception. Early cells called

stem cells can later transform into any type of neuron. The _____ of neurons

form a lot of connections with other neurons. A _____ baby has more of these

connections than an adult, and, after birth, _____ of connections occurs as the

child attunes to their environment.

8 Explain how a child's brain develops after birth. Include the role of the environment. **[4]**

Nature and Nurture

1 Which of the following explanations of personality development is **not** associated with the nurture side of the debate? Shade **one** box only. **[1]**

A Parenting ◯ **B** Education ◯

C Life experiences ◯ **D** Genetics ◯

2 Which of the following is **not** associated with biological development? Shade **one** box only. **[1]**

A DNA ◯ **B** Education ◯

C Genes ◯ **D** Epigenetics ◯

3 Complete the sentences by choosing the best words from the selection below. You do not have to use all the words. **[3]**

| nature | nurture | DNA | chromosome | upbringing | expression | cells |

The _____ side of the nature versus nurture debate places a strong emphasis on

the role of genes. A gene is a sequence of _____ and is held within every cell

in the body. The _____ of a gene is a term meaning that it causes the body to

produce a protein, a process which is essential for all aspects of development.

4 Which side of the nature versus nurture debate states that intelligence is largely innate? **[1]**

5 Describe how genes and the environment interact during development. **[2]**

6 Draw lines to match the terms with their definitions. **[3]**

A | Epigenetics   i) | The study of how gene expression and the environment interact

B | Twin study   ii) | How a person is looked after and raised, e.g. by parents

C | Upbringing   iii) | Comparison of the psychological traits of one or more pairs of twins

7 Read the following example. Then explain some of the factors that could affect why Maryam is different from her sister. **[6]**

> Maryam and Aneesa are twin sisters who have recently left school. Maryam is chatty and has an extroverted personality, while Aneesa is quiet and prefers to spend time alone. Maryam got really good A-Level grades and has gone to university to study psychology at one of the country's top university departments along with one of her best friends. Aneesa got lower grades, and decided to stop studying and look for a job. Both girls were always told to work hard by their parents, and given lots of support throughout school.

Piaget's Theories 1 and 2

1 What process means linking new information to an existing schema? **[1]**

2 What is the name for the fourth stage of Piaget's theory? **[1]**

3 Draw lines to match the terms with their definitions. **[4]**

A | Accommodation   i) | Focusing only on one aspect of a problem

B | Centration   ii) | Thinking which focuses on the self

C | Egocentrism   iii) | Understanding that properties remain the same despite a superficial transformation

D | Conservation   iv) | Changing a schema or developing a new one

4 What is the name of the developmental stage where the child focuses on interacting with physical objects? Shade **one** box only. **[1]**

A Sensorimotor ◯   B Pre-operational ◯

C Concrete operational ◯   D Formal operational ◯

5 What is the name of the developmental stage where the child becomes less egocentric? Shade **one** box only. **[1]**

A Sensorimotor ⬭   B Pre-operational ⬭

C Concrete operational ⬭   D Formal operational ⬭

6 Describe **one** experiment that has been used to criticise Piaget's theories. **[4]**

7 Discuss likely reasons behind the following situation, according to the theories of Piaget. **[3]**

> Stella is four years old. She has been playing with Fiona, who is the same age as herself, using colourful bricks to represent cars in a game. When Stella saw that her friend was playing with her favourite blue brick, she grabbed it. Her dad told her to apologise, but she cried and refused to do so.

The Effects of Learning on Development

1 What name is given to the controversial theory that everyone has their own most effective way of learning (verbal, visual or kinaesthetic)? **[1]**

2 An important developmental theory includes the concepts of growth and fixed mindsets.

a) Explain the theory. **[4]**

b) Briefly explain one piece of supporting evidence. **[2]**

3 Give **two** reasons why Willingham does not agree with learning styles theory. **[2]**

4 What term means a person's belief about how good or bad they are at something? **[1]**

5 Mehul says, "I'm not good at drawing, but I plan to take an art class and improve my skills." Which type of mindset is shown in this example? Give a reason for your answer. **[2]**

6 Read the following text. What factors or theories could help to explain Andy's study behaviour? **[3]**

> Andy is a Year 10 student. He has been told that he is a visual learner, and is therefore trying to learn a Shakespeare play using a flow chart on a large piece of paper. His psychology teacher has told him that while he might prefer visual information, using this alone will not help him to learn better. Instead, it would be best to combine his flow chart with verbal information such as quotations from the play. Andy replies that there is no point in trying too hard at it, because he's bad at English anyway.

Sampling Methods

1 Which type of sampling involves selecting participants who are easily available? **[1]**

2 Read the text. Which sampling method is being used? **[1]**

> A researcher decides to select participants from a university corridor. She randomly chooses a starting point and time, and then selects every 20th person who walks along, asking them if they are willing to take part.

3 Complete the sentences by choosing the best words from the selection below. You do not have to use all the words. **[3]**

representative	generalising	small	large	inferring	reminiscent

It is important to be able to conclude that findings from a sample will also be true of the

target population. Researchers call this _____ the results from the sample to

the population. This is only valid when a sample is _____ of the target

population as whole – in other words, it has similar characteristics. A _____

sample helps to reduces the effect of variation within the sample.

4 What term is used to describe the group of people from which a sample is selected? **[1]**

5 Student researchers sometimes select a sample by asking their friends to take part in an experiment. Explain **two** ways in which such a sample might be biased. **[2]**

Variables and Hypotheses

1 What is the name of the prediction that a researcher makes at the outset of an experiment? **[1]**

2 Complete the following sentence. **[1]**

Researchers manipulate one variable – the _____ variable – and measure the

level of another variable, which is known as the _____ variable.

3 Explain what is meant by experimental control. **[3]**

4   Draw lines to match the terms with their definitions.   **[3]**

A	Normal distribution	**i)**	Any variable that the researcher aims to keep constant/controlled
B	Cause and effect	**ii)**	Set of data where the middle values are common, while more extreme ones are rarer
C	EV	**iii)**	A relationship where changing one variable results in another variable changing

5   A researcher makes the prediction below at the start of an experiment. What term is used for this type of prediction?   **[1]**

> If listening to classical music has a beneficial effect on memory, then participants who study with background classical music will remember more facts in a test than participants who do not.

Design of Experiments 1 and 2

1   Name the research design where all participants take part in every condition of the experiment.   **[1]**

2   Tick (✓) or cross (✗) the statements about research ethics to indicate whether they are true or false.   **[4]**

Statements about research ethics	True (✓) or false (✗)?
Participant data must be kept confidential.	
Once participants have given consent, they can't back out.	
Harm can include psychological harm, distress or embarrassment.	
The usual practice is to get informed consent at the end of a study.	

3   A researcher wishes to study the memory of university students, and carries out a memory experiment in a university library. What kind of experiment is this?   **[1]**

4 Complete the sentences by choosing the best words from the selection below. You do not have to use all the words. **[3]**

order	conditions	experiments	control	counterbalancing	ethical

With a repeated measures design, ＿＿＿＿＿＿＿＿＿ effects could bias the results. This is

when participants improve or get worse at a task as they complete two or more conditions.

To avoid this happening, the order of conditions is balanced so participants do not all complete

the conditions in the same order as each other. This is known as ＿＿＿＿＿＿＿. An equal

proportion of the participants is divided among the ＿＿＿＿＿＿＿, each doing them in

a particular assigned order.

Non-experimental Methods

1 Which non-experimental research methods involve asking questions about people's thoughts and behaviour? **[2]**

2 Complete the sentences by choosing the best words from the selection below. You do not have to use all the words. **[3]**

reliability	naturalistic	validity	categories	examples	participant

Observation involves studying behaviour as it happens. Often this involves a ＿＿＿＿＿＿＿

observation in an everyday context such as a participant's workplace. An observation study will

typically set out ＿＿＿＿＿＿＿ of behaviour in advance, and the observer will use a

checklist to record these when they occur. However, a single observer may make errors, so studies

often use two or more observers. Inter-observer ＿＿＿＿＿＿＿ means the extent to

which different observers record the same data from the same observation.

3 "What do you like to do in your free time?" What type of data would be obtained from answers to this question? **[1]**

4 Define the following types of data that are gathered in psychology research. [4]

   a) Quantitative data   b) Qualitative data

   c) Primary data   d) Secondary data

5 Name the **two** types of questions that are used in interviews and questionnaires, and write an example of each. [4]

Correlation and Data Handling

1 Briefly explain how the mean is calculated. [1]

2 Describe how a bar chart might be used in psychology research. [2]

3 Complete the sentences by choosing the best words from the selection below. You do not have to use all the words. [4]

along	stronger	closed	upward	spread	direction

A scatter graph shows the strength of the correlation between two variables – the

_____ the relationship, the closer the points are to forming a line on the

graph, while weaker correlations appear _____ out. It also shows the

_____ of a relationship. If one co-variable increases as the other decreases, this is

called a negative correlation. A positive correlation will appear as a pattern on the graph which

moves _____ from left to right.

4 Describe the correlations shown in Graphs A–C. [3]

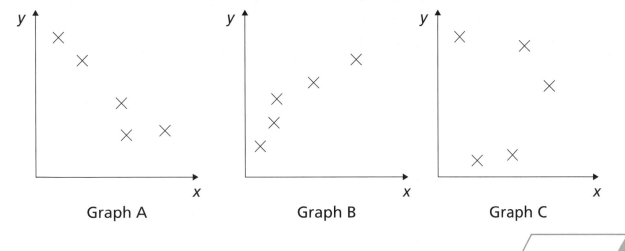

Graph A   Graph B   Graph C

Conformity

Quick Recall Quiz

You must be able to:

- Explain how social factors (group size, anonymity and task difficulty) affect conformity to majority influence
- Explain how dispositional factors (personality, expertise) affect conformity to majority influence
- Describe dispositional factors affecting conformity
- Describe Asch's study of conformity.

Factors Affecting Conformity to Majority Influence

- Conformity is a type of social influence involving a change in belief or behaviour in order to fit in with a group.
- In the line study conducted by Asch (1951), it was discovered that people are likely to give the obviously wrong answer to a question if the majority also give the same wrong answer.
- However, a number of factors can affect levels of conformity.
  - Dispositional factors:

The presence of an ally	Asch found that it often took only one of the confederates to agree with the participant for them to go against the majority's inaccurate judgements. The more allies there were, the less likely the participant was to conform to the group. This lack of unanimity reduces the chances of the participant succumbing to normative conformity (seeking the approval of the group or the 'desire to be liked').
The size of the majority	The more confederates there were who made incorrect judgements, the more likely the participant was to conform.
Anonymity	If participants were allowed to give their answers in private, then they were less likely to conform to the majority.
Task difficulty	When a task becomes more difficult or the answer more ambiguous, levels of conformity increase because people are much more likely to adopt the views of others in the group.

  - Social factors:

Personality	People who were introduced to the concept of rebellion prior to the experiment were less likely to conform, indicating that personality might play a role.
Expertise	If people were considered an expert in the field relating to the task, conforming with the expert was more likely, regardless of whether they were giving the correct answer.

Asch's Study of Conformity

- **Aim:** The line study was conducted by Asch in order to investigate the extent to which social pressure from a majority could influence the likelihood that a person would conform.
- **Procedure:** Participants were required to look at a 'target' line drawn on a card and compare it to three lines drawn on another card. They had to say which line was the same length as the target line.
  - Two of the lines on the comparison card were obviously wrong and one was obviously right.
  - Only one of the participants was genuine; the others were confederates of the experimenter who had been told to give the wrong answer.
  - The genuine participant was usually one of the last to give their judgement so that they could hear the answers given by the confederates.
- **Results:** 75 per cent of participants gave the wrong answer at least once. If one or more of the confederates gave the same answer as the participant, the participant was less likely to give the wrong answer.
- **Conclusions:** Participants often conformed to the group's answers even though they were obviously wrong.

Strengths
• The study was highly controlled and was therefore able to establish a very clear pattern of conformity by most of the participants in one or more of the trials. • Results have been replicated several times, so the study is reliable.

Weaknesses
• The study can be criticised on ethical grounds because the participants often displayed stress reactions as they struggled to decide what answer they were going to give. • The study was carried out in a laboratory setting, in order to control variables. We cannot be sure that the behaviour displayed is typical of that seen in real life.

Key Point

Asch used deception in his study. This raises ethical issues.

Quick Test

1. What is meant by conformity to majority influence?
2. Who conducted the 1951 study into conformity to majority influence?
3. What percentage of participants conformed at least once?

Key Words

conformity
confederate
normative conformity

Obedience

Quick Recall Quiz

You must be able to:

- Describe Milgram's agency theory of social factors, including agency, authority, culture and proximity
- Explain dispositional factors affecting obedience, including Adorno's theory of the authoritarian personality.

Social Factors Affecting Obedience

- Obedience to authority is defined as responding as instructed to a direct order.
- Milgram (1963) was interested in researching how far people would go to obey an instruction if it involved harming another person. He deceived participants into thinking that they were administering dangerous electric shocks to people because an authority figure told them to.
- Milgram found that the majority of people were willing to follow instructions given by an authority figure, even when those instructions involved inflicting harm on another. He found that 65% of participants were willing to administer the highest level of electric shock (450 volts) and all participants continued to 300 volts.
- There were, however, a number of factors that impacted this behaviour.

> **Key Point**
>
> Obedience might involve doing something that you would prefer not to do, or even something you believe to be wrong.

Proximity	People are more likely to harm another person when given an instruction to do so if they cannot see the other person. For example, Milgram found that if a learner and the teacher were in separate rooms, the teacher was more likely to obey an instruction to shock the learner. However, if the learner was seated directly opposite them, obedience levels dropped.
Authority	People are more likely to inflict harm on another person if they believe the person giving the instruction is an authority figure. In the Milgram study, the teacher was much more likely to shock the learner if the researcher wore a lab coat.
Culture	Levels of obedience change between cultures. For example, studies have found higher levels of conformity in more authoritarian cultures (e.g. Japan) and lower levels in less authoritarian cultures (e.g. Australia).
Agency theory	Milgram suggests that people have two states of behaviour when they are in social situations: **autonomous** and **agentic**. Agency theory suggests that people go into an agentic state when they feel they are acting on behalf of others. The person assumes the person giving the orders will take responsibility and therefore they take none and follow blindly. Acting autonomously is where people behave independently and do take responsibility for their own actions.

Autonomous and Agentic States

- In an autonomous state, people feel personally responsible for their actions.
- In an agentic state, people allow others to direct their actions and they no longer feel responsible for their behaviour, as their actions are attributed to the person giving the instructions.
- In the Milgram experiment, many of the participants felt that they were simply carrying out the instructions given to them. In other words, they were only following orders.

  - Agency theory could be seen as excusing people for their behaviour and it has been claimed that survivors of the Holocaust could have been offended that the behaviour of the Nazis was minimised in this way.
  - The suggestion that all of the soldiers carrying out orders was because someone told them to do it and they simply obeyed feeling no responsibility for their own actions, could be offensive.
  - This reason of acting as an agent, was used in some of the war crime trials, but Milgram's theory is questioned as to whether that many Nazis were all following orders, without examining the role of prejudice and racism that was prevalent in Germany at that time.

Dispositional Factors Affecting Obedience

- Dispositional factors are factors about the individual, such as personality.
- **Adorno** (1950) suggested that people who have an **authoritarian** personality display higher levels of obedience to authority.

  - Adorno developed a questionnaire known as the F-scale (F for fascist) to identify those with an authoritarian personality.
  - Adorno claimed personality and attitudes stem from childhood influences, with parents who enforce high levels of discipline more likely raising children with an authoritarian personality.

- Elms and Milgram (1966) replicated Milgram's original study with participants who had completed the F-scale finding a correlation between obedience and authoritarian personality type.

  - As this was a correlational study, we cannot be sure that personality type was the cause of higher levels of obedience.
  - The questionnaire is easily manipulated and it's likely that many people will be able to second guess the questions to avoid being categorised as authoritarian.
  - The F-scale correlates highly with levels of education, so the results can also be explained on an educational level rather than a dispositional one.

Quick Test

1. What is meant by obedience to authority?
2. Who conducted the 1963 study into obedience?
3. Who developed the theory of the authoritarian personality?

Key Words

autonomous
agentic
Adorno
authoritarian

Crowd Psychology and Collective Behaviour

You must be able to:

- Describe and explain bystander behaviour
- Describe and explain prosocial and antisocial behaviour in crowds
- Explain how social factors and dispositional factors affect collective behaviour
- Describe and evaluate the Piliavin *et al.* (1969) study.

Prosocial Behaviour

- Prosocial behaviour refers to the positive impact of human actions.
- One particular form of prosocial behaviour is **bystander intervention**.

Factors Affecting Bystander Intervention

Presence of Others

- Presence of others can affect bystander intervention as the more people present, the less likely they are to help. This is called **bystander effect**.

Expertise and Similarity to Victim

- If other people present do not perceive the situation to be an emergency, people are less likely to help.
- People are more likely to help if the victim is similar in a number of ways to the helper (e.g. race, gender).
- People are more likely to help if they feel they have the expertise to deal with the situation (e.g. an off-duty medical professional).

Cost of Helping

- If the cost of helping outweighs the benefits, people are less likely to help (e.g. if helping is time-consuming or it could put the helper in danger).

Piliavin's Subway Study

- Piliavin *et al.* (1969) investigated bystander behaviour on the New York subway.
- Students acted out a scene where one of them (the 'victim') collapsed on a subway train.
- The victim was sometimes black and sometimes white, acted drunk, or used a cane, or appeared to be ill.
- In some versions, one of the team would go and help the victim.
- Two members of the team observed the reactions of the other passengers on the train.
- Piliavin found that people were more likely to help if the victim was ill or carried a cane and less likely to help if they were drunk.
- There was also a slight tendency to help those of the same race.

> **Key Point**
>
> Bystander behaviour refers to the way a person acts when they witness an emergency.

Bystander behaviour

- The presence of others does not always have a negative effect on helping behaviour.
- When real-life emergencies occur lots of people get involved and help out. The cost of helping may be affected more by the seriousness of a situation, if it's deemed an emergency, rather than a cost to the helper.
- Similarity to the victim is also questioned as to whether that does influence someone helping or not. Again in emergency situations, such as 9/11, people helped regardless of potential similarities.
- Expertise of helpers can affect the quality of help given in an emergency, but the decision to help in real-life situations does not seem to be affected by the level of expertise.

How Social and Dispositional Factors Affect Collective Behaviour

Identification: This is when people act collectively because they identify with a group in some way. For example, because they all support the same football team or like the same music and have a 'dress code' where the identification comes into play.

Deindividuation: This is when the presence of a crowd or group leads to the loss of sense of individual identity. Deindividuation leads people to follow group norms rather than individual norms. It can lead to people acting more aggressively when they are part of a crowd.

Social loafing: This is where individuals put in less effort when there's a larger group than when they are on their own. For example, students singing in assembly don't put in much effort which they would if they were singing solo or in a duet.

Culture: This refers to the ideas and customs of a group or society that influence the behaviour of the people that are part of that group.

How a Social Factor's Deindividuation Affects Collective Behaviour

- **Deindividuation** is when the presence of a crowd or group leads to the loss of sense of individual identity.
- Deindividuation leads people to follow group norms rather than individual norms. It can lead to people acting more aggressively when they are part of a crowd.
- Zimbardo (1969) replicated Milgram's electric shock study into obedience but participants either wore a name badge or had their faces concealed with a hood. Those wearing the hoods gave more shocks than those with name badges, supporting the idea of deindividuation.
- The theory of deindividuation can also be used to reduce aggression, e.g. by installing CCTV cameras at football matches.
- Deindividuation in crowds can also lead to prosocial behaviour, for instance at religious gatherings.
- People might also exert less effort when part of a crowd than when they are acting as an individual, a process known as **social loafing**.
- Dispositional factors play a role in how people will behave.
  - For example, people with aggressive personalities are more likely to engage in acts of violence when in a group situation.

Key Point

Crowds can act in both prosocial and antisocial ways, depending on the circumstances. For example, personality can impact on pro- and antisocial behaviour. People with an internal locus of control take responsibility for their own behaviour and are less likely to act in an antisocial way. Someone who is highly moral may be more likely to act upon their own volition regardless of the group behaviour.

Key Point

Social loafing is likely to be affected by culture. For example, in collectivist cultures the needs of the group are taken into account when making decisions. The opposite may be true in individualistic cultures where self-interest may impact on decisions, without thinking of others.

Quick Test

1. What is meant by bystander behaviour?
2. Who conducted the subway study?
3. Define deindividuation.
4. Name one way a government might try to reduce the incidences of antisocial behaviour at football matches.

Key Words

bystander intervention
bystander effect
deindividuation
social loafing

Where space is not provided, write your answers on a separate piece of paper.

Sampling Methods

1 Explain what is meant by a sample being biased. **[2]**

2 State **one** important principle that must be met in order for a sample to be truly random. **[1]**

3 Complete the following sentences. **[2]**

One flaw with systematic sampling is that there could be pre-existing biases in the target

population/list of names that stop the sample from being ....

To select a random sample from a numbered list of everyone in the target population,

a researcher might use a computer to pick ....

4 Explain what is meant by a stratified sample, and give a strength and a weakness of this sampling method. **[4]**

5 Which of the following sampling methods is likely to involve numbering members of the population? Shade **one** box only. **[1]**

A Random sampling ⬡　　　B Opportunity sampling ⬡

C Systematic sampling ⬡　　　D Stratified sampling ⬡

6 Which of the following sampling methods is simplest to carry out? Shade **one** box only. **[1]**

A Random sampling ⬡　　　B Opportunity sampling ⬡

C Systematic sampling ⬡　　　D Stratified sampling ⬡

7 Write down the terms that best match the statements. **[4]**

Statement	Term
a) Selecting participants to take part in a study	
b) The group of people who are studied	
c) Concluding that findings also apply to the target population	
d) Flaws in a sample, which mean some characteristics are not representative of the target population	

Variables and Hypotheses

1 What term is used to refer to different parts of an experiment, each of which links to a different value of the independent variable? **[1]**

2 What is the name of the variable that a researcher measures? Give an example. **[2]**

3 Complete the sentences by choosing the best words from the selection below. You do not have to use all the words. **[4]**

manipulates	blocks	IV	DV	cause-and-effect	bias	correlational

In psychology experiments, a researcher _____ or changes the value of the

independent variable and measures the value of the dependent variable. An experiment

therefore looks for a _____ relationship between these two variables. The values

of the _____ relate to the two or more conditions of the experiment. The scores

on the _____ form the data that a researcher gathers and analyses.

4 State **two** characteristics of a normally distributed variable. **[2]**

5 Read the text. Then state what the **three** conditions of the independent variable are. **[3]**

> In an experiment into the spacing effect in memory, 24 Year 8 students learn a set of French words on Monday. Eight of them revise the words later the same day, eight revise the words the following day, and the remaining eight pupils revise them the following Monday. All of them are tested later that month.

6 What is the name of the variable that a researcher manipulates in an experiment? Shade **one** box only. **[1]**

A Independent variable ○   B Dependent variable ○

C Extraneous variable ○   D Controlled variable ○

7 What is the name of the prediction of what will be found if the alternative hypothesis is **not** supported by the data in an experiment? Shade **one** box only. **[1]**

A Extraneous prediction ○   B Cause-and-effect prediction ○

C Null hypothesis ○   D Experimental hypothesis ○

8 Discuss the likely extraneous variables which could affect the following experiment. **[4]**

> A researcher is studying the effect of pictures on memory by giving students visual and verbal tasks. The experiment is carried out in the school cafeteria.
>
> Students are given a set of sentences to study. One group is given sentences only. The other is given the same sentences but each one has a picture that goes with it. Some sentences are about planets of the solar system, and others are about famous sports stars – the choice of sentences is random.
>
> Both groups are given as long as they like to study the items, and then given a short memory test.
>
> Some participants take part in the experiment when they first arrive at school in the morning, and others take part during their lunch hour.

Design of Experiments 1 and 2

1 What term is used in research to mean treating participants fairly and in accordance with their rights? **[1]**

2 Which ethical consideration means that participants cannot be given incomplete information at the start of a study? Shade **one** box only. **[1]**

A Informed consent ◯ B Right to withdraw ◯

C Avoiding harm ◯ D Debriefing ◯

3 Which of the following is **not** an ethical issue in research? Shade **one** box only. **[1]**

A Right to withdraw ◯ B Avoiding harm ◯

C Confidentiality ◯ D Control ◯

4 A researcher carries out a study into perception, where participants are asked to view an illusion with or without a backing colour. Everyone does condition 1 first and then condition 2. What problem could occur, and how could the researcher have avoided this? **[2]**

5 A researcher wishes to study the effects of caffeine on how well university students can concentrate when watching a lecture. Explain how this could be done either as a field experiment or as a lab experiment. Give your view on which experimental design should be used. **[4]**

6 Complete the table. [4]

Design	Description	Weakness
Repeated measures design		
Independent groups design		

7 Why is it important to randomly allocate participants to conditions in an independent groups design? [2]

8 What name is given to an experimental condition that is used purely for comparison? [1]

Non-experimental Methods

1 Explain what is meant by a closed question and state a research method that might use one. [2]

2 Researchers gather different types of data in psychology.

    a) Name a research method that gathers primary data. [1]

    b) Name a research method that gathers secondary data. [1]

3 Give a strength and a weakness of the observation method. [2]

4 Tick (✓) or cross (✗) the statements about non-experimental methods to indicate whether they are true or false. [4]

Statements about non-experimental methods	True (✓) or false (✗)?
Non-experimental methods always obtain qualitative data.	
For ethical reasons, it is important to inform and gain consent from participants who are being observed.	
Surveys only used closed questions.	
Case studies only use secondary data.	

5 Which of the following is an example of secondary data? Shade **one** box only. [1]

A School reports   ◯   **B** Observations   ◯

C Brain scans   ◯   **D** Ability tests   ◯

6 Which of the following research activities would obtain qualitative data? Shade **one** box only. **[1]**

A A survey with closed questions ⬚ **B** A checklist used in an observation ⬚

C An interview with open questions ⬚ **D** An IQ test ⬚

7 A researcher is studying an individual with an accidental brain injury. Discuss the different research methods or techniques that might be involved, and any other data that should be gathered. **[3]**

8 Explain why observation studies often use more than one observer. **[2]**

Correlation and Data Handling

1 How is the range calculated, and what does it show? **[2]**

2 A researcher placed all of the scores from one experimental condition in order. Then he identified which score was at the midpoint of this set of data. Which statistic was he calculating? Shade **one** box only. **[1]**

A The mean ⬚ **B** The mode ⬚

C The median ⬚ **D** The range ⬚

3 What term is used to describe the correlation that is shown when dots on a scatter graph are randomly spread out, with no discernible pattern? Shade **one** box only. **[1]**

A Strong correlation ⬚ **B** Zero correlation ⬚

C Weak correlation ⬚ **D** Negative correlation ⬚

4 Explain the difference between a bar chart and a histogram. **[2]**

5 Explain the difference between a weak correlation and a negative correlation. **[2]**

6 Read the following text. Explain the **two** types of data used and how they would be analysed. Give a possible hypothesis for the study. **[5]**

> A researcher is studying the relationship between the number of books read per year and a child's grades at school. After gaining parental consent, the research team surveys 50 school children about their reading habits. They also obtain school grades via the head teacher.

7 On the graph below, sketch a strong (but not perfect) positive correlation. Label the axes 'Study time' and 'Average grade'. [2]

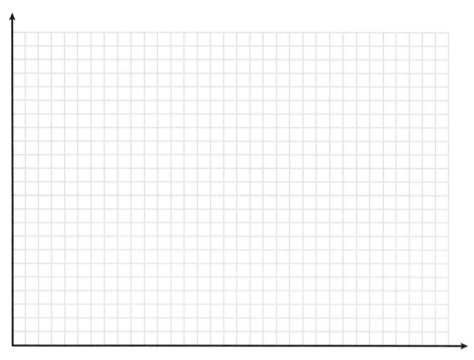

8 Complete the sentences by choosing the best words from the selection below. You do not have to use all the words. [5]

multiplying	middle	four	dividing	two	mean	common

It is important to be able to express an average score from a set of data. The

_____ is calculated by adding up the sum of all scores in a set of data and

then _____ by the number of scores. The median is calculated by placing all

the scores in order, from low to high, and then selecting the _____ score.

With even numbers of scores, the mean of the _____ middle scores is calculated.

Finally, the mode is obtained by identifying the most _____ score in a set

of data.

Where space is not provided, write your answers on a separate piece of paper.

Conformity

1   Why are people less likely to conform if they give their answers in private?   [2]

_____

2   Your maths teacher asks the class a difficult question. Susan, who is very good at maths, gives an answer that you know is wrong but when the teacher asks another student they give the same wrong answer. When it comes to your turn to answer, you give the same answer as Susan. Using your knowledge of conformity, explain why you gave the wrong answer.   [4]

_____

_____

3   Asch conducted his study of conformity in 1951.

a) Describe the procedure of Asch's line study.   [6]

_____

_____

b) The participants in the Asch study often displayed stress reactions as they struggled to decide what answer they were going to give. Why is this a weakness of the study?   [2]

_____

c) What was the advantage of carrying out the study in a laboratory setting?   [1]

_____

d) What was the conclusion of the Asch study?   [2]

_____

Obedience

1   A researcher ran an experiment about obedience. An actor asked people to pick up litter in a park: in Condition A the actor wore a uniform and in Condition B the actor wore casual clothes. Levels of obedience were higher in Condition A than in Condition B.

Use your knowledge of psychology to explain why the level of obedience was different in Condition A and Condition B. **[2]**

2 In Milgram's experiment, levels of obedience were higher when the study was conducted at the university than in a venue in town. Why might this be? **[2]**

3 What did Milgram discover about proximity? **[1]**

4 Describe what Milgram meant by agency. **[2]**

5 What does the F-scale measure? **[1]**

6 What did Elms and Milgram discover about the link between authoritarian personality and obedience? **[1]**

Crowd Psychology and Collective Behaviour

1 Outline what is meant by the term bystander behaviour. **[1]**

2 Identify **one** factor that can influence bystander behaviour. **[1]**

3 Describe the procedure of Piliavin and Rodin's subway study into bystander behaviour. **[4]**

4 Describe **one** study that investigated deindividuation. **[4]**

5 Deindividuation is universal. What is meant by this statement? **[2]**

The Possible Relationship Between Language and Thought

Quick Recall Quiz

You must be able to:

- Explain Piaget's theory of language and thought
- Explain the Sapir-Whorf hypothesis
- Describe how language and thought affect our view of the world.

Language Depends on Thought (Piaget)

- We discussed Jean Piaget (1896–1980) in the Development section, pages 36–39. He indicated that development takes place in a number of stages and that language development is the result of cognitive (or thought) development.
- According to Piaget, a child must first be able to use ideas and concepts before being able to use language. A child might use and repeat words before understanding the concepts behind these words. Piaget called this egocentric speech.
- The purpose of adult communication is to convey ideas and information. A child must be able to understand what specific words are used for before applying them to communication.
- This can be seen in the link between impaired cognitive development in children and impaired language development.
- However, some children have severe learning difficulties but normal language development, suggesting that language development isn't dependent on cognitive development.
- Some studies have found that language development can accelerate cognitive development.

Thinking Depends on Language (Sapir-Whorf Hypothesis)

- Language influences the way people perceive and think about the world.
- There are two types of Sapir-Whorf hypothesis:
  - The strong version says that language determines thought.
  - The weak version says that language influences thought.
- Differences between languages determine the types of thoughts people are able to have.
- There are certain thoughts an individual has in one language that cannot be understood by those who live in a society that uses a different language.
- The way people think is strongly affected by their native language.

> ### Key Point
>
> There are two main theories concerned with the relationship between language and thought. Piaget's theory states that language determines thought, while the Sapir-Whorf hypothesis suggests that thinking is dependent on language.

Language and Memory

- The Sapir-Whorf hypothesis suggests that language influences the way in which people remember events.
- Carmichael (1932) showed a series of nonsense pictures to two groups of participants.
  - The pictures were paired with a label but the label was different for each group.
  - When asked to draw the picture from memory, it was found that the label had influenced the participants' memory of it.

Colour Recognition

Zuni Tribe

- The Zuni (a Native American tribe) only use one term for the yellow-orange region of the colour spectrum.
- When Zuni participants were shown a coloured chip and asked to locate the chip amongst other chips, they performed better if there was a simple colour name (e.g. red) rather than a mixture of red and blue.

Himba Tribe

- Goldstein studied the Himba tribe of northern Namibia, who have the same word for green and blue (bura).
- However, the Himba use different words to distinguish between shades of green (dambu for light green; zuzu for dark green).
- When members of the Himba were shown 11 green squares and 1 blue square, they had difficulty indicating which square was the odd one out.
- When they were shown 12 green squares, 1 of which was a lighter green, they had no problem identifying the odd one out.
- These studies support the Sapir-Whorf hypothesis because they show if the tribes had no words for the colours they were shown, they were unable to think about which colour was the odd one out.
- This was the case for the Himba people suggesting that language comes before thinking, as the hypothesis suggests.

> **Key Point**
>
> Language can influence other cognitive functions such as memory and perception.

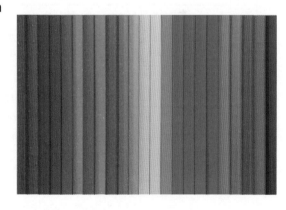

Quick Test

1. What are the two main theories of language and thought?
2. What is meant by egocentric speech?
3. Who studied the Himba tribe?

Differences Between Human and Animal Communication

Quick Recall Quiz

You must be able to:

- Describe the limited functions of animal communication
- Describe Von Frisch's bee study
- Explain the difference between animal and human communication.

Limited Functions of Animal Communication

- Non-human animals use communication as a survival tool, which results in greater simplicity of use.
- For non-human animals, communication is necessary for aspects of survival such as:
  - mate selection
  - defending or expanding territory
  - finding food
  - warning against danger.

Reproduction	Communication is used to attract the attention of a future mate for reproduction or to solidify pair-bonds. Many non-human male animals communicate their superiority over other males through their plumage (e.g. peacocks) or other attributes. Male birds of paradise engage in a complex dance in order to attract females.
Territory	Signals are used to defend or to claim territory. Territorial signals include song in birds, leaving markings on trees (e.g. the wild boar) or scenting territory using urine (e.g. dogs).
Food	Food calls are used to inform the group that food has been found (e.g. the 'waggle dance' of the honeybee).
Survival	For example, wolves howl to both let the pack know where they are and to signal that the pack should stay away.
	Signals are used to communicate the threat of a predator. One example is the magpie, who uses its distinctive 'chattering' to warn other magpies against predators, while rabbits thump with their paws.

Key Point

Non-human animals use communication for survival.

Von Frisch's Bee Study

- As mentioned earlier, honeybees communicate information about the location of pollen-rich flowers via what is known as the 'waggle dance'.
- The movements involved in the waggle dance were first translated by Karl Von Frisch.

- Aim: To describe dances performed by bees to show how they use this to communicate with each other.
- Procedure: Von Frisch observed bees in their natural environment, over a twenty-year period making over 6000 observations. He also manipulated the environment by moving food both closer and further away from the hives to see if this affected the bees' behaviour.
- Results: Von Frisch observed that when a foraging honeybee returned to the hive after finding pollen and nectar, it performed a series of intricate movements that are collectively known as the 'waggle dance'. Through body movements and vibrations, the bee communicates the direction and distance of the food relative to the position of the sun. The more plentiful the food source, the longer the duration the the dance.
- Conclusions: Von Frisch's research demonstrated that honeybees are capable of communication, providing information about the location of food sources to other members of the colony.
- Evaluations: Von Frisch advanced our understanding of animal communication, navigation, and sensory perception which has wider implications for the study of communication in animals.

Properties of Human Communication not Present in Animal Communication

- Human communication consists of both signals and **symbols**.
- Symbols are sounds, **gestures**, material objects or written words that have a specific meaning to a group of people.
- Key differences between human communication and that of other primates is that humans have an **open vocal system** and a larger bank of symbols to use in communication.
- Communication in non-human animals tends to occur within the present tense and is related to real-world information such as status, food, territory and mate availability.
- Human communication, on the other hand, generally uses past, present and future tense, allowing them to talk about past events, plan ahead and discuss future events.
- Human communication also allows for the discussion of possible future outcomes based on present situations and expected outcomes.

> **Key Point**
>
> Communication in both animals and humans consists of signals. Symbols are sounds or gestures that have meaning to those using them.

Quick Test

1. What is the main purpose of communication in non-human animals?
2. Who conducted the study into communication in honeybees?
3. What is the name of the behaviour honeybees use to communicate the location of food?

> **Key Words**
>
> symbols
> gestures
> open vocal system

Non-verbal Communication

You must be able to:

- Describe the differences between verbal and non-verbal communication
- Explain the importance of eye contact, including regulating flow of conversation, signalling attraction and expressing emotion
- Describe other types of non-verbal communication, including open and closed postures, and postural echo and touch
- Explain the factors that affect personal space, including cultural status and gender differences.

Verbal and Non-verbal Communication

- Verbal communication is a type of communication that uses words.
  - Words can be spoken, written or produced using sign language.
- Non-verbal communication is a type of communication that doesn't rely on spoken or written words.
  - It can include body posture or gestures.
  - It can also include certain aspects of language such as tone of voice (rather than the meaning of the words spoken). These are known as **paralinguistics**.

> **Key Point**
>
> Non-verbal communication doesn't rely on spoken or written words.

Functions of Eye Contact

- The functions of eye contact include regulating the flow of conversation, signalling attraction and expressing emotion.
- According to Argyle, eye contact regulates the flow of information in a number of ways.
- **Information seeking:** During a conversation, we obtain immediate feedback on the reactions of the listener by gazing at the face, and the eyes in particular.
  - Looking away can signal to the speaker that the listener isn't interested.
  - Breaking eye contact when listening can mean that the listener wishes to speak.
  - Looking away from the listener can help the speaker to filter out unnecessary information.
- **Signalling attraction:** Eye contact is used to let someone know we may find them attractive. It is often one of the first ways we can communicate our attraction towards someone. Researchers have suggested that eye contact is an evolutionary behaviour to attract a mate.
- **Expressing emotions:** Eye contact is linked to emotional intimacy. Rubin found that couples who scored highly on measures of love also spent longer in mutual eye contact.

Body Language

- Body language involves a number of **postural** behaviours, including open and closed posture, postural echo and touch.

An **open posture**	Revealing and leaves sensitive areas vulnerable. The head is usually slightly back, the chin slightly raised, arms by the side and the legs uncrossed.
A **closed posture**	Often seen as defensive and protecting. Hands are held up to the chin or the head is lowered to protect the throat; arms and legs are crossed.
Postural echo	The mirroring or the adoption of the same posture as the person doing the talking. This encourages mutual positive feelings.
Touch	Communicates emotion. Studies have found that when nurses speak to patients they also touch them. This shows sympathy and understanding.

Personal Space

- Personal space is an imaginary area that people view as their own territory.
- When personal space is invaded, people react to it in a number of ways, including feeling uncomfortable and adjusting their own position in order to regain territory.
- Factors affecting personal space include cultural norms, gender and status.

- Hall (1914–2009) found that personal space differs between cultures (e.g. people in South America stand closer to each other than those in the United States).
- Heshka and Nelson (1972) found that when they are strangers, females stand further apart than males.
- People of a similar status tend to stand closer together, while those of a different status stand further way.

> ### Key Point
> Personal space can differ from culture to culture. It can also vary between men and women. The status of an individual also plays a role in personal space.

> ### Key Point
> Elements of non-verbal communication include eye contact, body language and the use of personal space.

> ### Key Words
> paralinguistics
> posture
> open posture
> closed posture
> postural echo

Quick Test

1. What is meant by non-verbal communication?
2. What are the main functions of eye contact?
3. What is meant by open posture?
4. What is meant by closed posture?

Explanations of Non-verbal Behaviour

Quick Recall Quiz

You must be able to:

- Understand Darwin's evolutionary theory of non-verbal communication
- Describe evidence that supports the view that non-verbal behaviour is innate
- Describe evidence that supports the view that non-verbal behaviour is learned
- Discuss Yuki's study of emotions.

Darwin's Evolutionary Theory of Non-verbal Communication

- Charles Darwin (1809–1882) believed that non-verbal communication was an **evolutionary** mechanism; in other words, it is evolved and **adaptive**. He said that species that adapt in order to fit an ever changing environment, are the ones most likely to survive and reproduce.
- All mammals (both human and non-human) show emotions through facial expression and that non-verbal communication has evolved as a way of expressing emotions. This behaviour is universal and, therefore, evolutionary.
- Types of non-verbal behaviour persist in humans because they have been acquired for their value throughout evolutionary history.
- Non-verbal behaviour is therefore **innate** – it is something that we are born with.
- Darwin's theory takes the side of nature in the nature–nurture debate because it argues that non-verbal behaviour is not learned from the environment.
- Facial expressions such as anger and happiness have been shown to be universal, which shows support for Darwin's theory as it would suggest they are innate.
- Our nervous system has been shown to be responsible for some non-verbal communication such as pupil dilation, which supports the theory that these non-verbal behaviours are innate.
- However social learning theory would propose that humans imitate through observation and therefore non-verbal behaviour would be transmitted culturally, as seen in the study of emoticons (Yuki *et al.*, 2007).

Evidence that Non-verbal Behaviour is Innate

- Some scientists believe that non-verbal behaviour is innate.
- Children who have been blind since birth still display the same facial expressions as sighted children.

Key Point

Charles Darwin suggested that all non-verbal communication is evolutionary, but other scientists believe that non-verbal communication is learned.

- Matsumoto and Willingham (2009) studied sighted and blind judo athletes and found that both groups produced the same facial expressions in certain emotional situations.
- This supports the evolutionary theory of non-verbal behaviour.

Evidence that Non-verbal Behaviour is Learned

- Other scientists believe that non-verbal behaviour is a learned response.
- In other words, non-verbal behaviour develops as a response to observing and imitating people within one's own culture (e.g. shaking hands, kissing on the cheek or bowing).
- Yuki *et al.* (2007) conducted a cross-cultural study using American and Japanese participants.

  - Each participant was shown a number of emoticons with different emotional expressions and asked to rate them from very sad to very happy.
  - Japanese participants gave higher ratings to those emoticons with happier eyes while Americans rated happy mouths higher.
  - This indicates that non-verbal communication is affected by cultural experience. In other words, it is learned.

- Yuki's study suggest a nurture orientation (rather than a nature one, as with Darwin), so it positions itself on the nurture side of the nature–nurture debate.
  - Yuki's results lack ecological validity because the study used computer-generated faces and not real ones.
  - Yuki used students to test the hypothesis. Results might have been different if the study used older or younger participants.
  - Findings cannot be generalised to other emotions because Yuki only examined happy and sad faces.

Quick Test

1. What did Charles Darwin believe about non-verbal behaviour?
2. What did Matsumoto and Willingham's study find?
3. Who conducted the study into non-verbal behaviour using American and Japanese participants?

Key Words

evolutionary
adaptive
innate

Where space is not provided, write your answers on a separate piece of paper.

Conformity

1 Describe what Asch discovered in his study of conformity.   [2]

2 Explain why the presence of an ally might reduce levels of conformity.   [2]

3 What did Asch discover about the size of the majority in his study?   [2]

4 Name **one** other factor that might affect levels of conformity.   [1]

5 How did Asch use deception in his study?   [2]

6 Suggest **one** strength and **one** weakness of Asch's study into conformity.   [2]

Obedience

1 How does obedience differ from conformity?   [2]

2 What was the aim of Milgram's study? [2]

3 Name **two** factors affecting obedience. [2]

4 Describe **one** factor that might lead to someone developing an authoritarian personality. [1]

5 Name **one** weakness of the F-scale. [1]

6 Why can't we be sure that an authoritarian personality is the cause of high levels of obedience in some people? [1]

Crowd Psychology and Collective Behaviour

1 Fatima is doing her Christmas shopping. The town is really busy and she sees a man fall over in the street. Nobody tries to help him or ask him if he is okay. Fatima wonders why this might be, especially as there are so many people around. Fatima doesn't stop to help.

a) Explain to Fatima, using your knowledge of psychology, why nobody stopped to help the man. [2]

b) Under what circumstances might this have been different? [2]

2 In Pilivan's subway study, who were people more likely to help? [2]

3 Why might trick or treaters get more on Halloween if their faces are covered? [2]

4 a) Using your knowledge of crowd psychology, explain why violence often occurs at football matches. [4]

b) How could we reduce violence at football matches? [1]

c) Referring to your answer in **b)**, why might this strategy work? [1]

Where space is not provided, write your answers on a separate piece of paper.

The Possible Relationship Between Language and Thought

1 a) Briefly describe Piaget's theory of language and thought. **[3]**

b) According to Piaget, what is the purpose of human communication? **[1]**

2 Describe the weak Sapir-Whorf hypothesis. **[1]**

Differences Between Human and Animal Communication

1 Outline **one** difference in animal and human communication. Use an example to explain your answer. **[2]**

2 Give **one** example of food-related animal non-verbal communication. **[1]**

3 Describe **two** forms of non-verbal communication in animals, related to territory. **[2]**

4 How do bees tell the rest of the colony how far the food source is from the hive? **[1]**

5 What is meant by the word 'symbol' in relation to communication? **[2]**

6 What does human communication allow for that animal communication doesn't? **[2]**

Non-verbal Communication

1. Read the text and then answer the question that follows.

> Abi and Rebecca are best friends but their teacher doesn't allow them to sit together in class. When Abi enters the classroom, Rebecca smiles at her and Abi waves to her. When the teacher isn't looking, Rebecca passes a note to Abi and after Abi reads the note she laughs out loud. This annoys the teacher. The teacher tells both girls to stop being silly and to pay attention. Abi frowns at the teacher.

From the passage above, identify two examples of verbal behaviour and two examples of non-verbal behaviour. [4]

2. During a conversation, what can looking away indicate? [1]

3. Why might a person break eye contact during a conversation? [1]

4. Describe a closed posture. [3]

5. a) What is personal space? [1]

   b) What can happen when someone invades your personal space? [1]

Explanations of Non-verbal Behaviour

1. Briefly describe Darwin's theory of non-verbal communication. [4]

2. Evaluate Yuki *et al.*'s study of emoticons. [4]

3. What is the difference between something being innate and something being learned? [2]

The Structure and Function of the Brain and Nervous System

Quick Recall Quiz

You must be able to:

- Describe the divisions of the nervous system: central and peripheral (somatic and autonomic), and their basic functions
- Describe the role of the autonomic nervous system in the fight or flight response
- Understand the James-Lange theory of emotion.

The Divisions of the Human Nervous System

- The central nervous system (CNS) comprises the brain and spinal cord.

  - The brain is involved in psychological processes and the maintenance of life.
  - The spinal cord is involved in the transfer of messages to and from the brain to the peripheral nervous system (PNS). It is also involved in reflex actions such as the startle response.

- The PNS transmits messages to the whole body from the brain, and vice versa.
- The PNS has two divisions: the **somatic** system and the autonomic system.

  - The somatic system transmits and receives messages from the senses (e.g. visual information from the eyes and auditory information from the ears).
  - The somatic system also directs muscles to react and move.
  - The somatic nervous system consists of sensory and motor neurons.

  - The autonomic system helps to transmit and receive information from the organs and is divided into the sympathetic (which increases activity) and the parasympathetic (which decreases activity) systems.

The Autonomic Nervous System and The Fight or Flight Response

- The fight or flight response is triggered from the autonomic nervous system (ANS), most notably the sympathetic branch.
- The fight or flight response is designed to help an individual manage physically when under threat. It is also activated in times of stress when the body perceives a threat.

> **Key Point**
>
> The nervous system in humans is divided into the central nervous system (CNS) and the peripheral nervous system (PNS).

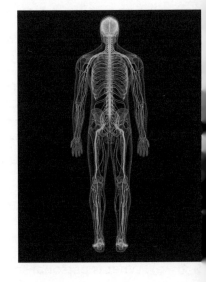

> **Key Point**
>
> Adrenaline is the key to the fight or flight response. It is the release of this hormone that sets in motion the bodily effects experienced, such as increased heart rate.

- The fight or flight response helps a person react quicker than normal and ensures that the body is able to tackle the threat by either attacking or running away.
- The fight or flight response occurs in a number of steps, or stages.
  - In the first stage of the fight or flight response, the hypothalamus recognises that there is a threat and sends a message to the adrenal gland.
  - The adrenal medulla then triggers the release of adrenaline to the endocrine system and noradrenaline to the brain.
- These stages lead to a number of bodily changes, including:
  - increased heart rate
  - muscular tension
  - faster breathing rate
  - pupil dilation
  - reduced function of the digestive and immune system.

Key Point

The autonomic nervous system is responsible for the fight or flight response.

The James-Lange Theory of Emotion

- The James-Lange theory, proposed by William James and Carl Lange, suggests that emotional experience is the result, not the cause, of perceived bodily changes.
- James illustrated the theory with the following example. We might think that if we meet a bear we become frightened and we run. The James-Lange theory, however, would suggest that we are frightened *because* we run. In a similar way, we feel sad because we cry or afraid because we tremble.
- People require feedback from bodily changes and they label their subjective experience based on this feedback: I am trembling, therefore I must be afraid.
- An alternative explanation (Cannon-Bard theory) argues that the ANS responds in the same way to all emotional stimuli, as explained by the fight or flight response.

Key Point

The James-Lange theory suggests that without physiological changes in the body, no emotion occurs.

Quick Test

1. What are the two systems contained within the human nervous system?
2. The brain and spinal cord are part of which system?
3. Which system controls the fight or flight response?
4. Who developed the James-Lange theory of emotion?

Key Word

somatic

Neuron Structure and Function

Quick Recall Quiz

You must be able to:

- Describe the functions of the three different types of neuron
- Describe Hebb's theory of learning and growth
- Explain the process of synaptic transmission (release and reuptake of neurotransmitters), including excitation and inhibition.

Sensory, Relay and Motor Neurons

- Different types of neurons serve different functions and are specialised to carry out particular roles.

  - **Sensory neurons** tell the rest of the brain about the external and internal environment by processing information taken from one of the five senses (sight, hearing, touch, smell, taste).
  - The **motor neuron** carries an electrical signal to a muscle, which will cause the muscle to either contract or relax.
  - **Relay neurons** carry messages from one part of the central nervous system to another. They connect motor and sensory neurons.

Hebb's Theory of Learning and Neuronal Growth

- Hebb's theory states that when one neuron sends a signal to another neuron, and that second neuron becomes activated, the connection between the two neurons is strengthened.
- The more one neuron activates another neuron, the stronger the connection between them grows.
- Hebb described this using the phrase 'what fires together, wires together'. In other words, with every new experience, the brain rewires its physical structure. This is commonly known as Hebbian learning.
- It is thought that Hebbian learning occurs through a mechanism known as long-term potentiation (LTP).
- LTP results in stronger connections between nerve cells and leads to longer lasting changes in synaptic connections.
- These changes in connections are thought to be responsible for learning and memory.
- Hebb's theory has scientific support from recent research and advances in cognitive neuroscience. His theory has provided useful application to everyday life such as in education where some of his ideas are utilised, such as practising information (rehearsal) to strengthen neural pathways which form memories.
- However, Hebb's theory only looks at structural changes in the brain during learning, whilst ignoring cognitive processes.

> **Key Point**
>
> Different types of neurons carry out different functions.

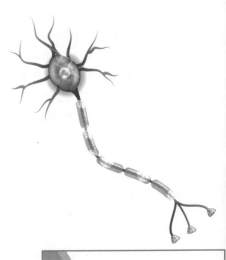

> **Key Point**
>
> The more often connections are made between neurons, the stronger that connection becomes.

- This reductionism is seen as a weakness of his theory because it attempts to explain the complexity of learning by mainly focusing on brain activity.

The Process of Synaptic Transmission: Release and Uptake of Neurotransmitters

- The **synapse** is a specialised gap between neurons through which the electrical impulse from the neuron is transmitted chemically.
- Synaptic transmission refers to the process whereby messages are sent from neuron to neuron.

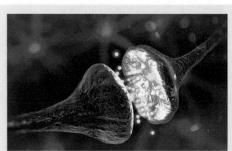

- During synaptic transmission, the electrical nerve impulse travels down the neuron, prompting the release of brain chemicals called neurotransmitters at the pre-synaptic terminal. These chemicals are then released into the synaptic fluid in the synapse.
- Examples of neurotransmitters are serotonin and dopamine.
- The adjacent neurons must then quickly take up the neurotransmitters from the fluid and convert them into an electrical impulse to travel down the neuron to the next synaptic terminal. The procedure is then repeated.

Excitation and Inhibition

- Not all messages prompt activation in the same way because it depends on the action potential of the post-synaptic neuron and the message type received. Only certain neurotransmitters can unlock a message channel in certain receptors in the post-synaptic neuron.
- We can think of this as a lock and key system whereby the right key (neurotransmitter) has to fit into the right lock (receptor) in order to open up the specific ion channel. Ions then flow through the membrane into the neuron along the specific pathways.
- This flooding of ions can cause a potential in the dendrites. This potential can be **excitatory** or **inhibitory**.

Excitatory potentials	Make it more likely for the neuron to fire. If the synapse is more likely to cause a post-synaptic neuron to fire, it is called an excitatory synapse.
Inhibitory potentials	Make it less likely to fire. If the message is likely to be stopped at the post-synaptic neuron, it is called an inhibitory synapse.

Quick Test

1. What are the three types of neuron?
2. How did Hebb describe the action of neuronal growth?
3. What is a synapse?

Key Words

synapse
excitation
inhibition

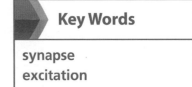

Localisation of Function in the Brain

Quick Recall Quiz

You must be able to:

- Describe the main brain structures and their functions (frontal lobe, temporal lobe, parietal lobe, occiptal lobe and cerebellum)
- Describe what is meant by localisation of function
- Describe the function of the motor, somatosensory, visual, auditory and language areas of the brain
- Explain Penfield's study of the interpretive cortex.

Brain Structures

- The brain consists of a number of structures, including the frontal lobe, temporal lobe, parietal lobe, occipital lobe and cerebellum.

Frontal lobe	Situated at the front of the brain and responsible for carrying out higher mental functions such as thinking, decision making and planning.
Temporal lobe	Situated behind the temples and responsible for processing auditory information from the ears (hearing).
Parietal lobe	Located at the back of the brain and responsible for processing sensory information that is associated with taste, temperature and touch.
Occipital lobe	Situated at the lower back of the brain and responsible for processing visual information from the eyes.
Cerebellum	Located in the lower brain and responsible for balance and coordination.

Localisation of Function in the Brain

Localisation of function refers to the view that particular areas of the brain are responsible for specific functions, such as vision and language.

- **Motor area:** the primary motor cortex is responsible for movement, whereby it sends messages to the muscles via the brain stem and spinal cord.
  - The motor cortex is important for complex movement but not basic functions like coughing or crying.
  - Within the motor cortex there are areas which control specific parts of the body.
- **Somatosensory area:** this is concerned with the sensation of the body and is situated next to the motor cortex.
  - The somatosensory cortex perceives touch. The amount of somatosensory cortex required dictates the amount needed for that area of the body.

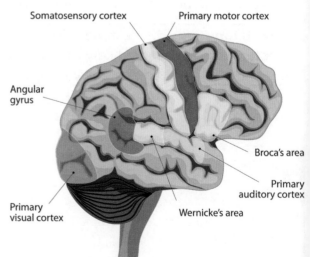

Main areas of the brain

Somatosensory cortex

Primary motor cortex

Angular gyrus

Broca's area

Primary auditory cortex

Wernicke's area

Primary visual cortex

- **The visual area:** this has two visual cortices, one situated in each hemisphere of the brain. The primary visual cortex is the occipital lobe. This is the main visual centre.
  - An area of the visual cortex known as Area V1 is thought to be specifically necessary for visual perception, and people with damage to this area report no vision of any kind (including in dreams).
  - The visual information is transmitted along the pathways, one containing the components of the visual field and the other being involved in the **localisation** within the visual field.
- **Auditory area:** the human brain has two primary auditory cortices, one in each hemisphere. The auditory cortices in both hemispheres receive information from both ears via two pathways that transmit information about what the sound is and its location.
  - If the primary auditory cortex is damaged, it does not lead to total deafness. However, if the sounds require complex processing (such as music) then this ability is lost.
- **Language area:** most language processing takes place in Broca's and Wernicke's areas. In most people, both areas are situated in the left hemisphere.

Penfield's Study of the Interpretive Cortex

- Penfield, a neurosurgeon, was the first person to map the brain's sensory and motor cortices using a technique known as neural stimulation.
- Often, in order to study the brain, it is necessary to surgically remove parts of the cortex. However, it is also possible to study the brain by using microelectrodes that can stimulate certain areas.
- While employing neural stimulation to epilepsy patients, Penfield discovered that the amount of cortical tissue involved in certain functions differs.
- This means that the more sensitive areas (e.g. the face) require a larger proportion of the cortex than others (such as the trunk), which do not require high levels of sensitivity.
- This is represented in an image known as the **Penfield homunculus**.

Penfield homunculus

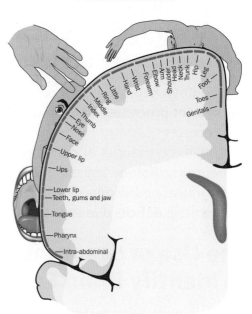

Key Point

The amount of cortical tissue required differs for different functions. The more sensitive the area, the more cortical tissue is required.

Key Words

frontal lobe
temporal lobe
parietal lobe
occipital lobe
cerebellum
somatosensory
localisation
Penfield homunculus

Quick Test

1. What is meant by localisation of function?
2. What is the temporal lobe area responsible for?
3. What is the cerebellum responsible for?

An Introduction to Neuropsychology

Quick Recall Quiz

You must be able to:

- Describe what is meant by cognitive neuroscience
- Describe the main scanning techniques for studying the brain (CT, PET and fMRI scans)
- Describe Tulving's 'gold' memory study
- Understand how neurological damage can affect motor abilities and behaviour.

Cognitive Neuroscience: How the Structure and Function of the Brain Relates to Behaviour and Cognition

- Cognitive **neuroscience** focuses on the biological basis of thought processes – specifically, how neurons explain thought processes.
- It relies on theories of cognitive science, and evidence from **neuropsychology** and computer modelling.
- Cognitive neuroscience includes the study of patients with cognitive deficits due to brain damage or strokes.

The Use of Scanning Techniques to Identify Brain Functioning

- Modern scanning techniques rely on matching behavioural actions with physiological activity.
- Because the person is usually conscious while being scanned, they can be directed to produce a particular action, such as performing a memory task.
- A number of scanning techniques are used to identify brain functioning.
  - **fMRI (Functional Magnetic Resonance Imaging):** MRIs record the energy produced by molecules of water after the magnetic field is removed, producing a static picture. fMRIs can show activity as it occurs. This is done by measuring the energy released by haemoglobin (the protein content of blood). When haemoglobin has oxygen, it reacts differently to when it does not have oxygen.
  - **CT or CAT (Computerised Axial Tomography) scan:** CAT scans use an X-ray beam to produce a picture of the physiology of the brain. The picture is not moving like an fMRI but is capable of identifying lesions (damage) and any unusual physiology.
  - **PET (Positron Emission Tomography) scan:** PET scans produce a moving picture of brain activity using radioactive glucose injected into the bloodstream. The scanner picks up the places in the brain where the most glucose is being consumed because these indicate which areas are most active.

> ### Key Point
> Cognitive neuroscience is concerned with the biological basis of thought processes.

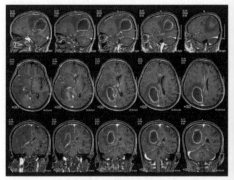
MRI scan

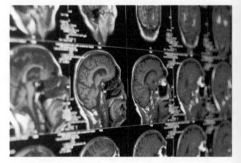
CAT scan

> ### Key Point
> Brain scanning techniques help neuroscientists pinpoint particular areas of the brain responsible for specific functions.

Tulving's Gold Memory Study

- Tulving's study (1989) is a good example of how brain scans help scientists understand cognitive processes.
- The study was conducted for two reasons:

  1. To investigate the difference in the processing of episodic memory and semantic memory tasks.
  2. To assess the effectiveness of neuroimaging as a means of investigating mental processes.

- Participants, including Tulving himself, were first injected with a small amount of radioactive gold and then asked to retrieve two types of memory – an episodic memory (that is, a personal experience) and a semantic memory (a general knowledge memory).
- Brain scans revealed that episodic memories resulted in greater activation in the frontal lobes, while semantic memories showed greater activation in the posterior region of the cortex.
- This study indicated that brain scans provide a useful means of identifying cognitive functioning.

Neurological Damage, Motor Abilities and Behaviour

- Damage to the brain can cause a number of deficits in both motor ability and behaviour.
- A stroke occurs when there is not enough oxygen going to the brain. Lack of oxygen can be due to blood vessels becoming blocked or a reduction in blood flow due to the narrowing of blood vessels.
  - The abilities that are affected by a stroke depend on where in the brain the damage has occurred.
  - If the damage occurs in the motor cortex, for example, the stroke victim might not have any movement. This could include reflex actions. Reflex actions can return but recovery varies between patients.
- Damage to the brain due to other factors (e.g. disease or damage caused by an accident) can impact other brain functions. For instance, damage occurring in the part of the brain responsible for short-term memory can result in the sufferer being unable to form new memories.

> **Key Point**
>
> A case study on a man, KC, showed that different memories were in different parts of the brain. After suffering damage to his temporal lobes and hippocampus, KC's semantic memory was intact but his episodic memory was impaired. This study provides more evidence of localisation of function.

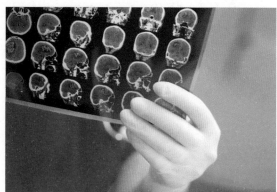

> **Key Words**
>
> neuroscience
> neuropsychology
> fMRI
> CT scan
> PET scan

> **Quick Test**
>
> 1. What is meant by cognitive neuroscience?
> 2. Name the main types of scanning techniques.
> 3. What causes a stroke?

Where space is not provided, write your answers on a separate piece of paper.

The Possible Relationship Between Language and Thought

1 How does Piaget's theory of language and thought differ from the Sapir-Whorf hypothesis? **[2]**

2 How does some evidence challenge Piaget's theory? **[3]**

3 **a)** Name the **two** types of the Sapir-Whorf hypothesis. **[2]**

   b) How do these **two** types differ? **[2]**

Differences Between Human and Animal Communication

1 How do animals use non-verbal communication to attract a mate? Give **two** examples. [2]

2 Describe how **two** non-human animals might warn others of their species about danger, such as the presence of a predator. [2]

3 How do honeybees communicate the whereabouts of pollen-rich flowers to the rest of the hive? [4]

4 What are the main differences between human and non-human animal communication? [2]

5 What do human communication systems allow humans to do that is absent in non-human behaviour? [2]

Non-verbal Communication

1 In what ways does verbal communication differ from non-verbal communication? **[4]**

2 Describe the difference between open and closed postures. **[4]**

3 a) What is meant by postural echo? **[1]**

b) What is the purpose of postural echo? **[1]**

4 How might a person use touch to show empathy? **[1]**

5 What factors affect personal space? **[3]**

Explanations of Non-verbal Behaviour

1 According to Darwin, why did humans develop methods of non-verbal communication? **[2]**

2 Why is Darwin's theory associated with nature rather than nurture? **[3]**

3 Children who have been blind since birth still display the same facial expressions as sighted children. Why does this provide evidence for Darwin's evolutionary theory of non-verbal communication? **[2]**

4 What do we mean when we claim that non-verbal behaviour is learned? **[2]**

5 a) In Yuki *et al.*'s 2007 study, how did American and Japanese people differ in terms of their non-verbal communication? **[4]**

b) Why does Yuki *et al.*'s study support a nurture theory of non-verbal communication? **[3]**

Where space is not provided, write your answers on a separate piece of paper.

The Structure and Function of the Brain and Nervous System

1 Which **one** of the statements about the human nervous system is correct? Shade **one** box only. **[1]**

A   The autonomic nervous system is responsible for thinking. ⃝

B   The central nervous system is part of the peripheral nervous system. ⃝

C   The peripheral nervous system consists only of relay neurons. ⃝

D   The somatic nervous system consists of sensory and motor neurons. ⃝

2 What is the function of the peripheral nervous system? **[1]**

3 Name the **two** branches of the autonomic nervous system (ANS). **[2]**

4 Read the text and then answer the question. **[6]**

> Jake was walking home at night alone when, suddenly, he heard a sound behind him. His heart started to beat fast as he began to run towards the bus stop. From behind him, he heard a voice shout, "Wait for me Jake". As he turned around he saw his friend Will running along the road to catch up with him. Jake stopped and his breathing began to slow down.

Use your knowledge of the central nervous system and the autonomic nervous system to explain Jake's experience.

5 Describe the James-Lange theory of emotion. **[4]**

Neuron Structure and Function

1 Which **one** of the statements about neurons is correct? Shade **one** box only. **[1]**

A   Motor neurons carry information to the spinal cord. ⃝

B   Relay neurons carry information from the motor cortex. ⃝

C   Sensory neurons carry information to the brain. ⃝

D   Sensory neurons always have longer axons than motor neurons. ⃝

2 Briefly explain the function of a motor neuron.   [2]

3 What is meant by Hebbian learning?   [3]

4 Name **one** neurotransmitter.   [1]

5 Describe the lock and key system.   [2]

Localisation of Function in the Brain

1 Briefly describe the function of the motor centre of the brain.   [2]

2 What does the somatosensory cortex perceive?   [1]

3 What is anomia?   [1]

4 What is neural stimulation?   [1]

An Introduction to Neuropsychology

1 What kinds of people might cognitive neuroscientists study?   [2]

2 Describe how modern scanning techniques have increased our understanding of the relationship
   between brain and behaviour.   [4]

3 a) What did Tulving inject into his participants?   [1]

   b) In Tulving's study, which part of the brain was activated when participants were asked to
       recall an episodic memory?   [1]

4 During a stroke, what causes the blood vessels to become blocked?   [1]

5 Following a stroke, different abilities can be affected. What determines the ability affected?   [1]

An Introduction to Mental Health

You must be able to:

- Describe the main characteristics of mental health
- Explain cultural variations in beliefs about mental health problems
- Describe how mental health is linked to the increased challenges of modern living
- Describe how society is challenging the stigma related to mental health problems.

Quick Recall Quiz

Characteristics of Mental Health

- Some behaviour can prevent people from functioning adequately, such as the inability to cope with everyday life.
- If behaviour causes distress leading to an inability to function properly, e.g. an inability to work or to engage in satisfying interpersonal relationships, this can be viewed as a mental health problem.
- Ideal mental health is said to consist of a number of factors:
  - a positive attitude towards oneself
  - personal growth and development (**self-actualisation**)
  - feelings of independence (autonomy)
  - resisting stress
  - an accurate perception of reality
  - being able to cope with life and the changing environment (environmental mastery).
- If these factors are absent, people often suffer from mental health problems.

> **Key Point**
>
> Ideal mental health includes positive engagement with society and coping effectively with challenges.

Cultural Variations in Beliefs about Mental Health Problems

- Social norms are unwritten rules that people are expected to abide by.
  - Social norms include appropriate public behaviour, control of aggression, politeness, and control of culturally and socially offensive language.
- Social norms change between cultures and over time. What might be considered as a mental illness in one culture or point in time might not be the same in other cultures or at a different historical period. For instance, homosexuality was once thought to be a mental illness but today few countries view it as such.
- Some cultures might consider hearing voices as divine, as talking with spirits or conversing with God.
- Some governments have been known to label political opponents as mentally ill and confine them to mental institutions.
- Some behaviours might be thought of as abnormal in some cultures but not in others (e.g. public nudity).

> **Key Point**
>
> Mental health changes over time and within different cultures.

Increased Challenges of Modern Living

- Modern society has led to geographical isolation from family and emotional support networks. This can increase levels of loneliness and the feeling of not knowing who to turn to in times of crisis.
- The increase in people living alone has led to a rise in disorders such as depression and anxiety.
- It has been suggested that the rise in technology and the internet has been responsible for higher levels of mental health problems, although there is little evidence to support this view at present.
- Increased pressure at work and at school has also been blamed for the rise of disorders such as depression and anxiety.

Increased Recognition of the Nature of Mental Health Problems

- In recent years there has been a greater emphasis on the normalising of mental health issues.
- Employers are now encouraged to take into account the wellbeing of their employees and to support them through **recovery**.
- With the recognition of men's mental health problems and the high level of suicide amongst men, more organisations are beginning to direct their attention towards this group (e.g. The Campaign Against Living Miserably, or CALM).
- A number of charities have been formed over the past few years (e.g. Time To Change) to reduce the **stigma** attached to mental health problems.
- Many high-profile celebrities and politicians have spoken openly about their mental health problems in an attempt to reduce stigma.

Quick Test

1. What is meant by ideal mental health?
2. How can modern life affect mental health?
3. Name one organisation that is trying to end mental health stigma.

Key Words

self actualisation
recovery
stigma

Effects of Mental Health Problems on Individuals and Society

Quick Recall Quiz

You must be able to:

- Describe how poor mental health can affect individuals (e.g. damage to relationships)
- Describe how poor mental health can affect wider society, such as crime rates and the economy.

Individual Effects

- Mental health issues can cause problems for people on an individual basis.
- Living with a person with significant mental health problems can put a strain on relationships.
  - For example, living with a person who has a mental illness can lead to the partner experiencing feelings of **guilt** and **shame**, and **blaming** themselves.
- In romantic relationships, social life and physical intimacy might change.
  - For example, the couple might not socialise as often as they used to, or engage in other social activities.
- A survey was conducted by the mental health charity Mind (2013). Sixty three per cent of people with mental health problems who told their partner about their condition said that their partners "weren't fazed" and were "really understanding".
- Mental health issues can:
  - impact day-to-day living, such as personal hygiene and generally looking after yourself
  - lead to loss of interest in socialising and engaging in activities that were once considered enjoyable
  - have a wider impact on physical wellbeing by reducing the function of the immune system and leading to a greater susceptibility to infection.

Social Effects

- Like any illness, sufferers require care and treatment.
- This leads to a greater need for social care, including social workers and mental health professionals.
- If social care is lacking or under stress through shortages in trained staff, this has an impact on the treatment that can be offered to patients.
- More funding for social care would increase patient care but put greater strain on the economy in general, as there would be less money to invest elsewhere.
- Some mental illnesses can lead to sufferers breaking the law, leading to increased crime rates.
  - Drug addiction, for example, can result in people stealing in order to raise money to sustain their addiction.
  - Alcohol addiction can increase acts of aggression in some individuals.
- However, people with mental health issues (especially those with mood disorders) are rarely violent and are much more likely to be a danger to themselves than to members of the public.
- When people are diagnosed with conditions such as depression and anxiety, work absence due to mental health issues increases. This results in a negative impact on businesses and consequently the economy in general.
- While there is less stigma today surrounding mental illness, many people might be concerned about divulging their illness to their employer.

 Key Point

Mental health issues can impact negatively on health services and the economy.

 Key Point

Mental health problems can affect both individuals and society in negative ways.

 Quick Test

1. How might mental health problems affect a person on an individual level?
2. How can mental health problems negatively impact society?
3. How might businesses be negatively affected by mental health problems?

Key Words

guilt
shame
blame

Characteristics of Clinical Depression

You must be able to:

- Explain the differences between bipolar and unipolar depression, and sadness
- Describe the characteristics of unipolar depression
- Describe how unipolar depression is diagnosed using the ICD criteria.

Clinical Depression

- Depression is one of the mood (or affective) disorders.
- Mood disorders involve a prolonged and major disturbance of mood and emotions.
- Depression and **sadness** differ in **duration** (how long the episodes last). Depression lasts for a long time while sadness does not.
- There are two main types of depression: **unipolar** depression and **bipolar** depression.
- Both types differ in terms of how the **symptoms** present themselves and can be distinguished from sadness by their duration and the resulting changes in mood and behaviour.

    - When clinical depression (also known as major depressive disorder) occurs on its own, it is called unipolar depression.
    - If **mania** occurs with depression, then it is called bipolar disorder or bipolar depression (it is also sometimes referred to as manic depression).
    - Mania can also occur on its own (manic disorder) but is still often referred to as bipolar disorder.

- Mania can be described as a sense of euphoria or elation.

    - People with mania tend to have a great deal of energy and rush around, but rarely get anything done.
    - They lack a sense of purpose in their actions and survive on very little sleep.

- People with bipolar depression alternate between mania and depressive episodes.

> **Key Point**
>
> Depression can be categorised as either bipolar or unipolar.

Classification and Diagnosis of Unipolar Depression

- A person suffering from depression experiences a general slowing down and loss of energy.
- Depression can begin at any time of life but is rarely seen in pre-adolescent children.
- The average age of onset is the late twenties, but the age of onset has decreased over the last fifty years, during which time depression's prevalence has increased (i.e. there are more people being diagnosed with depression and they are getting younger).
- Depression is more prevalent in women than in men, although this could be because men are less likely to seek help.
- The International Classification of Diseases (ICD) identifies three main behaviours that must be present for a diagnosis of unipolar depression:
  - persistent sadness/low mood
  - loss of interest/pleasure
  - fatigue/low energy.
- In addition, the ICD identifies a number of symptoms that often accompany the key behaviours. These include:
  - disturbed sleep
  - poor concentration
  - low self-confidence
  - poor or increased appetite
  - suicidal thoughts or acts
  - agitation
  - guilt/self-blame.

 Key Point

The ICD criteria identify a number of symptoms that must be present for a diagnosis of depression to be made.

Quick Test

1. What is depression?
2. What is mania?
3. What is bipolar depression?
4. What are the three main behaviours associated with unipolar depression?

 Key Words

sadness
duration
unipolar
bipolar
symptoms
mania

Theories of Depression and Interventions

Quick Recall Quiz

You must be able to:

- Describe both biological and psychological explanations of depression
- Explain the use of biological therapies in the treatment of depression
- Explain the use of psychological therapies in the treatment of depression.

Biological Explanations of Depression – The Influence of Nature, Imbalance of Neurotransmitters

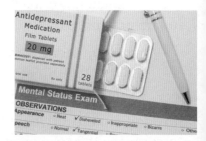

- Biological explanations of depression indicate that depression is caused by internal factors (the influence of nature rather than nurture), including brain chemicals and genes.
- It has been found that people suffering from clinical depression have lower levels of the neurotransmitter **serotonin**.
- Most modern anti-depressant medication helps to alleviate symptoms by regulating the levels of serotonin in the brain.

  - A strength of the biological explanation of depression is its emphasis on the role of neurotransmitters and brain chemistry.
  - Imbalances in neurotransmitters such as serotonin are associated with depression, which has led to the development of effective drug treatments, such as selective serotonin reuptake inhibitors (SSRIs). These target imbalances and help to treat symptoms in many individuals.
  - However, cause and effect is difficult to establish. It could be that depression results in lower levels of serotonin, rather than lower levels leading to depression.
  - The biological explanation also simplifies the complex nature of depression by focusing on biological factors and neglecting the influence of other explanations.
  - Biological causes overlook other vitally important reasons for the depression.

Psychological Explanations of Depression – The Influence of Nurture, Negative Schemes and Attributions

- Aaron Beck (1967) believed that depression was the result of a negative outlook.
  - According to this view, depressed people acquire a schema – a blueprint by which they view the world. Depressed people develop a view of the world (schema) that is pessimistic.
- Attributional style is another explanation.
  - This view states that people with depression will often attribute negative events to sources that are internal (their fault), stable (their circumstances won't change, even with effort) and global (their depression is the result of some personal defect or personality characteristic).
- Seligman (1967) believed that depression is the result of learned helplessness.

> **Key Point**
>
> Depression can be explained as both biological and psychological.

– When people continually fail, or bad things happen to them, they begin to believe that this is the way it will always be, no matter what they try to do to change it. They learn to be helpless.

Interventions and Therapies

- Interventions and therapies for depression are often seen as **reductionist**. They reduce the causes of depression down to, for example, brain chemicals, and improve mental health by treating the symptoms.
- Other interventions, such as CBT, are seen as **holistic** – they treat the symptoms but also tackle the causes of depression – e.g. poverty, home life and lack of meaning in life.
- The most common treatment is antidepressant medication.
- There are two main types of antidepressants: tricyclic antidepressants and **SSRI** antidepressants.

  – Tricyclic antidepressants block the transporter mechanism that absorbs both serotonin and another neurotransmitter called noradrenaline.
  – SSRI (selective serotonin re-uptake inhibitors) work in a similar way to tricyclic antidepressants but mainly block serotonin only. The best-known SSRI antidepressant is Prozac (fluoxetine).

- A number of psychotherapies are used to help alleviate depression.
- Psychotherapy is a term used for a number of different treatments for mental illness that involve talking with a specially trained therapist.
- One of the most popular types of psychotherapy is cognitive behavioural therapy (**CBT**) which is holistic.
- CBT is based on the premise that the way we think about things impacts our psychological wellbeing.
  – CBT emphasises the role of **maladaptive** thoughts and beliefs as the main cause of depression. When people think negatively about themselves and their lives they become depressed.
- Wiles (2013) compared the effectiveness of CBT and antidepressant medication (sertraline) in the treatment of depression. Participants (469 adults diagnosed with depression aged 18-75) were randomly assigned to one of three treatment groups: CBT, antidepressants or a combination of both. All groups showed significant improvements in depressive symptoms at 12 months, showing that a holistic approach to treatment should be considered. Patients who did not respond to medication alone did benefit from the addition of CBT.

> **Key Point**
>
> Depression can be treated with medication, or by psychotherapy, such as CBT.

> **Key Words**
>
> serotonin
> reductionist
> holistic
> SSRI
> CBT
> maladaptive

> **Quick Test**
>
> 1. What is a schema?
> 2. What does SSRI stand for?
> 3. What is CBT?

Characteristics of Addiction

Quick Recall Quiz

You must be able to:

- Define addiction
- Explain the difference between addiction/dependence and substance misuse/abuse
- Describe the criteria for diagnosing addiction.

Addiction

- **Addiction** or dependence refers to a behaviour that leads to dependency.
  - For example, an addiction to alcohol results in a dependency where individuals feel that they are unable to survive without it.
- Addictions also lead to other changes, including changes in behaviour (psychological changes) and in levels of brain chemicals.
- Addiction differs from substance misuse or **abuse** in that the substance is taken to excess but does not necessarily lead to addiction.
  - For example, a person might drink large amounts of alcohol but never feel that they couldn't live without it.

> **Key Point**
>
> Addiction includes a dependence on substances and activities.

Classification and Diagnosis of Addiction

- The International Classification of Diseases (ICD) describes addiction as "A cluster of physiological, behavioural, and cognitive phenomena in which the use of a substance or a group of substances takes on a much higher priority for a given individual than other behaviours that once had greater value".
- A diagnosis of dependence syndrome is made if three or more symptoms have appeared together for at least one month, or have occurred together repeatedly within a twelve-month period.
- These symptoms include, but are not limited to:
  - a strong desire or sense of compulsion to take the substance despite harmful consequences
  - impaired capacity to control substance-taking behaviour
  - pre-occupation with substance use and the giving up of activities once deemed important.
- Many psychologists suggest that addiction need not be centred around a substance, but can also include an experience which becomes addictive.

> **Key Point**
>
> Symptoms of addiction include compulsions, loss of control and pre-occupation.

- This suggestion leads to a broadening of the definition to include behaviours such as shopping and gambling.
- Walters (1999) argues that addiction can be defined as "the persistent and repetitive enactment of a behaviour pattern". This behaviour pattern includes:
  - *progression* (increase in severity)
  - *pre-occupation* with the activity
  - *perceived* loss of control
  - *persistence* despite negative long-term consequences.
- Griffiths (1999) argues that addiction can be extended to other activities, including watching TV, playing computer games and using the internet. Such behaviours are *potentially* addictive.
- According to Griffiths, these behaviours share the same core components as addiction:

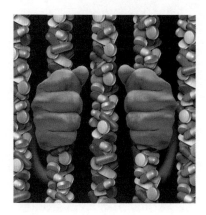

Salience	The activity becomes the most important one in the person's life.
Mood modification	The activity produces an arousing 'buzz' or 'high'.
Tolerance	Increasing amounts of activity are needed to achieve the same effects.
Withdrawal symptoms	Discontinuation or sudden reduction of the activity produces unpleasant feelings and physical effects.
Conflict	Conflict between the addict and the people around them, such as family and friends, or with other activities and interests.
Relapse	Reverting to earlier patterns of addiction soon after giving up.

Griffiths argues that mobile phone use is potentially addictive

 Quick Test

1. What is meant by addiction?
2. What is meant by substance abuse?
3. What are the main symptoms of addiction?

 Key Words

addiction
abuse
withdrawal

Theories of Addiction and Interventions

Quick Recall Quiz

You must be able to:

- Describe biological theories of addiction, including heritability
- Describe Kaij's twin study of alcohol abuse
- Describe psychological theories of addiction
- Explain one biological intervention and one psychological intervention for addiction.

Biological Theories of Addiction

- Biological explanations of addiction concentrate on areas that can be viewed on the nature side of the nature–nurture debate.
- Family and twin studies indicate that genes contribute to the development of addictive behaviour.
- **Heritability** (the extent to which traits are inherited) estimates range from between 50% and 60% in both men and women.
- Kaij (1960) studied the rates of alcohol abuse in identical and **fraternal** twins in Sweden.
  - He found that the concordance rate (the presence of the same trait in both twins) for identical twins was 54% and that for fraternal twins it was only 28%.
  - Kaij concluded that there are genetic and hereditary factors involved in alcohol addiction.
  - This means that children with parents who are alcohol dependent have a much greater chance of developing dependence disorders.

> **Key Point**
>
> Addiction can be explained in terms of biology (e.g. genes) and psychology (e.g. peer pressure).

  - This study suggests that genes play a big part in addiction.
  - However the concordance rates for the identical twins being 54% suggests the influence of other factors. As they are identical we would expect the other twin to also be an alcoholic as they share 100% of their genes.
  - So although 54% was higher than 28% for the non-identical twins, it still shows evidence for the role of both biological factors and environmental factors.

- Research indicates a link between the D2 dopamine receptor (DRD2) and severe alcoholism. More specifically, two-thirds of deceased alcoholics had the A1 variant of the DRD2 gene.

Psychological Theories of Addiction

- **Social learning theory** (SLT) proposes that learning occurs through observation and communication. It explains addiction in terms of how and why addictive behaviour is caused through social interaction.
- DeBlasio and Benda (1993) found the influence of peers to be a primary factor in the uptake of alcohol and drugs in adolescents.
- Young people who smoke are more likely to associate with other young people who smoke, indicating that they are attempting to conform to the norms of the reference group, or to peers whom they admire.

Interventions and Therapies for Addiction

Aversion Therapy

- **Aversion therapy** works by conditioning the individual into experiencing an unpleasant reaction when engaging in the unwanted activity.

  - When an unpleasant stimuli is paired with the unwanted behaviour, the behaviour becomes associated with the unpleasant feeling.
  - Drugs can be used that, when combined with an addictive substance (e.g. alcohol), result in a feeling of nausea. The individual then associates the activity (drinking alcohol) with feeling sick.
  - People can be taught to use **negative visualisation** or to focus on unpleasant thoughts when their mind wanders towards the undesirable activity.

Self-management Programs

- People often benefit from self-help groups where they can gain support from other people who are struggling with addiction.
- The most well-known of these is the 12-step program used by Alcoholics Anonymous.

  - The 12-step program of personal recovery involves a number of milestones on the journey to breaking the addiction.
  - Steps begin with an acceptance of the addiction. Steps are taken with the help of a sponsor – an experienced member who can offer individual support.
  - The 12-step program has proved useful for other addictions, including drugs and gambling.

- As mentioned on page 115, while some therapies and interventions can be thought of as reductionist (talking about one aspect of addiction and mental health), others are more holistic and can be combined with several treatments for improved outcomes.

  - Aversion therapy appears to work well short term but not so well long term. This could suggest using more than one therapy at a time such as support from CBT or the self-help groups, alongside the aversion therapy, to remain addiction free.
  - This approach to therapy is more of an holistic one rather than just focusing on one treatment, such as aversion therapy, which is reductionist and only targeting reducing the urge for the behaviour.
  - Not everyone responds positively to each treatment, which could be demotivating for the person and they could abandon the treatment plan they are on.

> ### Key Point
>
> Treatment for addiction can involve biological and psychological interventions.

> ### Key Words
>
> heritability
> fraternal
> **social learning theory**
> **aversion therapy**
> **negative visualisation**

Quick Test

1. What is meant by heritability?
2. Where were the participants from in the Kaij study?
3. Who studied the effect of peer pressure on addiction?

Where space is not provided, write your answers on a separate piece of paper.

The Structure and Function of the Brain and Nervous System

1 **a)** Name the components that make up the central nervous system. [2]

b) Explain the functions of the components you named in a). [2]

2 Describe the peripheral nervous system. [2]

3 What is meant by the fight or flight response? [4]

4 What is the function of the autonomic nervous system? [1]

5 How does the James-Lange theory differ from other explanations of human emotion? [3]

Neuron Structure and Function

1 Describe the purpose of sensory neurons. [2]

2 What did Hebb mean by the phrase "what fires together, wires together"? [2]

3 What is the result of long-term potentiation, or LTP? [2]

4 Describe the process of synaptic transmission. [6]

5 What are neurotransmitters? [1]

6 Explain the difference between excitation and inhibition. [2]

Localisation of Function in the Brain

1   Using the example of memory, explain what is meant by localisation of function.   **[4]**

2   Describe the function of the somatosensory centre of the brain.   **[3]**

3   Describe the function of the visual centre of the brain.   **[3]**

4   **a)**   How can neurosurgeons study the brain without having to remove parts of the cortex?   **[2]**

     b)   What did Penfield discover?   **[2]**

An Introduction to Neuropsychology

1   What do cognitive neuroscientists study?   **[1]**

2   Describe the main difference between MRI and fMRI scans.   **[2]**

3   How does a CAT scan produce an image of the brain?   **[1]**

4   Describe the procedure of Tulving's 'gold' memory study.   **[3]**

5   What would happen if a person suffered a stroke in their motor cortex?   **[2]**

6   Apart from a stroke, what else might cause damage to the brain?   **[1]**

Where space is not provided, write your answers on a separate piece of paper.

An Introduction to Mental Health

1. What kind of behaviour can prevent people from functioning adequately? [1]

2. Some behaviour can cause distress to the person experiencing it. One example is the inability to work. Name **one** other example. [1]

3. A positive attitude towards yourself and personal growth and development are two factors that encourage ideal mental health. Name **two** other factors. [2]

4. Social norms are unwritten rules that people are expected to abide by. Name **two** social norms. [2]

5. What kinds of mental health problems might loneliness and feelings of isolation lead to? [2]

6. Name **two** organisations that exist to help people cope with mental health problems or reduce stigma. [2]

Effects of Mental Health Problems on Individuals and Society

1. Living with a person with significant mental health problems can put a strain on relationships. Give **one** example of how the problems might do this. [2]

2. Living with a mental health problem can lead to poor physical health. Explain why this might be the case. [2]

3. What can impact on the ability to treat and care for people with mental health problems? [1]

4. Some conditions, such as addiction, can lead to sufferers becoming aggressive and breaking the law. What other criminal activity might they engage in, and why? [2]

5. Why might people be reluctant to tell their employer about their mental health problem? [2]

Characteristics of Clinical Depression

1   What is the difference between sadness and depression?   [1]

2   What is clinical depression also known as?   [1]

3   What symptom of bipolar depression isn't present in unipolar depression?   [1]

4   State **two** symptoms often seen in people who are diagnosed with unipolar depression.   [2]

5   At what stage of life does unipolar depression usually develop?   [1]

Theories of Depression and Interventions

1   What do biological explanations of depression indicate?   [2]

2   Which neurotransmitter is most commonly associated with depression?   [1]

3   Depression has been linked to a mutated gene. How might this cause depression?   [1]

4   a) What is the most common treatment for depression?   [1]

   b) What two types of drugs are used to treat depression?   [1]

5   Name **one** type of psychotherapy used to treat depression.   [1]

Characteristics of Addiction

1 What is meant by addiction? [1]

_____

2 Give **one** example of a substance addiction. [1]

_____

3 How is substance abuse different from addiction? [1]

_____

4 One symptom of addiction is a strong desire or sense of compulsion to take the substance despite harmful consequences. Name **two** other symptoms. [2]

_____

_____

_____

Theories of Addiction and Interventions

1 Describe **one** study into the heritability of addiction. [4]

2 What is the role played by peers in the development of addictions? [2]

3 Katie has been diagnosed with an addiction to alcohol. When Katie is with her friends they encourage her to drink more. Her father and older sister have also been diagnosed with an addiction to alcohol.

Which of the following statements are true? Shade **two** boxes. [2]

A One treatment that might be offered to Katie is aversion therapy. ◯

B Katie might have a genetic vulnerability to alcohol addiction. ◯

C One biological explanation for Katie's addiction could be peer pressure. ◯

4 How would a psychologist use aversion therapy to cure someone of alcohol addiction? [3]

5 **a)** What is meant by a self-management program? [2]

b) What is the most well-known self-management program? [1]

Where space is not provided, write your answers on a separate piece of paper.

An Introduction to Mental Health

1 What behaviours might suggest that a person is not coping well with everyday life?   **[3]**

2 What factors indicate ideal mental health?   **[6]**

3 **a)** In what ways might culture affect attitudes towards mental illness?   **[2]**

   b) Suggest **one** behaviour that was once thought of as abnormal but is no longer considered
   to be by much of society.   **[1]**

4 How might being geographically closer to family help prevent the onset of mental health
   problems?   **[2]**

5 How might stigma surrounding mental health problems make some conditions worse?   **[2]**

Effects of Mental Health Problems on Individuals and Society

1 How can living with a partner with a mental illness put strain on the relationship?   **[3]**

2 How might mental illness affect a person's day-to-day life?   **[2]**

3 How does mental illness increase the possibility of poor physical health?   **[2]**

4 An increase in mental health issues can put a strain on a number of social services.
   What specific services might this include?   **[2]**

5 Why might some mental health conditions lead people to engage in criminal activities?   **[1]**

6 How might mental illness put a strain on employers?   **[2]**

Characteristics of Clinical Depression

1 Depression is a mood disorder. What are the main characteristics of mood disorders?   **[1]**

2 What is bipolar depression also known as?   **[1]**

3 Explain the main difference between unipolar and bipolar depression.   **[2]**

4 What are the main characteristics of mania?   **[4]**

5. a) List the **three** main behaviours that are characteristic of unipolar depression. [3]

   b) List **three** additional symptoms that are also often present in depression. [3]

Theories of Depression and Interventions

1. a) What is the relationship between serotonin and depression? [1]

   b) How might the relationship in **a)** be criticised? [2]

2. What did Beck believe caused depression? [2]

3. How do SSRI antidepressant drugs work? [2]

4. How does CBT reduce the symptoms of depression? [2]

Characteristics of Addiction

1. Describe the difference between addiction and substance abuse. [2]

2. Explain why addiction can be related to behaviours and habits and not just substances. [2]

3. Describe Walters' behaviour pattern of addiction. [4]

4. What is meant by salience in relation to addiction? [1]

5. What is meant by relapse? [1]

6. You are concerned that your friend, Ella, might be addicted to playing computer games. Briefly describe the symptoms she is displaying that gave rise to your concerns. [3]

Theories of Addiction and Interventions

1. What do Kaij's results tell us about the nature of alcohol abuse? [2]

2. What is the link between the D2 dopamine receptor and addiction? [2]

3. Why are young people who smoke more likely to have friends who also smoke? [2]

4. a) What is aversion therapy? [2]

   b) How do self-management programs differ from aversion therapy? [3]

Mixed Questions

Where space is not provided, write your answers on a separate piece of paper.

Cognition and Behaviour

1 State a possible alternative hypothesis for an experiment that aims to study the effect of background noise levels on stress. **[4]**

2 Explain the role of rehearsal in memory, according to the multi-store model. **[2]**

3 Besides the eye, name **one** other body area involved in the perception of vision and explain what it does. **[2]**

4 Briefly explain the interview and survey methods of research. **[4]**

5 Explain **one** brain development change that occurs before birth and **one** that occurs after birth. **[4]**

6 Discuss the capacity and duration of the memory stores known as STM and LTM. **[4]**

7 Complete the following two sentences. **[2]**

a) A .... chart is one of the most important ways of displaying data in

psychology. It can be used to show the mean scores of different conditions in an experiment.

b) Correlation is used to analyse primary data gathered from a survey, or secondary data. It

shows the direction and .... of a relationship between two co-variables.

8 Which theory of perception thinks that illusions are important examples of how complex and difficult perception truly is? Why? **[3]**

9 Briefly explain **one** of the binocular cues to depth. [3]

10 What **three** terms are used to mean putting information into a memory store, keeping it there, and then taking it out when needed? [3]

11 Complete the sentences by choosing the best words from the selection below. You do not have to use all the words. [4]

areas	set	language	people	motivation	languages

Perception varies between individuals and is affected by a number of factors including

_____, emotion and expectations. Together, these factors are called the

perceptual _____. Another factor that can play a role is culture – the beliefs

and behaviour of a particular group of _____, usually associated with specific

_____.

12 What is this statement describing? A stimulus that causes a person to see something different from what is actually there, or where there are two or more possible interpretations of the same image. [1]

13 Explain how the encoding and storage of human memories is different to recording and saving a video or computer file. [2]

Mixed Questions

14 Tick (✓) or cross (✗) the statements about factors affecting memory to indicate whether they are true or false. **[4]**

Statements about factors affecting memory	True (✓) or false (✗)?
Information is better remembered if it is unusual and distinctive.	
Participants in the War of the Ghosts study forgot things because the cultural concepts in the story were unfamiliar.	
It's easier to remember things in a different location from where we first learned them.	
Loftus found that false memories could be generated within an experiment.	

15 In a random sample, every member of the target population must have the same chance of being selected. Explain why this is not the case if a sample is chosen by asking passers-by on a school corridor during the school day. **[3**

....

....

....

....

16 Explain **two** things that could happen to a child's schemas when they see a type of vehicle that they have never seen before. **[4**

17 Complete the following **two** sentences. **[2**

   a) Experimental design means the way that participants are .... to the conditions of a study.

   b) In a repeated measures design, ... must be used to avoid order effects biasing the results.

18 To what extent could the **two** sides of the nature versus nurture debate *both* be true? Explain your answer. **[3**

19 Briefly explain **two** things that Willingham has said about how learning works best. **[2**

....

....

Social Context and Behaviour

1 Name **two** methods used to treat depression. [2]

2 You are talking with a person you have just met and notice that they begin to mirror your actions. What are they doing and why are they doing it? [2]

3 What is the function of a relay neuron? [1]

4 What **four** factors affect conformity? [4]

5 Someone suffering with alcohol addiction could get help from a self-management program like the 12-step program. What other treatment is available? [1]

6 Why might a person break eye contact while engaged in a conversation? [1]

7 Which response is triggered from the autonomic nervous system? [1]

8 Why might you feel uncomfortable when someone stands very close to you? [2]

9 What **four** factors affect obedience to authority? [4]

10 How would you know if a person was addicted to alcohol? [3]

11 The brain and spinal cord are part of which division of the nervous system? [1]

12 What **four** factors affect bystander intervention? [4]

13 The sympathetic and parasympathetic branches are part of which division of the nervous system? [1]

14 Describe the posture of a person who is being defensive. [3]

15 How would you know if a person was suffering from depression rather than just sad? [1]

16 Name the scanning technique that produces a moving image. [1]

Answers

Pages 6–13 **Revise Questions**

Pages 6–7
1. Encoding
2. Retrieval

Pages 8–9
1. Attention
2. Semantic encoding
3. Short-term memory (STM)
4. Semantic

Pages 10–11
1. STM has a limited capacity.
2. **Possible strengths**: provides a basic outline which forms the basis of many later models; supported by serial position curve; supported by evidence of separate STM/LTM, e.g. brain damage patients. **Possible weaknesses**: over-simplistic; doesn't account for different types of STM or LTM; view of encoding based on rehearsal is not accurate.
3. Those in the middle.

Pages 12–13
1. The story was from a culture with which they were not familiar.
2. **Any two from**: cue, context, interference

Pages 14–15 **Practice Questions**

Processes of Memory
1. An active process
2. C
3. A
4. A Procedural B Episodic C Semantic

Structures of Memory 1 and 2
1. a) The serial position curve
   b) Murdock's serial position curve supports the model, **[1]** the primacy effect is explained by items being rehearsed into LTM, **[1]** the recency effect is explained by a few items remaining within a limited capacity STM. **[1]**
2. Encoding, semantic, words
3. No – often rehearsal alone is not enough.
4. C
5. Limited capacity, limited duration

Memory as an Active Process
1. Interference, distinctive, easier
2. Different mood, drugs such as caffeine, consumption of alcohol. Also accept a different physical location.
3. B

Pages 16–25 **Revise Questions**

Pages 16–17
1. Sensation
2. True
3. Colour constancy

Pages 18–19
1. Occlusion
2. Texture gradient
3. Convergence

Pages 20–21
1. The Kanizsa triangle
2. Ambiguity
3. They misinterpret the depth cue of linear perspective.

Pages 22–23
1. The direct/bottom-up theory of perception
2. The constructivist/top-down theory of perception

Pages 24–25
1. It caused participants to perceive food as looking brighter/more vivid.
2. A perceptual set

Pages 26–29 **Review Questions**

Processes of Memory
1. A–iii, B–i, C–ii
2. The three sections of the exam require recognition, cued recall and free recall respectively. **[3]** The best answers will compare two or more types, noting, for example, that cued recall is easier than free recall. **[1]**
3. **A** Hippocampus, LTM **B** Frontal lobe, STM

Structures of Memory 1 and 2
1. Up to approximately 30 seconds
2. A temporary store
3. Unlimited/it does not get full
4. Understanding the meaning (because it uses semantic encoding).

5.

Multi-store model

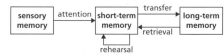

6. Atkinson & Shiffrin; sensory memory, short-term memory and long-term memory; attention; rehearsal; rehearsal
7. Reading out a list of random words to a group of participants. **[1]** Each participant would have to write down all of the words that they could remember. **[1]** The researcher would count how many times each word was recalled, with the expectation that words at the beginning and end of the list would be recalled more frequently on average. **[1]**
8. The student is able to access the question from the auditory store in sensory memory. **[1]** Now that they are paying attention, they can transfer this question to their short-term memory, where it can be held for a few seconds. **[1]** The student will also need to recall meaningful/factual information from their long-term memory in order to answer the question. **[1]**
9. Sensory memory is a very brief store. **[1]** The visual store was found by Sperling (1960) to have a large capacity but a duration of less than one second. **[1]** The auditory store is thought to last around two seconds. **[1]**

10. Curve, first, list, STM
11. A–iii, B–i, C–ii, D–iv
12. B
13. D
14. Repeating, understand, link, spaced
15. Information is only taken into memory if a person pays attention to it. **[1]** This typically happens when they find things interesting or emotional in some way/if they don't pay attention, things will not enter STM and therefore will not be processed and encoded to LTM. **[1]**
16. It is important for memory, as more exposure increases the chance of encoding. **[1]** However, simply repeating things does not always lead to encoding, particularly if information is hard to understand. **[1]** More important processes are active, such as linking new information to what is already known/ retrieving information from memory in a way that is spaced out over time helps to consolidate it. **[1]** Answers could also refer to the multi-store model of memory, which makes the over-simplistic claims that rehearsal is the only means of encoding items to LTM. **[1]**

Memory as an Active Process
1. a) Sir Frederic Bartlett
   b) Additions, subtractions, transformations (to familiar), preservation of detached detail
2. A
3. It came from a culture that was unfamiliar to the participants. **[1]** Therefore they lacked schema knowledge to connect it to. **[1]**
4. Culture, timing, interference, context
5. **Any two from**: the first letter, a question, an image, or an aspect of the learning context.

Pages 30–31 **Practice Questions**

Perception and Sensation
1. A neuron
2. Due to light constancy. **[1]** When people perceive objects, the brain makes allowances for lighting and therefore objects still appear the same to us. **[1]**
3. Visual cortex (or sensory cortex/occipital lobe of the cerebral cortex)

Visual Cues and Constancies
1. Depth perception is essential for survival. **[1] Accept two from the following**: environmental risks to species if they couldn't tell how far away a threat was, or how far they would fall if they jumped off something; predator species need to perceive how close a prey animal is before attacking; modern human examples such as sport and driving.
2. Cues should be named **[1 for each]** and given a brief but recognisable

explanation. **[1 for each]** Answers should focus on monocular cues such as occlusion (one object in front of another shows that it is closer, e.g. plants in front of the water); height in plane (further objects appear higher up, e.g. trees in background); linear perspective. Others are acceptable if accurate and relevant.
3. No (they look blurry and less detailed)

Visual Illusions
1. No. **[1]** There are illusions and distortions that can occur. **[1]**
2. The Kanizsa triangle
3. True, false, false, false

Theories of Perception
1. James Gibson
2. Direct, inferences, affordances
3. a) The constructivist theory
   b) An inference involves working something out from incomplete information. **[1]** Accept any appropriate example, e.g. seeing half of a bus that is partially obscured by another object such as a building, and working out that it must be a whole bus. **[1]**

Factors Affecting Perception
1. The perceptual set
2. Illusions, hallucinations (distortions to perception also acceptable)
3. Answers should focus on expectations and emotions. If a person is hungry or in a different mood, they can see something differently. **[1]** Seeing the scene with different expectations could also affect how they perceive it. **[1]** Culture and motivation do not tend to change as quickly, but could do so over long time periods. **[1]** Answer should back up one point with Bruner and Minturn/Gilchrist and Nesberg's research. **[1]**

Pages 32–41 **Revise Questions**

Pages 32–33
1. Receiving signals from other brain areas and passing signals on.
2. a) Brain stem
   b) Cerebral cortex
   c) Cerebellum
3. Regulating involuntary behaviours such as breathing, heart rate, etc.

Pages 34–35
1. Any appropriate answer, e.g. personality, intelligence, crime, mental health
2. Parenting, culture
3. It is not expressed. (Accept epigenetics.)

Pages 36–37
1. Assimilation, accommodation
2. Centration
3. Pre-operational

Pages 38–39
1. Education/schooling
2. McGarrigle and Donaldson's (1974) naughty teddy study

Pages 40–41
1. No
2. Growth mindset

Pages 42–45 **Review Questions**

Perception and Sensation
1. Receptor cells
2.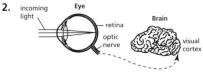

3. Answers must explain that sensation is the process of receiving information from the outside world to the senses, e.g. vision, hearing, **[1]** while perception involves interpreting that information, automatically filtering it and making use of memories and assumptions. **[1]**
4. **Any two from:** colour constancy, light constancy, size constancy, shape constancy.
5. No. **[1]** The perceptual system is very complex. The human brain automatically adjusts for things like lighting conditions and objects moving around – it is possible but difficult to program a computer to do this. **[1]** Also, human sensation relies on very complex networks of receptor cells that help us to build up an image of the world/could mention real-world examples, e.g. self-driving cars, facial recognition software. **[1]**

Visual Cues and Constancies
1. Occlusion is a monocular depth cue, **[1]** whereby one object partially covering another allows people to perceive that it must be closer. **[1]**
2. Answers (top to bottom): linear perspective, texture gradient, retinal disparity, height in plane
3. a) Using binocular cues to depth gives more precise depth perception, and for predators this is very important to survival (more important than peripheral vision from side-facing eyes).
   b) It would be less likely to hunt successfully, e.g. misjudging a pounce on the animal or running after it when it was too far away.
4. Monocular, relative, occlusion
5. a) Vanishing point
   b) It makes paintings look more realistic, so that a two-dimensional picture can give a sense of depth and distance.

Visual Illusions
1. Perception
2. It is a two-dimensional shape that tends to be interpreted as a cube **[1]** but there are two possible ways that it could be facing, making it possible for a person to mentally 'flip' the way they perceive the shape. **[1]**
3. Rubin's vase
4. A–ii, B–iii, C–i
5. Depth cues guide us to distance but can be misinterpreted/misleading. **[1]** Various supporting points could be made, e.g. explanation of example(s) of illusions where depth cues are an issue, e.g. Ponzo illusion, Müller-Lyer/ examples from art – artists use depth cues to indicate depth and distance in

paintings, such as by drawing clouds at different heights above the horizon (height in plane) and in different levels of detail (texture gradient). **[1 per explained point]**

Theories of Perception
1. James Gibson – direct theory; Richard Gregory – constructivist theory
2. The direct theory (bottom-up processing). **[1]** Animals have simpler thought processes than humans, so if they perceive the world in similar ways to us, then perception can't be based to a large extent on cognitions such as memories, inferences, etc. **[1]**
3. B
4. D
5. Visual cliff, hollow face
6. It is a cue in the environment that allows a person or animal to perceive their surroundings. **[1]** The existence of affordances supports the direct (bottom-up) theory of perception, **[1]** because it suggests that the environment provides enough information for organisms to perceive it without the need for using inferences or schema knowledge (or could give examples of affordances such as depth cues). **[1]**

Factors Affecting Perception
1. Individual differences
2. D
3. B
4. Demonstrates that depth cues can be interpreted in different ways by different cultures. **[1]** This shows one aspect of perceptual set – that culture influences how people perceive the world, due to experiences and expectations. **[1]** However, any conclusions from images like this are limited in that they are only based on pictures. **[1]** They don't show that people from different cultures perceive real-world environments differently. **[1]**
5. Gilchrist and Nesberg (1952) study **[1]** where people were asked to judge the brightness of food colours, such as the red of a tomato, and found it more vivid when they were hungry. **[1]** Bruner and Minturn (1955), **[1]** where people were shown an ambiguous figure that could either be perceived as a letter 'B' or the number '13'. The context (other numbers or other letters) affected their expectations. **[1]** Also accept relevant studies such as the Hudson/Deregowski research on culture.

Pages 46–47 **Practice Questions**

Early Brain Development
1. **Any two from:** axon, cell body, nucleus, axon terminal, etc.
2. True
3. The ability of the brain to respond to circumstances and modify its neural structure, **[1]** even after childhood/ adolescent brain development processes are complete. **[1]**

4. The brain stem is a region of the brain, responsible for autonomic functions, whereas a stem cell is an individual cell that develops early in pregnancy and can later turn into a neuron. **[1 mark for each correct definition, does not need to be fully explained.]**

Nature and Nurture
1. Nature
2. A twin study
3. From top to bottom: true, false, true, true
4. Nurture side puts more emphasis on parenting/upbringing and life experiences rather than genetics when explaining personality, intelligence, mental health, etc. **[1]** Answer should include the role of parents/environment/social background (rather than genetics), e.g. in educational success. **[1]** Study of epigenetics suggests that life experiences can impact on gene expression, so the two are interlinked. **[1]** Could also mention the importance of an enriched rather than deprived environment, or the role of culture in behaviour. **[1]**

Piaget's Theories 1 and 2
1. Schemas
2. Egocentrism/egocentric
3. The child starts to make logical operations, **[1]** is less egocentric **[1]** and no longer shows centration/can conserve volume in the 'tall glass' task. **[1]**
4. Assimilation. **[1]** The boy does not yet have a schema for antelope, so he mentally links it to the closest schema that he has – horse. **[1]**

The Effects of Learning on Development
1. Verbalisers and visualisers
2. Influencing, styles, visual, coding
3. **Any one from**: praise, success and failure, feedback and messages from teachers and parents
4. Yes **[1]** because learning facts provides essential schema knowledge to which new learning can be connected. **[1]**

Pages 48–49
1. Random sampling
2. Bias

Pages 50–51
1. The dependent variable, or DV
2. **Any suitable answer, such as:** If caffeine harms people's ability to fall asleep, then participants in the 500 mg caffeine condition will take longer to fall asleep than those in the 0 mg of caffeine condition.

Pages 52–53
1. Independent groups (or matched pairs)
2. Background noise/distractions

Pages 54–55
1. Order effects, e.g. they may improve due to practice.
2. It breaches the ethical principle of confidentiality.
3. Counterbalancing

Pages 56–57
1. Quantitative data
2. The case study method

Pages 58–59
1. A bar chart
2. A strongly positive correlation

Early Brain Development
1. Autonomic functions. **Any one example from**: breathing, heartbeat
2.

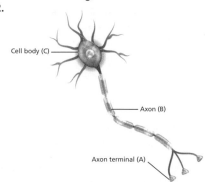

Cell body (C)

Axon (B)

Axon terminal (A)

3. Because without neurons, the brain has not yet developed the structures that are required for sensory processing (thalamus and visual cortex), thinking, memory (cerebral cortex), etc.
4. The thalamus
5. D
6. B
7. Brain, axons, newborn, pruning
8. The child's brain continues to develop through to adolescence and beyond, **[1]** and this occurs mainly through the strengthening of connections and pruning of unnecessary ones. **[1]** It is important to have a stimulating environment that challenges the child and allows for creative play. **[1]** A deprived environment can set back brain development and take years to recover from, or even have permanent effects. **[1]**

Nature and Nurture
1. D
2. B
3. Nature, DNA, expression
4. The nature side
5. Genes do not have a direct effect on development but instead are modified by life experience, a process known as epigenetics. **[1]** If a certain environmental condition is present then the gene will be expressed; if not, then it won't be. **[1]**
6. A–i, B–iii, C–ii
7. Consider whether the girls are identical twins. If they are not, then Maryam may have a higher level of intelligence than her sister, helping to explain her higher grades according to the nature side of the nature versus nurture debate. **[2]** Both seem to have a similar background – they have the same parents, are the same age, and were both encouraged to study hard. **[1]** If the girls are identical twins, then their different personality and achievement can't be explained via genes. **[1]** It could be that Maryam's friends have

encouraged her to work hard and do the same university course (experiences/nurture) or that she was lucky enough to get better teachers. **[1]** Good answers could also discuss possible interactions between genes and the environment, e.g. perhaps the school was more encouraging to extroverted students. **[1]**

Piaget's Theories 1 and 2
1. Assimilation
2. The formal operational stage
3. A–iv, B–i, C–ii, D–iii
4. A
5. C
6. Must describe a suitable study, e.g. the policeman doll study or the naughty teddy study. **[1]** Answer should include researcher name(s) and year. **[1]** Should describe procedure as well as findings/results, e.g. policeman doll: 90 per cent of four year olds succeeded; naughty teddy: majority of children under the age of six were correct. **[2]**
7. Stella is in the pre-operational stage of development. **[1]** In this stage, children can represent one object with another, such as making a brick represent a car. **[1]** However, children are also very egocentric at this stage, so Stella doesn't realise that taking the blue brick away from Fiona would upset her. **[1]**

The Effects of Learning on Development
1. Learning styles
2. a) In a growth mindset, abilities are seen as open to improvement and mistakes are viewed as useful feedback, **[2]** whereas for someone with a fixed mindset, abilities are not seen as open to change/improvement with effort/practice, and mistakes are viewed as a threat (to self-efficacy). **[2]**
   b) Blackwell *et al.*'s (2007) study of maths learning in school, or any other appropriate answer.
3. **Any two answers from**: no scientific evidence that learning style makes a difference to learning; it makes no sense to try to learn items in a way that doesn't fit the material; it is best to combine the senses where possible, e.g. via dual coding
4. Self-efficacy
5. Growth mindset, **[1]** because Mehul thinks that a skill is not fixed but can be improved. **[1]**
6. Andy appears to have a fixed mindset regarding his English ability. **[1]** He thinks he is a visual learner, but as learning styles theory lacks supporting scientific evidence, he would be best to try other strategies. **[1]** His teacher has told him that he should combine his chart with verbal information, a strategy known as dual coding (or could mention that Andy may be a visualiser – someone who prefers to learn with visual information). **[1]**

Sampling Methods
1. Opportunity sampling
2. Systematic sampling
3. Generalising, representative, large

4. The target population
5. Any appropriate answers, e.g.: As with any opportunity sample, the people who are available have particular characteristics. [1] Friends of the researcher might all be of similar ages, or have similar personalities and interests. If they are also students, they might be above average on intelligence and other cognitive abilities. [1]

Variables and Hypotheses
1. Hypothesis (also accept alternative hypothesis/experimental hypothesis/ null hypothesis)
2. Independent, dependent [half a mark for each correct answer]
3. Control means manipulating one variable (the IV) while keeping extraneous variables from impacting on the results. [1] This means ensuring that everything other than the IV is exactly equal across all conditions. [1] Could give an example, such as giving all participants the same time/instructions, or discuss the role of lab/field experiments in terms of controlling the research environment. [1]
4. A–ii, B–iii, C–i
5. Alternative hypothesis

Design of Experiments 1 and 2
1. A repeated measures design
2. From top to bottom: true, false, true, false
3. A field experiment
4. Order, counterbalancing, conditions

Non-experimental Methods
1. Interviews and surveys
2. Naturalistic, categories, reliability
3. Qualitative data (accept primary)
4. a) Numerical data
   b) Verbal or other non-numerical data
   c) Data directly obtained by researcher, e.g. interviewing a participant
   d) Indirectly obtained data that was originally used for another purpose
5. Open [1] and closed questions. [1] The open question should allow the participant to answer in any way they want; [1] the closed question should allow only limited answer options, e.g. yes/no. [1]

Correlation and Data Handling
1. Adding up all the numbers and dividing by how many numbers there are.
2. The mean of each condition (such as scores on a test) could be displayed on a separate bar along the x-axis, [1] with the DV shown on the y-axis. [1]
3. Stronger, spread, direction, upward
4. Graph A shows a negative correlation, Graph B a positive correlation (both strong), Graph C zero/no correlation at all (or very weak)

Pages 68–73 Revise Questions

Pages 68-69
1. Conformity is a type of social influence involving a change in belief or behaviour in order to fit in with a group.
2. Asch
3. 75%

Pages 70–71
1. Responding as instructed to a direct order
2. Milgram
3. Adorno

Pages 72–73
1. The way a person acts when they witness an emergency
2. Piliavin (et al.)
3. When the presence of a crowd or group leads to the loss of sense of individual identity
4. Any one from: use CCTV cameras; restrict access to alcohol; increase policing

Pages 74–79 Review Questions

Sampling Methods
1. A biased sample is one which is not representative of the target population [1] because certain characteristics are more or less likely to occur, such as a higher or lower age range, a distribution of socio-economic or ethnic background that differs from the target population, etc. [1]
2. Every member of the target population must have the same chance of being selected.
3. Representative, random numbers
4. Involves selecting a sample that has the same proportions as the target population; e.g. an equal mix of sexes, or people of different religious backgrounds in the same ratio as the target population. [2] Strength: ensures that selected characteristics are representative of the target population. [1] Weakness: only ensures representativeness of some characteristics; others are ignored. [1]
5. A
6. B
7. a) sampling, b) the sample, c) generalising, d) bias

Variables and Hypotheses
1. Conditions
2. The dependent variable. [1] Any appropriate example, e.g. the score on a test in a memory experiment. [1]
3. Manipulates, cause-and-effect, IV, DV
4. Any two from: the normal distribution is symmetrical; the mean, mode and median are all equal; scores near the mean are very common, and get rarer as they get more extreme
5. Same day revision/short spacing; next day revision/medium spacing; next week revision/long spacing
6. A
7. C
8. This is not a fair test/extraneous variables are not well controlled. [1] Using the school cafeteria (field experiment) will lead to background noise, which might distract students. It could be especially noisy for students who take part at lunch time, leading to bias in the results. [1] Students might do better or worse in the experiment depending on how interested they are in sports stars or planets. These variables should have been kept constant for all participants.

[1] It is a bad idea to test some people in the morning and some at lunchtime, as they may vary on important EVs such as tiredness/hunger. [1]

Design of Experiments 1 and 2
1. (Research) ethics/ethical standards
2. A
3. D
4. Order effects – when a participant does condition 2, everyone has already seen the illusion in condition 1. [1] Could have been avoided by counterbalancing conditions or using an independent groups design. [1]
5. Field experiment: could go to a real lecture and give half of the participants caffeine and half none as the control condition (or placebo, e.g. decaffeinated drink). [1] Lab experiment: would have to be conducted in controlled conditions, perhaps by testing students viewing a video of a lecture one at a time in a lab. [1] An appropriate design should be chosen [1] and justified [1] e.g. independent groups design should be used, because watching the same lecture twice would lead to significant order effects.
6. Repeated measures: every participant does every condition; order effects. Independent groups: participants complete only one condition; participant variables.
7. Random allocation helps to ensure that participant variables are randomly divided among the conditions, [1] and avoids systematic bias. [1]
8. A control condition

Non-experimental Methods
1. Questions with a limited selection of possible answers, such as in a multiple choice question. [1] Research method: surveys or interviews [1]
2. a) Any one from: experiment, observation, survey, interview
   b) Case study (accept correlation)
3. Strength: gathers real-life behaviour as it happens. Weakness: any one from: Can risk invasion of privacy; if participants are informed about the observation, this can affect their behaviour
4. From top to bottom: false, true, false, false
5. A
6. C
7. The case study method would be used, but this could involve a number of other techniques. [1] Brain scans would be necessary in this case, and probably also personality tests, ability/IQ tests, etc. [1] It would be useful to gain secondary data in the form of scores on tests or descriptions of the patient's behaviour prior to the injury, e.g. any tests that were done while at school. [1]
8. Data from a single observer can be unreliable. [1] Therefore, studies tend to train observers, and get two or more people to observe the same behaviour. This increases the reliability of results. [1] Inter-observer reliability could also be mentioned.

Correlation and Data Handling

1. The difference between the lowest and highest score. [1] Shows how spread out the data are overall, but is not a very sensitive/powerful statistic. [1]
2. C
3. B
4. Visually, a histogram does not have gaps between the bars. [1] The graphs are used for different purposes: a bar chart usually represents the conditions of an experiment; a histogram shows survey responses from groups that vary along a specific variable, e.g. different age groups. [1]
5. A weak correlation means that the two co-variables are not closely linked; this can be either in a positive or a negative direction. [1] A negative correlation means that as one variable increases, the other decreases; this relationship can be either weak or strong. [1]
6. The survey provides primary data while the school grades are secondary data (also acceptable: one of them could be referred to as quantitative data). [2] The two variables would be analysed using a correlation study. Each variable would be shown along one axis of a scatter graph. This would display a pattern, allowing interpretation of the relationship between reading level and school grades. [2] A possible (correlational) hypothesis: the number of books read is positively correlated with/has a strong relationship with school grades. Accept other appropriate answers. [1]
7.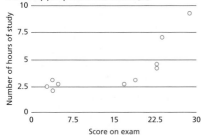

   Accept other appropriate graphs.
8. Mean, dividing, middle, two, common

Pages 80–81 **Practice Questions**

Conformity

1. Anonymity reduces the desire to conform [1] because others are unaware of this non-conformity. [1]
2. Susan is well known for her skill in maths so you're surprised that she gave an incorrect answer. [1] When the second student is asked and also gives the incorrect answer you assume that you are wrong. [1] Rather than look stupid or incompetent you conform to the group norm, [1] even though you know the answer to be incorrect. [1]
3. a) Participants were first asked to look at a 'target' line drawn on a card. [1] They then had to compare it to three lines drawn on another card and say which one was the same length as the target line. [1] Two of the lines on the comparison card were obviously wrong and one was obviously right. [1] Only one of the participants was genuine – the others were confederates of the experimenter

   who had been told to give the wrong answer. [1] The genuine participant was usually one of the last to give their judgement [1] so that they could hear the answers given by the confederates. [1]
   b) Researchers have to abide by ethical guidelines [1] that include a duty of care to their participants. Participants shouldn't be put under undue stress. [1]
   c) In a laboratory setting, variables can be controlled.
   d) Participants often conformed to the group's answers [1] even though they were obviously wrong. [1]

Obedience

1. In condition A, the level of obedience was higher because the actor wore a uniform. [1] Wearing a uniform suggests legitimate authority. [1]
2. The university is seen as having a higher status than the venue in town [1] and therefore the experiment is seen as more legitimate and important. [1]
3. Proximity influences levels of obedience – when participants could see their victims, levels of obedience fell.
4. When people are in an agentic state they allow other people to direct their actions. [1] Their actions are attributed to the person giving the instruction and are not seen to be the responsibility of the person carrying out the instruction. [1]
5. Authoritarian personality type
6. They discovered a correlation between obedience and authoritarian personality type.

Crowd Psychology and Collective Behaviour

1. How a person acts when they witness an emergency
2. **Any one from:** similarity to victim (e.g. race, gender), number of people present and low cost of helping
3. Piliavin et al. (1969) investigated bystander behaviour on the New York subway. Students acted out a scene where one of them (the 'victim') collapsed on a subway train. [1] The victim was sometimes black and sometimes white, acted drunk, or used a cane, or appeared to be ill. [1] In some versions, one of the team would go and help the victim. [1] Two other members of the team observed the reactions of the other passengers on the train. [1]
4. Zimbardo (1969) replicated Milgram's electric shock study [1] but participants either wore a name badge or had their faces concealed with a hood. [1] Those wearing the hoods gave more shocks than those with name badges, [1] supporting the idea of deindividuation. [1]
5. It means that deindividuation is seen across cultures [1] so it isn't influenced by social or cultural differences. [1]

Pages 82–89 **Revise Questions**

Pages 82–83

1. Piaget's theory (language determines thought) and the Sapir-Whorf hypothesis (thinking is dependent on language)

2. When a child uses and repeats words before understanding the concepts behind them
3. Goldstein

Pages 84–85

1. Survival
2. Von Frisch
3. Waggle dance

Pages 86–87

1. A type of communication that doesn't rely on spoken or written words
2. Regulating the flow of conversation, signalling attraction and expressing emotion
3. A posture that is revealing and leaves sensitive areas vulnerable
4. A posture that is defensive and protecting

Pages 88–89

1. That it is evolutionary
2. Matsumoto and Willingham studied sighted and blind judo athletes and found that both groups produced the same facial expressions in certain emotional situations.
3. Yuki et al.

Pages 90–91 **Review Questions**

Conformity

1. People are likely to give the obviously wrong answer to a question if the majority also give the same wrong answer, [1] but a number of factors can affect levels of conformity. [1]
2. Lack of unanimity [1] reduces the chances of the participant succumbing to normative conformity (seeking the approval of the group). [1]
3. The more confederates who made the incorrect judgements, [1] the more likely the participant was to conform. [1]
4. **Any one from**: anonymity, task difficulty, expertise, personality
5. He made participants believe that all the people in the experiment were volunteers [1] when, in fact, they were confederates of the experimenter and were told to give an incorrect answer. [1]
6. **One strength from**: The study was highly controlled and was therefore able to establish a very clear pattern of conformity by most of the participants on one or more of the trials; results have been replicated several times so the study is reliable. [1]
   One weakness from: The study can be criticised on ethical grounds because the participants often displayed stress reactions as they struggled to decide what answer they were going to give; the study was carried out in a laboratory setting in order to control variables, so we cannot be sure that the behaviour displayed is typical of that seen in real life. [1]

Obedience

1. Conformity involves changing your behaviour in order to be accepted by the majority, [1] whereas obedience refers to responding as directed to an order being given by an authority figure. [1]

2. To see how far people would go in obeying an instruction from an authority figure, [1] even if it involved harming another person. [1]
3. **Any two from**: proximity; symbols of authority (white coat); agency; culture; status of situation
4. Influence from authoritarian parents
5. **Any one from**: easily manipulated; can be explained in terms of educational level
6. Because the study is correlational – it could be that a tendency towards obedience caused people to be more authoritarian. We cannot establish cause and effect. [1]

Crowd Psychology and Collective Behaviour
1. a) This behaviour can be explained using the theory of diffusion of responsibility. [1] The more people who witness an emergency, the less responsible for helping they feel. [1]
   b) If Fatima had been on her own when she saw the man fall, she would have felt more responsible [1] and would have been more likely to help. [1]
2. People who appeared ill [1] or less able to help themselves, such as a person using a walking stick. [1]
3. Anonymity increases feelings of deindividuation [1] and leads to people acting more confidently. [1]
4. a) When people find themselves in crowds they begin to lose their sense of individuality (this is called deindividuation). [1] When we are a member of a crowd we also feel more anonymous [1] and are more likely to do things that go against our personal beliefs, [1] such as becoming involved in acts of aggression. [1]
   b) **One from**: install CCTV cameras; remove or restrict access to alcohol
   c) **Any one from**: using CCTV cameras at football matches decreases the feeling of anonymity; individuals know they might get caught on camera and punished for their actions; alcohol could influence the acts of aggression and so restricting it could minimise any potential effects.

Pages 92–93 **Practice Questions**

The Possible Relationship Between Language and Thought
1. a) Piaget thought that development takes place in a number of stages and that language development is the result of cognitive (or thought) development. [1] According to Piaget, a child must first be able to use ideas and concepts before being able to use language. [1] However, a child might use and repeat words before understanding the concepts behind these words. Piaget called this egocentric speech. [1]
   b) To convey ideas and information
2. The weak version of the Sapir-Whorf hypothesis suggests that language influences thought.

Differences Between Human and Animal Communication
1. Animals only communicate to pass messages about survival, reproduction, territory and obtaining food (such as a rabbit thumping to warn of predators for survival). [1] Humans communicate information about many aspects of their lives, such as how they are feeling, by smiling when they are happy or frowning when they are uncertain. [1]
2. The waggle dance of the honeybee
3. **Any two from**: song in birds; leaving marking on trees (e.g. wild boar); scenting territory using urine (e.g. dogs)
4. Distance is based on the duration of the dance.
5. Symbols are sounds, gestures, material objects or written words [1] that have a specific meaning to a group of people. [1]
6. The discussion of possible future outcomes [1] based on present situations and expected outcomes. [1]

Non-verbal Communication
1. Verbal: **any two from**: Rebecca passing a note; Abi laughing out loud; teacher telling off
   Non-verbal: **any two from**: Rebecca smiling; Abi waving; Abi frowning
2. Looking away can signal to the speaker that the listener isn't interested.
3. Because the listener wishes to speak
4. Hands held up to the chin [1] or the head is lowered to protect the throat; [1] arms and legs are crossed. [1]
5. a) An imaginary area that people view as their own territory.
   b) People react in a number of ways, including feeling uncomfortable and adjusting their own position in order to regain territory.

Explanations of Non-verbal Behaviour
1. Non-verbal communication is an evolutionary mechanism – it is evolved and adaptive. [1] All mammals (both human and non-human) show emotions through facial expression. [1] This behaviour is universal and, therefore, evolutionary. [1] Types of non-verbal behaviour persist in humans because they have been acquired for their value throughout evolutionary history. [1]
2. Lack of ecological validity because Yuki used computer-generated faces to test participants and not real faces. [1] Demand characteristics – participants were aware that they were taking part in a study so may not have given true responses. [1] Findings cannot be generalised because the study only looked at one element of emotion (happy/sad) and not any other emotions. [1] Yuki used students in the study – other groups might have reacted differently. [1]
3. If something is innate then we are born with it. [1] If something is learned we are not born with it but learn it through our experiences and observations. [1]

Pages 94–101 **Revise Questions**

Pages 94–95
1. Central nervous system and peripheral nervous system

2. Central nervous system
3. Autonomic nervous system
4. William James and Carl Lange

Pages 96–97
1. Sensory, motor, relay
2. 'What fires together, wires together'
3. A specialised gap between neurons through which the electrical impulse from the neuron is transmitted chemically.

Pages 98–99
1. It is the view that particular parts of the brain are responsible for specific functions.
2. Hearing
3. Balance and coordination

Pages 100–101
1. It is concerned with the biological basis of thought processes.
2. fMRI, CAT, PET
3. Insufficient oxygen going to the brain

Pages 102–105 **Review Questions**

The Possible Relationship Between Language and Thought
1. Piaget's theory states that language determines thought [1] and the Sapir-Whorf hypothesis suggests that thinking is dependent on language. [1]
2. Some children have severe learning difficulties but normal language development, [1] suggesting that language development isn't dependent on cognitive development. [1] Some studies have found that language development can accelerate cognitive development. [1]
3. a) Strong and weak version
   b) The strong version says that language determines thought and the weak version says that language influences thought.

Differences Between Human and Animal Communication
1. Peacocks attract a mate using their plumage. Male birds of paradise engage in a complex dance to attract females.
2. Magpies chatter; rabbits thump their paws on the ground
3. They engage in the waggle dance. [1] The direction the bee moves in relation to the hive indicates direction. [1] If the bee moves vertically, the direction to the source is directly towards the sun. [1] The duration of the waggle dance signifies the distance to the source from the hive. [1]
4. Humans have an open vocal system and a larger bank of symbols to use in communication.
5. To discuss the past, plan for the future and discuss future events.

Non-verbal Communication
1. Verbal communication relies on the use of words; [1] non-verbal communication doesn't rely on spoken or written words. [1] Non-verbal communication can include body posture or gestures. [1] It can also include certain aspects of language such as tone of voice. [1]

2. Open postures involve leaving the body vulnerable, [1] including having the chin raised, arms placed to the side (not folded) and legs uncrossed. [1] A closed posture ensures that vulnerable areas are protected by folding arms and crossing legs. [1] A closed posture is thought to be a defensive posture. [1]
3. a) The mirroring or the adoption of the same posture as the person doing the talking.
   b) Encourages mutual positive feelings
4. **Any appropriate answer, such as:** tapping somebody lightly on the shoulder; gently stroking their hand; hugging them; holding their hand
5. Cultural norms, gender, status

Explanations of Non-verbal Behaviour
1. Non-verbal communication is an evolutionary mechanism, [1] allowing species to adapt and evolve. [1]
2. It assumed that non-verbal behaviour is innate, [1] i.e. it is something we are born with rather than a behaviour we learn from the environment. [1] It is therefore nature rather than nurture. [1]
3. In order to learn facial expressions from others, it is necessary to see other people use those expressions. [1] A child who has been blind since birth is unable to learn from what they cannot see, so the expressions they make must have been present at birth. [1]
4. Learned behaviour arises through observing others. [1] Learning theories would argue that non-verbal behaviour is a learned response to watching other people display such behaviour. [1]
5. a) Americans responded to visual cues associated with the mouth [1] and Japanese people responded to eyes. [1] For example, while an American would identify a happy person from their upturned mouth, [1] a Japanese person would focus on creases around the eyes. [1]
   b) Yuki found that American and Japanese people focus on different areas of the face to identify emotional states. [1] If non-verbal behaviour was evolutionary, all cultures should identify emotions in the same way, [1] but because Yuki found a difference, non-verbal behaviour must be learned. [1]

The Structure and Function of the Brain and Nervous System
1. D
2. The PNS transmits messages to the whole body from the brain, and vice versa.
3. Sympathetic and parasympathetic
4. It is the CNS initially that would pick up the sound, the auditory cortex, [1] and this has stimulated the hypothalamus to sensing fear. [1] The ANS now takes over and Jake starts to run as his fight or flight response has been triggered increasing his heart rate at the same time. [1] When Jake recognises Will's voice, using his CNS again he slows down. [1]

5. The theory suggests that emotional experience is the result, not the cause, of perceived bodily changes. [1] For example, we might think that if we meet a bear we become frightened and we run. [1] James-Lange theory, however, would suggest that we are frightened *because* we run. [1] In a similar way, we feel sad because we cry or afraid because we tremble. [1]

Neuron Structure and Function
1. C
2. It carries an electrical signal to a muscle, [1] which will cause the muscle to either contract or relax. [1]
3. It is the theory that states when one neuron sends a signal to another neuron, and that second neuron becomes activated, the connection between the two neurons is strengthened. [1] The more one neuron activates another neuron, the stronger the connection between them grows. [1] With every new experience, the brain rewires its physical structure. [1]
4. **Any one from:** serotonin or dopamine
5. During synaptic transmission, [1] the right key (neurotransmitter) has to fit into the right lock (receptor) to open up the specific ion channel. [1]

Localisation of Function in the Brain
1. The primary motor cortex is responsible for movement [1] by sending messages to the muscles via the brain stem and spinal cord. [1]
2. Touch
3. When a person struggles to find the word that they need
4. The technique of using microelectrodes to stimulate parts of the brain

An Introduction to Neuropsychology
1. People with cognitive deficits [1] due to brain damage or strokes. [1]
2. Techniques such as fMRI rely on matching behavioural actions with physiological activity. [1] Because the person being scanned is usually conscious, [1] they can be directed to produce a particular action [1] such as performing a memory task while being scanned. [1]
3. a) Radioactive gold
   b) Frontal lobes
4. Lack of oxygen
5. The area in which the damage occurred

Pages 108–109
1. Positive engagement with society and coping effectively with challenges.
2. Geographical isolation from family and emotional support networks, which in turn increases levels of loneliness and the feeling of not knowing who to turn to in times of crisis; technology and internet usage; increased pressure at work and school
3. Any appropriate organisation, e.g. Time To Change

Pages 110–111
1. Living with a person with significant mental health problems can put a strain on relationships.
2. If social care is lacking, or under stress through shortages in trained staff, this has an impact on the treatment that can be offered to patients; can lead to higher crime rates; effect on economy through time off work
3. Increased staff absence

Pages 112–113
1. One of the mood (or affective) disorders – mood disorders involve a prolonged and major disturbance of mood and emotions
2. A sense of euphoria or elation
3. Depression with mania
4. Persistent sadness/low mood, loss of interest/pleasure, fatigue/low energy

Pages 114–115
1. A blueprint by which depressed people view the world
2. Selective serotonin re-uptake inhibitors
3. Cognitive behavioural therapy – a type of psychotherapy that helps people to think in more constructive ways

Pages 116–117
1. Addiction refers to a behaviour that leads to dependency.
2. When a substance is taken to excess but does not necessarily lead to addiction.
3. A strong desire or sense of compulsion to take the substance despite harmful consequences, impaired capacity to control substance-taking behaviour, pre-occupation with substance use and the giving up of activities once deemed important, a physiological withdrawal state when the substance is reduced or ceased.

Pages 118–119
1. The extent to which traits are inherited
2. Sweden
3. DeBlasio and Benda

The Structure and Function of the Brain and Nervous System
1. a) Brain and spinal cord
   b) The brain is involved in psychological processes and the maintenance of life [1]; the spinal cord is involved in the transfer of messages to and from the brain to the peripheral nervous system (PNS). [1]
2. The PNS transmits messages to the whole body from the brain, and vice versa. [1] The PNS has two divisions: the somatic system and the autonomic system. [1]
3. The fight or flight response is designed to help when we feel that we are under threat. [1] It helps a person react quicker than normal. [1] It is triggered from the autonomic nervous system, specifically the sympathetic branch, and gets the body ready to fight or run away from the threat. [1] It leads to a number of bodily changes, e.g. increased heart rate, faster breathing, pupil dilation, etc. [1]

4. Helps to transmit and receive information from the organs

5. It proposes that the way in which we experience an emotional event is triggered by our bodily response [1] rather than the other way around. [1] For example, we get anxious because our heart is beating very fast (or any other appropriate example). [1]

Neuron Structure and Function

1. They tell the rest of the brain about the external and internal environment [1] by processing information taken from one of the five senses (sight, hearing, touch, smell, taste). [1]

2. With every new experience, the brain rewires its physical structure [1]; the more often the activity occurs, the stronger the connection becomes. [1]

3. Stronger connections between nerve cells [1] and longer lasting changes in synaptic connections. [1]

4. The electrical nerve impulse travels down the neuron, [1] prompting the release of neurotransmitters at the pre-synaptic terminal. [1] The neurotransmitters are released into the synaptic fluid in the synapse. [1] The adjacent neurons must then take up the neurotransmitters from the fluid [1] and convert them into an electrical impulse to travel down the neuron to the next synaptic terminal. [1] The procedure is then repeated. [1]

5. Chemicals within the brain that transmit signals

6. Excitatory potentials make it more likely for the neuron to fire; [1] inhibitory potentials make it less likely to fire. [1]

Localisation of Function in the Brain

1. Refers to the view that particular parts of the brain are responsible for specific functions, [1] such as vision and language. [1] In the case of memory, a person could suffer memory impairment through infection or trauma and retain long-term memories but be unable to create new memories [1] due to damage to the part of the brain responsible for short-term memory. [1]

2. Concerned with the sensation of the body; [1] the somatosensory cortex perceives touch; [1] the amount of somatosensory cortex required dictates the amount of somatosensory cortex needed for that area of the body. [1]

3. The visual centre of the brain is concerned with visual perception. [1] More specifically, an area of the visual cortex known as Area V1 is thought to be specifically necessary for visual perception; [1] people with damage to this area report no vision of any kind (including in dreams). [1]

4. a) Neural stimulation; [1] microelectrodes are used to stimulate parts of the brain to test their function [1]
   b) The amount of cortical tissue required differs for different functions; [1] the more sensitive the area, the more cortical tissue is required. [1]

An Introduction to Neuropsychology

1. How the function of neurons affects thought and behaviour

2. Traditional MRI scans produce static images; [1] fMRIs can produce moving images captured in real time [1]

3. Uses an X-ray beam to produce a picture of the physiology of the brain.

4. Participants were injected with a small amount of radioactive gold [1] and then asked to retrieve two types of memory: an episodic memory (that is, a personal experience) [1] and a semantic memory (a general knowledge memory). [1]

5. They would lose at least some movement, such as reflex actions and the ability to walk or to lift their arms. [1] This movement can return over time but is sometimes permanently lost. [1]

6. Any appropriate answer, such as accidents; certain types of infection

Pages 123–125 **Practice Questions**

An Introduction to Mental Health

1. The general inability to cope with everyday life

2. The inability to engage in satisfying interpersonal relationships

3. **Any two from**: feelings of independence (autonomy); resisting stress; an accurate perception of reality; being able to cope with life and the changing environment (environmental mastery)

4. **Any two from**: appropriate public behaviour; control of aggression; politeness; control of culturally and socially offensive language

5. Anxiety; depression

6. Any appropriate answers, such as The Campaign Against Living Miserably (CALM) and Time To Change

Effects of Mental Health Problems on Individuals and Society

1. The partner may experience feelings of guilt and shame [1] and even blame themselves. [1]

2. Chronic mental health problems can lead to a weakened immune system [1] and make people more susceptible to infection. [1]

3. The number of trained mental health professionals and social workers

4. Theft [1] to obtain money to feed their addiction [1]

5. Stigma; [1] the employee might believe that people will treat them differently if they divulge their illness. [1]

Characteristics of Clinical Depression

1. Depression has a longer duration

2. Major depressive disorder.

3. Mania

4. **Any two from**: persistent lowering of mood, decrease in activity/energy, change in sleep pattern, reduced self-esteem or self-confidence, ideas of guilt or worthlessness, loss of pleasurable feelings, agitation, loss or increase in appetite, loss of concentration, suicidal thoughts or acts

5. It usually develops after adolescence/in adulthood.

Theories of Depression and Interventions

1. Depression is caused by internal factors (nature rather than nurture), [1] including brain chemicals and genes. [1]

2. Serotonin

3. The gene has been found to reduce levels of serotonin.

4. a) Antidepressant medication
   b) Tricyclics and SSRIs

5. Cognitive behavioural therapy (CBT)

Characteristics of Addiction

1. A behaviour that leads to dependency

2. Any appropriate answer, e.g. alcoholism, drug addiction

3. Abuse doesn't include dependency.

4. Any two from: impaired capacity to control substance-taking behaviour; pre-occupation with substance use and the giving up of activities once deemed important; a physiological withdrawal state when the substance is reduced or ceased

Theories of Addiction and Interventions

1. Kaij (1960) [1] studied the rates of alcohol abuse in identical and fraternal twins. [1] He found that the concordance rate for identical twins was 54% and that for fraternal twins it was only 28%. [1] He concluded that there are genetic and hereditary factors involved in alcohol addiction. [1]

2. DeBlasio and Benda found the influence of peers to be a primary factor in the uptake of alcohol and drugs in adolescents. [1] Young people who smoke are more likely to associate with other young people who also smoke. [1]

3. A and B

4. They could use a drug that reacts with alcohol [1] and makes the person feel nauseous. [1] The addict would learn to associate alcohol with the feeling of being sick. [1]

5. a) A group of people with the same or similar problem who come together for support and help in overcoming their addiction.
   b) The 12-step program

Pages 126–127 **Review Questions**

An Introduction to Mental Health

1. Feeling bad about yourself (including the way you look); [1] showing signs of stress or the inability to cope; [1] feelings of having no control over life [1]

2. A positive attitude towards yourself, [1] personal growth and development (self-actualisation), [1] feelings of independence (autonomy), [1] resisting stress, [1] an accurate perception of reality, [1] and being able to cope with life and the changing environment (environmental mastery). [1]

3. a) Different cultures have different norms and values, [1] so something that might appear ordinary or normal in one culture can be seen as abnormal in another. [1]
   b) Homosexuality

4. More support networks to fall back on in times of need. [1] Families can support people in a number of ways, including psychological support, comfort, understanding and feelings of belonging. [1]

5. Mental illness can lead some people to feel alienated because of the negative feelings towards it. People might equate mental illness to psychological weakness and associate it with violence and extreme unusual behaviour. [1] This leads to an awkwardness around sufferers and they could feel isolated because of it, making the condition worse. [1]

Effects of Mental Health Problems on Individuals and Society

1. It can lead to the partner experiencing feelings of guilt and shame. [1] They might even blame themselves for their partner's illness. [1] Behaviour can change, resulting in the relationship being less intimate. [1]

2. It can lead to some people neglecting themselves, such as their personal hygiene. [1] They might become less interested in activities they once found enjoyable and socialise less often. [1]

3. Certain conditions, such as chronic anxiety and depression, can put a strain on the immune system, [1] making people more susceptible to infections. [1]

4. Health services [1] and social services [1]

5. To obtain money to buy the addictive substances they crave

6. Some conditions, such as stress-related problems and depression, can lead to people having to take long periods off work. [1] This can lead to understaffing in some workplaces. [1]

Characteristics of Clinical Depression

1. A prolonged and major disturbance of mood and emotions.

2. Manic depression or bipolar disorder

3. Bipolar depression is characterised by periods of mania followed by periods of low mood. [1] Unipolar depression doesn't include manic episodes. [1]

4. A sense of euphoria or elation. [1] People with mania have a great deal of energy [1] and can survive on very little sleep. [1] Despite this, however, they have difficulty focusing and rarely get very much done. [1]

5. a) Persistent sadness, loss of interest and pleasure in activities, fatigue and low energy
   b) **Any three from:** disturbed sleep, poor concentration, low self-confidence, poor or increased appetite, suicidal thoughts or acts, agitation, guilt/self-blame

Theories of Depression and Interventions

1. a) People with depression often display low levels of the neurotransmitter serotonin.
   b) The assumption is that low levels of serotonin are responsible for depression. [1] However, there is a problem with cause and effect in that depression might lead to lower

levels of serotonin rather than be caused by it. [1]

2. Negative self-schemas [1] which lead people to think pessimistically [1]

3. They help to regulate the levels of serotonin in the brain. [1] They block the transporter mechanism that absorbs the serotonin. [1]

4. It helps people to think differently about how they perceive events – encourages more positive and adaptive ways of thinking. [1] Maladaptive thoughts can be challenged and held up to scrutiny where they are found to be false. [1]

Characteristics of Addiction

1. Addiction refers to a behaviour that leads to dependency; [1] abuse refers to taking the substance in excess but doesn't necessarily lead to dependency. [1]

2. Certain behaviours and habits can cause people to become dependent on them (such as playing computer games). [1] These behaviours share the same core components as addiction. [1]

3. Progression (increase in severity); [1] preoccupation with the activity; [1] perceived loss of control; [1] persistence despite negative long-term consequences [1]

4. The addictive activity becomes the most important aspect of the addict's life.

5. The reverting to the patterns of addiction that existed prior to recovery.

6. Ella will have become gradually more consumed by playing games and will find it difficult to think about anything else. [1] Activities she once found interesting and exciting (such as playing sports or socialising with friends) will have become far less important. [1] She might be spending large amounts of time on her own playing games. [1]

Theories of Addiction and Interventions

1. There is a genetic component to alcohol abuse [1] because identical twins had higher concordance rates (54%) than fraternal (non-identical) twins (28%). [1]

2. Research found that deceased alcoholics were more likely to possess the A1 variant of the DRD2 gene, [1] suggesting that the cause of alcoholism might be genetic. [1]

3. Addiction is learned through observation. [1] This would suggest that people are more likely to engage in potentially addictive behaviour if they witness the behaviour being carried out by others, especially peers. [1]

4. a) A technique that pairs the addictive behaviour with an unpleasant experience or sensation. [1] For example, drugs can be taken that cause nausea when a cigarette is smoked. [1]
   b) Self-management programs rely on group support and a series of steps on the path to recovery, [1] while aversion therapy attempts to apply the principles of conditioning. [1] Aversion therapy obtains faster results than self-management programs. [1]

Cognition and Behaviour

1. Any appropriate example, such as 'If noise has an effect on stress, then people who complete a task in a noisy environment will score higher on a measure of their stress level than people who complete the task in a quiet environment.' [4]

2. It has two main roles: it maintains information in STM [1] and encodes it into LTM. [1]

3. The brain/visual cortex; [1] this builds up an image of the world by combining information from a network of receptor cells and integrating it with memories/assumptions. [1]

4. Both are non-experimental methods which involve asking questions to participants. [1] Interview is done face-to-face; surveys via paper or on screen. [1] Both could use two types of question, but interviews tend to feature open questions and surveys closed questions. [1] Interviews allow follow-up to questions, whereas an advantage of surveys is that they are private, so could prompt a higher level of honesty in responses. [1]

5. Before – **any two from**: beginning of brain formation in week 3; development of stem cells; true neurons forming from day 42; brain areas largely complete by midway through pregnancy; many connections forming (axons/fibres linking cells). After – **any two from**: pruning of axonal connections; rapid learning and strengthening connections; structural changes until mid-20s; (neuro)plasticity throughout life.

6. Limitations of STM, i.e. 5–9 items in terms of capacity (two seconds of rehearsal time is also acceptable), [1] and a duration of up to 30 seconds before items decay. [1] In LTM, both capacity and duration should be described as unlimited. [2]

7. a) bar b) strength

8. The top-down/constructivist theory. [1] Illusions show that the world is sometimes ambiguous, and therefore people can't perceive it just from information that reaches the senses. [1] Therefore, according to constructivist theory, it is necessary to make inferences and use knowledge about the world stored in memory in order to build up a mental picture of the world. [1]

9. Retinal disparity: [1] differences between the images from the two eyes gives a cue to distance, [1] as the difference is larger when the object is close. [1] **Or** convergence/eye convergence: [1] a cue from the muscles that move our eyes, [1] as the eyes have to rotate slightly for closer objects. [1]

10. Encoding, storage, retrieval

11. Motivation, set, people, areas

12. An illusion

13. It is an active process, [1], which can be distorted by things such as prior knowledge/expectations. [1]

14. **From top to bottom**: true, true, false, true
15. Asking passers-by is an opportunity sample, not a random sample. [1] There are various ways that such a sample could be biased – accept any appropriate answer. For instance: some people might not be in school; some are more likely to be in the corridor while others are in class/in the school library, etc. People who take a particular school subject are more likely to be on a particular corridor (e.g. a science corridor). People who are missing class for various reasons are more likely to be in the corridor. Certain pupils are more likely to have a free period, e.g. older pupils with a lighter timetable. [2]
16. They could link it to an existing schema (e.g. "it's a type of train") [1] or create a new schema for this new category of vehicle [1], i.e. they could assimilate [1] or accommodate [1] the stimulus.
17. a) allocated
    b) counterbalancing
18. The two sides may be correct on different occasions. Some psychological attributes might be largely genetic, while others are linked to upbringing and culture. [1] Genetic aspects could also have an effect on later life experiences, meaning that the two interact. [1] Genes and the environment interact biologically (epigenetics) meaning that aspects of the 'nurture' side such as upbringing could affect things usually associated with the nature side, i.e. based on gene expression. [1]
19. **Any two answers from**: facts are necessary in order to connect new ideas; we shouldn't just teach skills; it's best to avoid teaching the theory of learning styles because there is no scientific evidence for it; it's important to combine different sensory inputs – dual coding; a style of learning needs to be appropriate to the material.

Social Context and Behaviour
1. Antidepressant medication; [1] cognitive behavioural therapy (CBT) [1]
2. Postural echoing; [1] to increase positive feelings between you [1]
3. They carry messages from one part of the central nervous system to another.
4. Presence of an ally, [1] size of majority, [1] anonymity, [1] task difficulty [1]
5. Aversion therapy
6. The listener wants to speak.
7. Fight or flight
8. They have invaded your personal space. [1] Personal space is an imaginary area around us that we think of as our territory. [1]
9. Proximity, [1] symbols of authority, [1] status of the situation, [1] agency [1]
10. They would feel unable to survive without it; [1] drinking would take priority over all other behaviours; [1] there would be specific behavioural changes. [1]
11. The central nervous system
12. Number of people present; pluralistic ignorance; similarity of victim to helper; cost of helping
13. The autonomic nervous system
14. They will be protecting vital parts of their body such as the chest and genital region. [1] Arms will most likely be folded across the chest [1] and if they are seated, legs will be crossed. [1]
15. The symptoms would last longer.
16. fMRI

Notes

Glossary

abuse – the use of a substance (often a drug) in amounts that are harmful to the user

accommodation – the process of changing a schema or developing a new one when faced with information that cannot be assimilated into a person's current schemas

acoustic encoding – encoding information to memory based on its sound

active process – a cognitive process that requires effort and attention, for example problem-solving or rehearsal in working memory

adaptive – a behaviour that evolves in order to increase the chances of reproductive success

addiction – a condition that results when a person ingests a substance or engages in activity that over time becomes compulsive and interferes with ordinary life responsibilities

Adorno – German philosopher and sociologist who developed the theory of the authoritarian personality

affordances – information from the environment that aids perception, for example depth cues

agentic – a state in which a person behaves as if an agent of another, assuming no responsibility for their actions or the consequences

(random) allocation – a basic principle of experimental design which states that the choice of condition or order of conditions that a participant completes must be random to avoid bias

alternative hypothesis – a scientific prediction of the effect that the IV will have on the DV, with a rationale based on past research

ambiguity – more than one possible interpretation; the basis of several illusions

Ames Room – a specially constructed room that appears ordinary when viewed from the front but is actually distorted, causing an illusion of size

assimilation – the process of fitting new information into an existing schema

attention – the cognitive function of focusing on a stimulus; people have a limited amount of attention which must be divided among active tasks

authoritarian – the favouring or enforcing of strict obedience to authority at the expense of personal freedom

autonomic – involuntary or automatic; referring to the autonomic nervous system

autonomous – having the freedom to act independently

aversion therapy – creates in the individual a strong aversive (i.e. dislike) response to the source of the addiction

axon – part of a neuron; the nerve fibre which carries signals to other neurons

bar chart – a graph displaying statistical results based on the height of two or more bars; commonly used to compare conditions of an experiment

Bartlett – memory researcher Sir Frederic Bartlett was the first professor of psychology in the United Kingdom

bias – ways in which data or judgements are distorted or skewed

binocular – a visual cue to depth/distance which depends on comparing the differences between what is sensed by the two eyes

bipolar – a disorder where people alternate between periods of depression and mania

blame – feeling responsible for a fault or a wrong; people who are close to individuals with mental health problems will often believe that they are somehow at fault for the illness

bottom-up processing – a type of perceptual processing based on the information received via sensation, considered to be primary by the direct theory

brain stem – part of the brain; responsible for autonomic functions such as breathing and heartbeat

bystander effect – the tendency for an individual to feel less responsible in the presence of others because responsibility is distributed among all the people present

bystander intervention – a psychological phenomenon in which someone is less likely to intervene in an emergency situation when others are present than when they are alone

capacity – in cognitive psychology, the amount of information that can be held in a memory store at one time

case study – an in-depth study of one individual or a small group

categories of behaviour – types of behaviour that might be recorded during observational research, generally phrased broadly so that many possible actions could fall within a single category

cause-and-effect relationship – relationship between two variables where a change in one variable directly causes a change in the other, i.e. there is causation

CBT – cognitive behavioural therapy; a type of psychotherapy that attempts to correct faulty thought patterns

cell body – part of a neuron; the central part of the cell containing the nucleus

centration – the tendency of children in Piaget's pre-operational stage to focus on one element of a problem and ignore others

cerebellum – part of the brain; responsible for precise physical movement and coordination

cerebral cortex – part of the brain; responsible for cognition, including thinking, perception and most memory processes

closed posture – a defensive posture involving the protection of vulnerable parts of the body

closed questions – questions that give participants a pre-determined choice of possible answers

colour constancy – the perceptual constancy where the brain makes allowances for the variable appearance of colours under different conditions

concrete operational stage – a developmental stage from Piaget's theory; children aged 8 and above can make logical operations and are able to conserve volume and other properties

conditions – parts of an experiment which are compared, each relating to a different value of the IV

confederate – a person hired by the researcher to act as a participant when they are, in fact, part of the experiment

confidentiality – ethical principle regarding the treatment of data and participant details; information must be held securely and personal information should not be released

conformity – the process of giving in to real or imagined pressure from a group

conservation – awareness that the appearance of an object or set of objects can transform without its properties fundamentally changing; Piaget believed that this emerges in the concrete operational stage of development.

constructivist theory – a psychological theory which states that a person's schemas can influence and distort what they remember and perceive

context – a factor that affects memory; it's easier to remember things in the same context as where they were first learned

control – keeping extraneous variables constant and minimised during experimentation, allowing the researcher to test for cause and effect between the experimental variables

control condition – a condition of an experiment which is conducted to form a baseline for comparison

convergence – a binocular cue to depth based on muscular movements; the eyes rotate inwards to a greater extent when viewing an object that is closer

correlation – a statistical analysis technique that aims to show how two variables are linked

correlation strength – how closely connected two co-variables are in a correlational study, in either a positive or negative direction

counterbalancing – varying the order of experimental conditions to balance out any possible order effects

co-variables – the variables studied in a correlation study

CT scan – a type of scanning technique that uses an X-ray beam to produce a picture of the physiology of the brain

cue – a piece of information which helps a memory to be retrieved

cued recall – retrieval from memory where the individual has a prompt or reminder of some kind

culture – the beliefs and behaviour of a particular group of people, usually associated with specific areas or countries; a factor that affects both memory and perception

debriefing – information given to participants at the end of a study

deception – an ethical flaw in research whereby a researcher will withhold details or give false information to participants

deindividuation – the tendency of people in a large, arousing, anonymous group to lose inhibitions, sense of responsibility and self-consciousness

dependent variable (DV) – the variable that is measured in an experiment, resulting in the data that a researcher analyses

deprivation – time spent in an environment which limits or harms a child's ability to develop healthily; a lack of suitable stimulation can harm intellectual development

depth cues – affordances in the environment that allow a person or animal to perceive depth or distance

depth perception – the perceptual process of interpreting how close or far away objects are

direct theory – a psychological theory which states that perception is based on sensation rather than on expectations and inferences

displacement – in cognitive psychology, forgetting from STM where items are pushed out because of its limited capacity

distortion – an aspect of a memory which differs from what was originally experienced

dual coding – the finding that combining both verbal and visual information during learning improves the rate at which people later remember information

duration – the length of time a memory store can retain information before it is forgotten

Dweck – Carol Dweck, a cognitive psychologist with an interest in education, and the originator of the theory of growth and fixed mindsets

effort after meaning – a term used by Bartlett to describe people's motivation to reconstruct and distort information in memory in order to make sense of it

egocentrism – inability to think about the feelings of others or to view situations from their perspective, or the tendency to avoid doing so

emotion – feelings such as happiness, worry and fear; bodily feelings such as hunger are sometimes included

encoding – taking new information into memory; an input process

epigenetics – the study of how the environment impacts on whether genes are – or are not – expressed

episodic memory – long-term memory for life events

ethical guidelines – code of conduct set out by a professional organisation such as the British Psychological Society, aiming to ensure that research meets ethical standards

ethical standards – set of principles which must be followed by researchers to ensure that research is ethically sound and does not harm participants

evolution – the process by which different kinds of living organism are believed to have developed from earlier forms during the history of the earth

excitation – a positive change in voltage that occurs when a neurotransmitter binds to an excitatory receptor site

expectations – a factor in the perceptual set; people's perceptions are influenced by what they expect, which is in turn influenced by past experience

extraneous variable (EV) – any variable other than the IV which could potentially affect the DV

false memory – events that appear in memory but didn't actually happen

fiction – the basis of some illusions, fictions are where something is perceived despite not being (fully) available to the senses

field experiment – any experiment which is conducted in a participant's natural environment

fixed mindset – a set of attitudes based around the idea that ability levels are fixed, and that how well someone does at a task is largely due to factors outside of their control

fMRI – a scanning technique that measures the energy released by haemoglobin; an fMRI scan produces a moving picture

formal operational stage – a developmental stage from Piaget's theory; children aged 11 and above can solve abstract problems

fraternal – non-identical twins

free recall – retrieval from memory where the stimulus is not present and there is no cue

frontal lobe – one of the four main lobes of the cerebral cortex; this area is essential for STM/working memory processes

gene expression – where a gene causes the body to produce a protein, potentially impacting on brain structure and behaviour

generalise – to conclude that the findings from a research study also hold true for the wider population

genes – sequences of DNA held within every cell in the body

genetics – the study of genes and their effects on the characteristics of living organisms

Gestalt approach – a psychological perspective which states that people have a tendency to perceive objects as wholes rather than many parts, and therefore to mentally connect objects that appear to belong together

gestures – movements of part of the body, especially a hand or the head, to express an idea or meaning

Gibson – J.J. Gibson, the main figure behind the direct theory of perception

Gregory – Richard Gregory, the main figure behind the constructivist theory of perception

growth mindset – a set of attitudes based around the idea that ability levels can be changed, and therefore how well someone does at a task is largely due to effort and learned skill

guilt – a feeling of responsibility or remorse for an offence, crime, wrongdoing, etc., whether real or imagined

hallucinations – perception in the absence of any relevant sensation

harm – ethical principle which states that research participants must be treated with respect and should come to no physical or psychological harm, including stress

height in plane – a monocular cue to depth; objects that are more distant appear closer to the horizon line

heritability – an estimation of how much variation in a phenotypic trait in a population is due to genetic variation among individuals in that population

hippocampus – an area of the brain essential to encoding new long-term memories

histogram – a graph displaying statistical results based on the height of a series of bars; commonly used to represent a continuous set of groups among a target population

holistic – the treatment of the whole person, taking into account mental and social factors rather than just the symptoms of a disease

hollow face illusion – an image of the back of a mask which tends to be perceived as a face, supporting the constructivist theory of perception

illusion – a stimulus which causes a person to see something different from what is actually there, or where there are two or more possible interpretations of the same image

independent groups – an experimental design where each participant takes part in only one experimental condition

independent variable (IV) – the variable that is manipulated in an experiment

individual differences – ways in which people differ from each other, for example culture

inferences – assumptions and problem solving which is done to convert sensations into a coherent perception of the world; the need for inferences implies that the information received by the senses is insufficient for perception to take place

informed consent – ethical principle which states that research participants must give their consent in full knowledge of what they are consenting to

inhibition – a negative change in voltage that occurs when a neurotransmitter binds to an inhibitory receptor

innate – something (such as an ability) that is present at birth

input process – a cognitive process such as encoding where information is entered for the first time

interference – a type of forgetting where information is forgotten because it gets confused with other information

internalise – when a belief or value is integrated with a person's identity

inter-observer reliability – the extent to which different observers record the same data from the same observation

interview – a research method which involves asking people questions about their behaviour or thoughts face-to-face

invasion of privacy – an ethical flaw in research whereby a researcher breaches a participant's right to privacy in terms of their actions or data

Kanizsa triangle – a fiction illusion where corners of a triangle are shown, and people tend to perceive a whole triangle

laboratory experiment – an experiment in a lab, i.e. any controlled environment that allows the effects of distractions to be minimised

leading question – a question that prompts inaccurate recall of memories

learning styles – a controversial educational theory which suggests that people learn best if a task suits their preferred modality: auditory, visual or kinaesthetic

light constancy – the perceptual constancy where objects are perceived as the same regardless of lighting conditions

linear perspective – a monocular cue to depth; parallel lines tend to appear closer together as they become more distant

localisation – the idea that different parts of the brain are responsible for specific behaviours, or that certain functions are localised to certain areas in the brain

Loftus – memory researcher Elizabeth Loftus is an expert in the formation of distorted or false memories

logical operation – a symbolic task involving making a deduction or calculation

long-term memory (LTM) – a permanent memory store which encodes information on the basis of meaning

maladaptive – not adjusting adequately or appropriately to the environment or situation

mania – a behaviour marked by great excitement, euphoria and overactivity

matched pairs – an experimental design where each participant takes part in only one experimental condition and is matched by characteristics such as age or gender with participants in the other conditions, rather than randomly allocated

mean – a statistic which shows the arithmetic average of a set of data

median – a statistic which shows the midpoint of a set of data by finding the centre-most score

mode – a statistic which shows the midpoint of a set of data by finding the most common score

monocular – cues to depth that are apparent using only one eye

motion parallax – the way that the visual scene world changes when a person or animal moves; closer objects appear to move more, and more distant ones move less

motivation – a desire to do, perceive or remember something; a factor in the perceptual set

Müller-Lyer illusion – an illusion of length which appears like a pair of arrowheads around a line

multi-store model – a theory of memory which states that the main stores of memory are separate, but connected together via attention and rehearsal

natural experiment – research method with the overall structure of an experiment but which lacks experimenter control over the independent variable and the allocation of participants to conditions.

naturalistic observation – observing a participant in an everyday context such as their workplace

nature – one side of the nature–nurture debate which states that genes are much more important than the environment, and that they largely determine what kind of personality and skills someone will develop

naughty teddy study – a task which was used to test for the conservation of number in children

Necker cube – an ambiguous figure of a cube

negative correlation – a correlational relationship between two variables, where increases in one variable are associated with decreases in the other

negative visualisation – a technique that involves imagining the worst possible outcome of a situation or an unpleasant result of a specific behaviour

neurons – the cells of the nervous system, which communicate via electrochemical signals and whose functioning underlies all sensory and brain processes

neuropsychology – a branch of psychology that involves the study of the brain and nervous system, and how these relate to behaviour

neuroscience – the scientific study of the nervous system; a multidisciplinary science, drawing from fields including anatomy, molecular biology, mathematics, medicine, pharmacology, physiology, physics and psychology

neurotransmitters – chemicals released by neurons, stimulating responses in other neurons

normal distribution – a distribution of data where the middle values are common while more extreme ones are progressively rarer, resulting in a bell-shaped curve

normative conformity – a type of conformity that arises due to the desire to be accepted by the group

null hypothesis – a baseline scientific prediction which assumes that the IV will not have an effect on the DV

nurture – one side of the nature–nurture debate which states that upbringing and life experiences are more important than genes, and that what happens to a person during their life will largely determine what kind of personality and skills they will develop

observation – research method which involves studying behaviour as it happens and recording data in the form of notes or videos

occipital lobe – one of the main lobes of the brain, located at the bottom, back part of the cortex. The occipital lobe is responsible for processing visual information from the eyes.

occlusion – a monocular cue to depth; objects that partially cover other objects tend to be perceived as closer

open posture – a form of non-verbal communication where the body is left vulnerable (such as arms unfolded and legs apart). It implies that the person adopting the posture is listening and receptive to the other person

open questions – questions that allow the participant to answer in any way they want

open vocal system – the vocal system found in humans that allows them to combine known symbols with new symbols in order to create new meanings

opportunity sampling – selecting research participants on the basis of convenient availability

order effects – any way in which the order of conditions completed by participants in a repeated measures experimental design could affect results

output process – a memory process such as retrieval where information is retrieved or used

paralinguistics – the study of vocal (and sometimes non-vocal) signals beyond the basic verbal message or speech

parietal lobe – one of the four main lobes of the brain; responsible for processing sensory information

Penfield homunculus – a physical representation of the human body, located within the brain, describing the proportion of cortex required by each area of the body

perception – the process where the brain interprets the information that reaches the senses and builds up a coherent mental representation of the world that allows us to function

perceptual constancy – way in which the perceptual system makes allowances for changes in the environment, adjusting the information that reaches the senses

perceptual set – a group of assumptions and emotions that affect perception, biasing how people perceive the world

PET scan – a scanning technique that produces a moving picture of brain activity using radioactive glucose injected into the bloodstream

Piaget – researcher Jean Piaget was a Swiss developmental psychologist responsible for a stage theory of cognitive development

plasticity – the ability of brain cells and structures to adapt their function to respond to new environmental conditions throughout life

policeman doll study – a variation on the three mountains problem which suggested that young children are less egocentric than previously thought

Ponzo illusion – an illusion based on misinterpreted depth cues, where images closer to a vanishing point look larger

positive correlation – a correlational relationship between two variables, where both increase and decrease together

postural echo – the mirroring of body postures between two or more participants

posture – a position of the body; in body language, posture can be open or closed (defensive)

pre-operational stage – a developmental stage from Piaget's theory; children aged 7 or below learn to use one object to represent another, but are egocentric and exhibit centration

primacy effect – part of the serial position effect, where words at the start of a list are better remembered than those in the middle

primary data – new data obtained directly from the participant(s)

procedural memory – long-term memory for skills

qualitative data – data in the form of spoken/written words or in another non-numerical form

quantitative data – data in the form of numbers

questionnaire – a research method which involves asking people questions about their behaviour or thoughts on paper or via a computer

random allocation – selecting participants to take part in experimental and/or control conditions using a random process in order to avoid bias

random numbers – a set of numbers in a random order; used to carry out random sampling

random sample – ensuring that every member of the target population has the same chance of being selected

range – statistic which shows the distribution of a set of data via the difference between the lowest and highest score

recency effect – part of the serial position effect, where words at the end of a list are better remembered than those in the middle

receptor cells – sensory cells such as rods and cones which respond to external cues such as light and sound

recognition – retrieval from memory where the information or stimulus is repeated and the person compares it to what is in their memory

reconstructive memory – the process of using schema knowledge to fill gaps when retrieving a memory

recovery – in addiction, the diminishing of the physical and psychological need for the addicted-to substance

reductionist – analysing and describing a complex phenomenon in its most simple form

rehearsal – the process of maintaining information in STM by repeating it again and again, potentially playing a role in encoding new information to LTM

relative size – a monocular cue to depth; smaller objects of the same type tend to be perceived as more distant

repeated measures – an experimental design where participants all take part in every condition of the experiment

representative – a sample which has the same characteristics as the target population as a whole

research methods – a group of techniques used to gather and analyse data in psychology

retinal disparity – a binocular cue to depth; the difference between the visual images to the eyes reduces as objects become more distant

retrieval – in memory, accessing stored information and bringing it back to mind when needed

right to withdraw – ethical principle in research ensuring that participants can stop their participation at any time

Rubin's vase – an illusion which can be interpreted as either two faces looking towards each other, or as a vase

sadness – an emotion associated with feelings of loss, despair or sorrow

sample – a group of people that takes part in an experiment or other research study, selected from among the target population

scatter graph – a graph that shows relationships in correlation studies via a pattern of points

schema – a memory structure based on a concept that people derive from life experience and which is influenced by their culture; forms the basis of long-term memories and also of children developing understanding of the world, as studied by Piaget

secondary data – data which has been generated before for a different purpose, and is obtained and analysed by a researcher

self-actualisation – the realisation of one's talents and potentialities

self-efficacy – a person's sense of whether they are good or bad at a task

semantic encoding – encoding information to memory based on its meaning

semantic memory – the term 'semantic' means meaning; long-term memory for facts and meanings; semantic memories are understood and can be explained to other people

sensation – the process which occurs when receptor cells in the senses process external cues such as light and sound

sensorimotor stage – a developmental stage from Piaget's theory; children up to the age of 2 focus on interacting with physical objects, and develop object constancy

sensory cortex – part of the cerebral cortex; the area responsible for processing sensory information and therefore essential for perception

sensory memory – a very brief memory store, allowing sensations such as sounds and images to be retained for up to two seconds without being processed

serial position curve – a U-shaped graph showing recall of a series/list, which tends to show better recall at the beginning and the end (the primacy and recency effects)

serotonin – a neurotransmitter associated with depression

shame – a painful feeling of humiliation or distress

shape constancy – the perceptual constancy where the brain makes allowances for changes in an object's apparent shape as it is viewed from different angles

short-term memory (STM) – a temporary memory store with limited capacity, which encodes information on the basis of sound; also known as working memory

size constancy – the perceptual constancy where the brain allows for changes in an object's apparent shape as it is viewed from different distances

social learning theory – proposes that learning is a cognitive process that takes place in a social context and can occur purely through observation or direct instruction

social loafing – the phenomenon whereby a person exerts less effort to achieve a goal when they work in a group than when they work alone

somatic – relating to body; distinct from the mind

somatosensory – part of the sensory system concerned with the conscious perception of touch, pressure, pain, temperature, position, movement and vibration, which arise from the muscles, joints, skin and fascia

SSRI – selective serotonin re-uptake inhibitors; a class of antidepressant drugs that increase the level of serotonin

standardised instructions – the presentation of standard information to all participants in a research study or experimental condition, in order to minimise random error or bias

state – a factor that affects memory; it's easier for people to remember things when they are in the same physical state as when it was first learned; includes their mood, arousal level and the consumption of drugs

statistics – mathematical operations used to interpret and make sense of data, and summarise it in a simplified form

stem cell – a type of bodily cell which plays a key role in the early development of the brain and other organs; can transform into different types of cell

stigma – a mark of disgrace associated with a particular circumstance, quality or person; with regards to mental illness, stigma occurs when people look negatively on those with psychological problems

storage – the process of maintaining information in memory over time, avoiding forgetting or distortions

store – an area of memory such as short-term memory, long-term memory and the sensory stores

stratified sampling – selecting research participants in a way which maintains the same proportions as the population, in categories that the researcher considers to be important

symbols – sounds, gestures, material objects or written words that have a specific meaning to a group of people

symptoms – physical or psychological features indicating the presence of a disease

synapse – the junction between the axon of one neuron and the cell body or dendrite of a neighbouring neuron

systematic sampling – selecting research participants according to a regular pattern

target population – the group of people who the researcher is interested in studying

temporal lobe – one of the main lobes of the brain responsible for processing auditory information

texture gradient – a monocular cue to depth; the texture of objects can be seen in less detail as they become more distant

thalamus – part of the brain; responsible for basic sensory processing and relaying signals to the cortex

theory of cognitive development – an explanation or model of how cognitive abilities such as thought and language develop through life, and especially during childhood

three mountains problem – an experimental task involving model mountains, used to test egocentrism

timing – a factor that can affect memory, with delays either harming or improving later memory performance

top-down processing – a type of perceptual processing involving inferences and prior knowledge, considered to be primary by the constructivist theory

twin studies – research studies which compare the psychology of identical and non-identical twins within the same families, or after adoption

unipolar – a type of depression that occurs in the absence of mania

upbringing – the way a child is looked after by their parents or guardians

vanishing point – the point towards which lines appear to converge as they become more distant

variable – any characteristic, attribute or environmental condition that can have different values

verbaliser – a person with a preference for learning via words

visual cliff – an experiment involving a sheet of glass which is safe to walk on but looks like a cliff edge; it was used to support the idea that perception is innate

visual encoding – encoding information to memory based on its appearance

visualiser – a person with a preference for learning via images

Willingham – Daniel Willingham, a cognitive psychologist with an interest in education, and a critic of learning styles

withdrawal – the unpleasant physical reaction that accompanies the process of ceasing to take an addictive drug

References

Adorno, T. W., Frenkel-Brunswik, E., Levinson, D. J. and Nevitt, S. R. (1950) *The Authoritarian Personality.* Oxford: Harpers.

Argyle, M. (1972) *Non-verbal communication in human social interaction*. In Hinde, R.A. (ed.) *Non-verbal communication*. Boston: Houghton Mifflin.

Asch, S. E. (1951) *Effects of group pressure upon the modification and distortion of judgement*. In Guetzkow, H. (ed.) *Groups, leadership and men*. Pittsburgh, PA: Carnegie Press.

Atkinson, R.C. and Shiffrin, R.M. (1968) *Human memory: A proposed system and its control processes*. In K.W. Spence and J.T. Spence (Eds) *The Psychology of Learning and Motivation*: Vol. 2. London: Academic Press.

Bartlett, F.C. (1932) *Remembering: A Study in Experimental and Social Psychology*. Cambridge: Cambridge University Press.

Beck, A. T. (1967) *Depression: Clinical, experimental and theoretical aspects*. Philadelphia: University of Pennsylvania Press.

Blackwell, L.S., Trzesniewski, K.H. and Dweck, C.S. (2007) 'Implicit theories of intelligence predict achievement across an adolescent transition: A longitudinal study and an intervention', *Child Development,* 78 (1), 246–263.

Bruner, J. S. and Minturn, A. L. (1955) 'Perceptual identification and perceptual organization', *The Journal of General Psychology,* 53 (1), 21–28.

Carmichael, L., Hogan, H.P. and Walker, A.A. (1932) 'An experimental study of the effect of language on the reproduction of visually perceived form', *Journal of Experimental Psychology*, 15 (1) 73–86.

DeBlasio, F.A. and Benda, B.B. (1993) 'Adolescent sexual intercourse: Family and peer influences', *School Social Work Journal*, 18 (1), 17–31.

Elms, A. C. and Milgram, S. (1966) 'Personality characteristics associated with obedience and defiance toward authoritative command', *Journal of Experimental Research in Personality*, 1 (4) 282–289.

Gilchrist, J. C. and Nesberg, L. S. (1952) 'Need and perceptual change in need-related objects', *Journal of Experimental Psychology*, 44 (6), 369–376.

Gregory, R. (1974) *Concepts and Mechanisms of Perception*, London: Duckworth.

Griffiths, M. (1999) 'Internet addiction: Fact or Fiction?' *The Psychologist*, 12 (5) 246–250.

Hall, E.T. and Hall, M.R. (2001) *Part 1: Key concepts: Underlying structures of culture*. In Hall, E.T. and Hall, M.R. *Understanding cultural differences: Germans, French and Americans*. London: Nicholas Brealey Publishing Company.

Heshka, S. and Nelson, Y. (1972) 'Interpersonal speaking distance as a function of age, sex and relationship', *Sociometry*, 35 (4) 491–498.

Hollinghurst, S., Jerrom, B., Kessler, D. and Kuyken, W. (2013) 'Cognitive behavioural therapy as an adjunct to pharmacotherapy for primary care based patients with treatment resistant depression: results of the CoBalT randomised controlled trial', *The Lancet*, 381 (9864) 375–384.

Hudson, W. (1960) 'Pictorial depth perception in sub-cultural groups in Africa', *Journal of Social Psychology*, 52 (2) 183–208.

Hughes, M. (1975) *Egocentrism in preschool children*. Unpublished doctoral dissertation. Edinburgh University.

International Classification of Diseases, *The ICD-10 Classification of Mental and Behavioural Disorders: Clinical descriptions and diagnostic guidelines*, available at https://www.who.int/publications/i/item/9241544228.

Kaij, L. (1960) *Alcoholism in twins: Studies on the etiology and sequels of abuse of alcohol*. Almqvist & Wiksell.

Kraemer, D. J., Rosenberg, L. M. and Thompson-Schill, S. L. (2009) 'The neural correlates of visual and verbal cognitive styles', *The Journal of Neuroscience,* 29 (12) 3792–3798.

Loftus, E.F. and Palmer, J.C. (1974) 'Reconstruction of automobile destruction: an example of the interaction between language and memory', *Journal of Verbal Learning and Verbal Behaviour*, 13, 585–589.

Matsumoto, D. and Willingham, R. (2009) 'Spontaneous facial expressions of emotion of congenitally blind individuals', *Journal of Personality and Social Psychology*, 96 (1) 1–10.

McGarrigle, J. and Donaldson, M. (1974) 'Conservation accidents', *Cognition,* 3, 341–350.

Milgram, S. (1963) 'Behavioural study of obedience', *The Journal of Abnormal and Social Psychology*, 67 (4) 371-378.

Mind (2013) *Mental health and romantic relationships research released today*, available at https://www.mind.org.uk/news-campaigns/news/mental-health-and-romantic-relationships-research-released-today/ (accessed 11 September 2023).

Murdock Jr, B. B. (1962) 'The serial position effect of free recall', *Journal of Experimental Psychology,* 64 (5) 482.

Piliavin, I. M., Rodin, J. and Piliavin, J. A. (1969) 'Good Samaritanism: An underground phenomenon?' *Journal of Personality and Social Psychology*, 13 (4) 289–299.

Rubin, Z. (1970) 'Measurement of romantic love', *Journal of Personality and Social Psychology*, 16 (2) 265–273.

Scoville, W.B. and Milner, B. (1957) 'Loss of recent memory after bilateral hippocampal lesions', *Journal of Neurology, Neurosurgery and Psychiatry,* 20, 11–21.

Seligman, M.E. and Maier S.F. (1967) 'Failure to escape traumatic shock', *Journal of Experimental Psychology*, 74 (1) 1.

Sperling, G. (1960) 'The information available in brief visual presentations', *Psychological Monographs,* 74 (11) 1–29.

Tulving, E. (1989) 'Remembering and knowing the past', *American Scientist*, 77 (4) 361–367.

Walters, G.D. (1999) *The addiction concept: Working hypothesis or self-fulfilling prophesy?* Boston: Allyn & Bacon.

Wiles, N., Thomas, L., Abel, A., Ridgway, N., Turner, N., Campbell, J., Garland, A., Hollinghurst, S., Jerrom, B., Kessler, D., Kuyken, W., Morrison, J., Turner, K., Williams, C., Peters, T. and Lewis, G. (2013) 'Cognitive behavioural therapy as an adjunct to pharmacotherapy for primary care based patients with treatment resistant depression: results of the CoBalT randomised controlled trial', *Lancet*, 381 (9864) 375–84.

Yuki, M., Maddux, W.W. and Masuda, T. (2007) 'Are the windows of the soul the same in East and West? Cultural differences in using the eyes and mouth as cues to recognize emotions in Japan and the United States', *Journal of Experimental Social Psychology*, 43 (2) 303–311.

Zimbardo, P.G. (1969) *The cognitive control of motivation*. Glenview, Il: Scott, Foresman and Co.

Index

Psychology

Workbook

Sally White

Contents

Cognition and Behaviour

Social Context and Behaviour

Exam Papers

Preparing for the GCSE Exam

Revision That Really Works

Experts have found that there are two techniques that help you to retain and recall information and consistently produce better results in exams compared to other revision techniques.

It really isn't rocket science either – you simply need to:

- **test yourself** on each topic as many times as possible
- **leave a gap** between the test sessions.

Three Essential Revision Tips

1. **Use Your Time Wisely**

   - Allow yourself plenty of time.
   - Try to start revising six months before your exams – it's more effective and less stressful.
   - Don't waste time re-reading the same information over and over again – it's not effective!

2. **Make a Plan**

   - Identify all the topics you need to revise (this Complete Revision & Practice book will help you).
   - Plan at least five sessions for each topic.
   - One hour should be ample time to test yourself on the key ideas for a topic.
   - Spread out the practice sessions for each topic – the optimum time to leave between each session is about one month but, if this isn't possible, just make the gaps as big as realistically possible.

3. **Test Yourself**

   - Methods for testing yourself include: quizzes, practice questions, flashcards, past papers, explaining a topic to someone else, etc.
   - This Complete Revision and Practice book provides seven practice opportunities per topic.
   - Don't worry if you get an answer wrong – provided you check what the correct answer is, you are more likely to get the same or similar questions right in future!

Visit **collins.co.uk/collinsGCSErevision** to download your free flashcards, for more information about the benefits of these revision techniques, and for further guidance on how to plan ahead and make them work for you.

Command Words Used in Exam Questions

This table shows the meanings of some of the most commonly used command words in GCSE exam questions.

Command word	Meaning
Calculate...	A calculation needs to be carried out
Compare...	Give a balanced answer of similarities and differences
Describe...	Give an account of
Evaluate...	A description is needed but with the emphasis on a conclusion
Explain...	Give detailed reasons for your answer
Identify...	Be able to recognise the answer, often from the information given
Name...	Be able to give a recognised technical term
Outline...	Give an overview of the main characteristics

Memory

Where space is not provided, write your answers on a separate piece of paper.

1 | Alina and George are revising for their GCSE Psychology exam. Alina finds revising much easier once she has mastered all the concepts in the topics and understands what they mean. George draws diagrams of information such as mind maps.

Which types of encoding are Alina and George using?

Alina .... **[1]**

George .... **[1]**

2 Define the following terms:

Encoding **[2]**

....

....

Storage **[2]**

....

....

Retrieval **[2]**

....

....

3 Which of the following statements about encoding are correct?
Shade **two** boxes. **[2]**

A An example of visual encoding is if you are asked to mentally picture your house. ⭕

B An example of semantic encoding is knowing the capital city of France. ⭕

C An example of visual encoding is repeating a poem you have read. ⭕

D An example of acoustic coding is storing information by meaning. ⭕

4 Outline **two** features of storage. **[2]**

....

....

Memory

5 Explain how different types of retrieval can be used, referring to the example below. **[6]**

> Bobby cannot remember all the names of the football teams in his league unless his friend gives him the first letter of the name. Anil, who plays in the same team, says he can easily pick out all of the teams in their league if he is shown a full list of all team names in all leagues. Nick suggests he needs no help whatsoever.

6 Using research evidence, evaluate semantic, procedural and episodic memories. **[5]**

7 Describe the multi-store model of memory. **[6]**

8 Explain **one** strength of the multi-store model of memory. **[2]**

....

....

9 According to the multi-store model, what is the duration of the short-term memory? **[1]**

....

10

> Dayna and Archie had both been taught the names of famous psychologists in chronological order of when they were influential. They were told by their teacher they would be tested the next day and they had to recall them in the correct order. They both revised that evening. Dayna had her psychology lesson first in the morning so she sat the test first. Archie did not sit his test until after break, after his Spanish lesson.

a) According to interference theory, who is more likely to have forgotten some of the names – Dayna or Archie?

....
 [1]

b) When analysing the class results, the teacher noticed there was a pattern of which names were easily recalled and which ones were forgotten. It was noted that the students were more likely to correctly recall the first few names and the last few names but the names in the middle were likely to be forgotten or mixed up.

What is the term used to describe this pattern of results?

....
 [1]

11 Outline **one** difference between short-term and long-term memory. **[2]**

....

....

12 Murdock investigated the effects of serial position on recall.

How does this study support the multi-store model of memory? **[4]**

13 Which of the following statements about Murdock's study are incorrect?
Shade **two** boxes.   **[2]**

A   Murdock randomly selected words from the 4000 most common words in English.   ◯

B   The independent variable (IV) was the position of a word in the list.   ◯

C   The dependent variable (DV) was the words recalled in serial position.   ◯

D   The study used an independent measures design.   ◯

E   The study was a field experiment.   ◯

14 What is meant by 'effort after meaning'?   **[2]**

15 Using an example, describe the reconstructive theory of memory.   **[3]**

16 Describe the findings of Bartlett's 'War of the Ghosts' study.   **[3]**

17 Emilia was telling her friend Ellie that she was asked to participate in a psychology experiment on memory. She told Ellie that the researchers were really strict with their instructions and all of the participants were asked to do exactly the same thing. However, whilst she was participating, she kept trying to work out what they were really testing.

a)   What type of experiment did Emilia participate in?   **[1]**

b)   What is **one** weakness of the method that Emilia is referring to?   **[2]**

18 What is meant by false memories? Give an example.   **[3]**

19 You have been asked to investigate accuracy of memory with reference to context of recall. Describe how you would design an experiment to do this.   **[6]**

You need to include:

• The procedure – what participants could do to test the accuracy of memory and context of recall

• A suitable hypothesis for your experiment

• The results that you expect to find.

Perception

Where space is not provided, write your answers on a separate piece of paper.

1 Outline the difference between sensation and perception. **[4]**

2 What are monocular depth cues? **[2]**

3 Which **two** of the following are monocular depth cues? Shade **two** boxes. **[2]**

   A Convergence ◯   **B** Linear perspective ◯

   C Retinal disparity ◯   **D** Height in plane ◯

   E Motion parallax ◯

4 What are binocular depth cues? **[2]**

5 Sketch the Ponzo illusion. **[1]**

6 Outline how psychologists would explain the Ponzo illusion. **[3]**

Perception

7 A researcher showed male and female participants the Kanizsa triangle (**Figure 1**). They were asked to write down their perception of what they saw – a white triangle on top of another triangle, incomplete circles or an incomplete triangle. The researcher split the results into male and female responses.

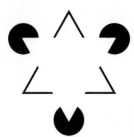

Figure 1.

The results are shown in **Table 1**.

	White triangle	Incomplete circles	Incomplete triangle	Total
Males	100	70	30	200
Females	140	60	20	220
Total	240	130	50	420

a) Draw a suitable graph to represent the data in **Table 1**.
   Provide a suitable title and fully label your graph. **[4]**

Perception

b) Calculate the ratio of males to females. Show your workings. **[2]**

c) 50% of the men in the study perceived **Figure 1** to be a white triangle. Calculate the percentage of women (to three significant figures) who also perceived the illusion to be a white triangle. Show your workings. **[2]**

d) Which of the following is the correct fraction of both males and females who saw **Figure 1** as a white triangle?
Shade **one** box only. **[1]**

A $\frac{1}{7}$ ⬜   B $\frac{3}{4}$ ⬜

C $\frac{1}{2}$ ⬜   D $\frac{4}{7}$ ⬜

E $\frac{2}{7}$ ⬜

8 What is meant by perceptual set? **[2]**

9 How is perceptual set affected by culture? **[2]**

10 Researchers advertised for a group of vegetarians to participate in a word search study. There were two conditions. Condition one included a word search of twenty food neutral words, such as crisps and pear. Condition two contained twenty words of food associated with meat, such as stew. Participants took part in both conditions on different days. Participants were timed on the time it took them to complete the task.

Using the theory of perceptual set and emotion, explain what results the researcher would expect to find. **[3]**

11 Why can findings of studies looking at the effects of emotions on perception be unreliable? **[2]**

12 Evaluate Gilchrist and Nesberg's study on how motivation affects perception. **[4]**

Perception

13 Describe the findings of the Bruner and Minturn study of perceptual set. **[6]**

14 Participants volunteered to take part in research where they were asked to look at pictures flashed on a screen. Some pictures, such as a piece of fruit, were neutral and some were more anxiety-inducing, such as a scene from a disaster. As soon as they saw the picture they had to say what it depicted out loud. Their anxiety was measured using a galvanic skin response machine which would record their anxiety through the amount of electrical activity caused by sweat. It was found that it took longer for participants to say what the anxiety-inducing pictures showed than the neutral pictures and they produced a higher skin conductance (more anxiety) with the anxiety-inducing pictures.

What is the name of the perceptual set?

Explain the findings of the above study. **[4]**

15 Explain why the data in this study is primary data. **[2]**

Development

Where space is not provided, write your answers on a separate piece of paper.

1 Which of the following is the part of the brain where all of our thinking and processing takes place? Shade **one** box only. **[1]**

A Brain stem ◯

B Cerebellum ◯

C Cortex ◯

D Thalamus ◯

2 What is meant by automatic functions? Give **one** example. **[3]**

3 Emilia is four and is learning to hop. Which part of the brain is involved in this activity? Shade **one** box only. **[1]**

A Brain stem ◯

B Cerebellum ◯

C Cortex ◯

D Thalamus ◯

4 Smoking is just one factor that may affect a growing brain. This is an example of nurture. What is meant by nurture? **[2]**

5 Give **one** other factor that could be considered nurture. **[1]**

6 A midwife is interested in brain development in the womb. She delivered information programmes warning women about the dangers of smoking, particularly if they were going to have children. She then conducted a study to find out if her information programme had had an effect. She asked women attending the clinic, who had attended her information programme, if they would take part in her study.

At the end of the study she found the following results in **Table 1**:

Table 1. Percentage of mothers who smoked before pregnancy and stopped during pregnancy.

Smoked before pregnancy	Stopped smoking during pregnancy
87	69

Calculate the percentage decrease of mothers who stopped smoking, to two significant figures. Show your workings. **[3]**

7 With reference to the above study, which sampling method did the midwife use? **[2]**

....

....

8 What is meant by nature? **[2]**

....

....

9 a) Label the areas of the brain A, B, C and D. **[4]**

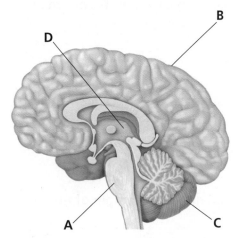

b) Write A, B, C and D in the boxes to match each area to its function.

Autonomic functions such as breathing and heartbeat	
Precise physical movement/coordinates actions	
Cognition/thinking/perception/memory processes	
Some sensory processing/relaying signals to the cerebral cortex	

[4]

10 Describe Piaget's concepts of assimilation and accommodation. **[4]**

11

Keshav was complaining that his teacher was unhelpful in class when he was struggling to understand the work. Another student, Seb, liked the teacher and felt Keshav had been messing around during the lesson and that was why he struggled. When Seb wanted the teacher's help but didn't get it, he changed his mind about the teacher.

Is Seb showing an example of assimilation or accommodation? Explain your answer. **[4]**

12

Daisy's aunt pours a drink for Daisy into a tall, narrow beaker. Daisy's sister, Maya, also wants a drink but her drink (the same amount as Daisy's) is poured into a short, wide beaker. Maya laughs and says she has more drink than Daisy. Daisy just smiles.

Development

a) Using your knowledge of conservation, which sister is the youngest? [1]

b) Using your knowledge of conservation, how old is the eldest sister likely to be? [1]

c) Which stage is the youngest sister likely to be at? [1]

13 Which **one** of the following suggests that development happens in stages? Shade **one** box only. [1]

A Willingham ◯

B Dweck ◯

C Piaget ◯

14 Evaluate McGarrigle and Donaldson's naughty teddy study. [5]

15 What is meant by egocentrism? [2]

16 Briefly describe how Piaget studied egocentrism in young children. [3]

17 Hughes investigated the development of conservation in the policeman doll study. Describe this study.

Evaluate the research method used in the Hughes study. [9]

18 Complete the table below by writing the stage or age of cognitive development according to Piaget. [4]

Stage	Age
Sensorimotor	
	2-7 years
	7-11 years
Formal operational	

19 Briefly outline the sensorimotor stage and the pre-operational stage of cognitive development. [4]

20 Outline the role of Piaget's theory in education. [4]

21 Outline **two** weaknesses of Piaget's theory. [4]

Development

22 According to Dweck, what is a fixed mindset? **[2]**

23 According to Dweck, what is a growth mindset? **[2]**

24

> Darragh believes he isn't very good at school and he doesn't worry when he is absent. Adam doesn't like being away from school as he knows he will have to catch up on missed work if he wants to do well.

Name the growth mindset that each student has. **[2]**

25 Discuss how praise and self-efficacy could be used to have an impact on both Darragh and Adam at school. **[6]**

26 A school asked their sixth form students which learning style they preferred.
Sketch a suitable diagram to represent the data in **Table 2**. **[4]**

Table 2.

A	B	C
Preferred listening and talking	Preferred diagrams, mind maps, images	No preference
45%	35%	20%

Research

Where space is not provided, write your answers on a separate piece of paper.

1 How can a random sample be selected? [2]

2 What is **one** advantage of a random sample? [2]

3 **a)** A researcher wanted to choose participants for a study using systematic sampling from an alphabetical register of adults aged over eighteen and working in a college. A colleague suggested stratified sampling would be better. Explain why stratified sampling should be more representative of the target population. [4]

b) The researcher gathered their stratified sample of participants but was now concerned about how they could allocate participants to an independent groups design study. Explain how they could do this. [2]

c) A different colleague then identified problems with using an independent groups design. Outline **one** problem the researcher might encounter and suggest **one** way this problem could be addressed. [4]

d) The researcher had allocated their participants into two experimental conditions. The study was looking at the effects of alcohol on driving performance. One condition had a 300ml bottle of beer and the other did not. Identify **one** ethical issue with this study and explain how this issue could be overcome. [4]

e) Identify the independent variable in this study. [2]

f) How could the dependent variable be operationalised? [2]

4 In both conditions the researcher used a driving hazard video test but was concerned about extraneous variables. What are potential extraneous variables in this study? [3]

5 Write a suitable hypothesis for the effects of alcohol on driving performance. [3]

Research

6 The results of the study were presented in **Table 1**.

Table 1.

	Alcohol	No Alcohol
Median	5	6.5
Range	6	3

[3]

a) What does the range tell us about the difference in the driving performance between the two conditions? [2]

b) Outline **one** problem in using the range to present results. [2]

7 A researcher gathered students for a study on memory. The students were gathered in the common room at break and asked if they would take part in the study. Those that agreed were asked to meet in the psychology lab at 1pm to participate. On arrival they were asked to sign a consent form.

a) What does a consent form include? [2]

b) Name the sampling technique that the researcher used. [1]

8 After signing the consent form, participants were asked to look at a set of photographs of people's faces. After twenty minutes they were shown a second set of photographs, including the faces they had already seen and some new ones. The participants were asked to identify if they had seen the faces previously. They had a 90% accuracy in recognition.

a) Which research method has been used in this study? [1]

b) Outline **one** strength and **one** weakness of using this method. [4]

Research

9 In a different study, a staged incident occurred, whereby participants witnessed a 'robbery' amongst an audience at a school play. A person entered the stage and 'stole' a valuable ring being used in a scene. The audience were individually interviewed about the description of the 'thief'. In this study, 25% accuracy was recorded regarding important features of the perpetrator.

    a) Which research method has been used in this study?   **[1]**

    b) Outline **one** strength and **one** weakness of using this method.   **[4]**

    c) Explain the main differences between the two studies.   **[4]**

10 Which **one** of the following is an example of a qualitative research method? Shade **one** box only.   **[1]**

    A Laboratory experiment ⬜

    B Correlational study ⬜

    C Case study ⬜

    D Field experiment ⬜

11 What is the purpose of random assignment in an experimental study? Shade **one** box only.   **[1]**

    A To ensure the sample is representative of the population ⬜

    B To increase the generalisability of results ⬜

    C To control for the effects of extraneous variables ⬜

    D To determine causation ⬜

12 A researcher is studying a relationship between two co-variables. What is this research method called? Shade **one** box only.   **[1]**

    A Correlation ⬜

    B Laboratory experiment ⬜

    C Case study ⬜

    D Field experiment ⬜

13 Outline **one** difference between primary and secondary data.   **[2]**

14 Some students completed a psychology test.

Their scores out of 100 were: 75, 82, 90, 88, 95, 64, 59, 67, 52, 41, 75, 53, 72

a) Work out the median score. Show your workings. **[2]**

b) Work out the range of the scores. Show your workings. **[2]**

c) Write down the mode of the scores. **[1]**

15 A different group of students completed another test.

Their marks out of 35 were: 25, 28, 24, 26, 23, 27, 26

a) Work out the mean of the marks achieved by the students. Show your workings and give your answer to two decimal places. **[2]**

b) Work out the percentage score for the student who achieved the lowest number of marks. Show your workings and give your answer to two significant figures. **[2]**

c) Draw an appropriate graph to represent the marks that each student achieved. Label the axes and provide a suitable title for your graph. **[4]**

Social Influence

Where space is not provided, write your answers on a separate piece of paper.

1 In Asch's conformity study, participants were shown a line and asked to identify which of the three comparison lines was the same length. Which of the following did the study aim to investigate? Shade **one** box only. **[1]**

   A   The effect of authority figures on obedience ⬭

   B   The impact of social facilitation on performance ⬭

   C   The role of group influence on conformity ⬭

   D   The relationship between personality traits and leadership ⬭

2 Describe the influence of group size on conformity. Use an example in your answer. **[3]**

3 Discuss how dispositional factors can affect conforming to a majority. Use an example in your answer. **[6]**

4 Describe and evaluate Asch's line study. In your description, include the method used, the results obtained and a conclusion drawn. **[9]**

5 Milgram's agency theory suggests that obedience to authority is influenced by several social factors. Which of the following is **not** one of the factors highlighted by the theory? Shade **one** box only. **[1]**

   A   Agency ⬭

   B   Authority ⬭

   C   Task difficulty ⬭

   D   Proximity ⬭

6 Use your knowledge of psychology to evaluate Milgram's agency theory of obedience. **[5]**

7 Briefly outline Adorno's theory of the Authoritarian Personality. **[3]**

8 As part of his Authoritarian Personality theory, Adorno suggested that obedience is influenced by which of the following? Shade **one** box only. **[1]**

   A   Genetic factors ⬭

   B   Cultural norms ⬭

   C   Childhood experiences ⬭

   D   Cognitive dissonance ⬭

Social Influence

9 Adorno used the F-scale to measure how authoritarian people were. Outline **one** weakness in using a questionnaire.   **[2]**

10 Outline **one** difference between using a questionnaire and an interview.   **[2]**

11 Piliavin's bystander study focused on which of the following? Shade **one** box only.   **[1]**

    A   Obedience to authority figures ◯

    B   Factors influencing bystander intervention in emergencies ◯

    C   The impact of group size on conformity ◯

    D   The relationship between personality traits and leadership ◯

12 Piliavin's study utilised a simulated emergency situation involving which of the following? Shade **one** box only.   **[1]**

    A   A staged argument between two actors ◯

    B   A fake electrical shock apparatus ◯

    C   A person appearing to be in need of medical assistance ◯

    D   A series of moral dilemmas presented to participants ◯

13 Explain how social factors (the presence of others and the cost of helping) affect bystander intervention.   **[4]**

14 Explain how dispositional factors (similarity to victim and expertise) affect bystander intervention.   **[4]**

15 Describe deindividuation, using an example in your answer.   **[3]**

16 Identify and explain **two** dispositional factors that influence collective behaviour.   **[4]**

Language, Thought and Communication

Where space is not provided, write your answers on a separate piece of paper.

1 According to Piaget's theory of language depends on which of the following? Shade **one** box only. **[1]**

A   Social interactions and imitation ⃝

B   Biological factors and innate abilities ⃝

C   Thought and cognitive processes ⃝

D   Cultural influences and exposure ⃝

2 What does the Sapir-Whorf hypothesis suggest? Shade **one** box only. **[1]**

A   Language determines our thoughts and perceptions ⃝

B   Language is influenced by cultural norms and values ⃝

C   Language is a universal human trait ⃝

D   Language acquisition is primarily a biological process ⃝

3 Explain the difference between Piaget's and Sapir-Whorf's theories regarding the possible relationship between language and thought. **[4]**

4 Describe how language variation can affect recall of events and recognition of colours. **[4]**

5 A researcher collected data from people speaking different languages around the world. They collected the data via a questionnaire. The following results show the total number of colours they have words for:

People	Colour
Zuni	5
Berinmo	5
Dani	2

What problems would individuals from these cultures encounter when shown a colour chart used in Western societies? **[3]**

6 Other than socially desirable responses, what problems might the researcher have encountered using a questionnaire? **[3]**

7 Describe Von Frisch's bee study. **[4]**

8 Evaluate Von Frisch's bee study. **[4]**

9 Animal communication has a limited number of functions when compared with human communication. Match each function of communication with its description. **[4]**

A To attract a mate   i) Food

B To mark their area, using urine for example   ii) Survival

C To draw attention to a source of nourishment   iii) Reproduction

D To make an alarm call as a warning   iv) Territory

10 Name **one** property of human communication that is not present in animal communication. Use an example in your answer. **[2]**

11 A researcher decided to carry out an observation on monkeys in captivity to record their communication with each other. Give **one** category of behaviour that the researcher could observe. **[1]**

12 The researcher was concerned about the reliability of the observation. Explain how this could be assessed and improved. **[4]**

13 Outline **one** strength and **one** weakness of carrying out an observation. **[4]**

14 Outline **one** difference between verbal and non-verbal communication. Give an example of each in your answer. **[4]**

15 Identify **three** functions of eye contact. **[3]**

16 A researcher wanted to investigate eye movement and whether it affected the flow of conversation. People who happened to be in the cafe were asked if they would participate in a study and if they were free to meet in the psychology lab at a given time. On arrival they were randomly paired with people they had never met and sat at a table. One pair at a time was asked to get to know each other. The researcher covertly observed their interaction in a one-way mirror. The eye movements were recorded. It was found that when a person was finishing speaking they would give a prolonged look to the other person. If they were about to speak, they would break eye contact. It was concluded that eye contact did provide non-verbal cues for conversing with someone else.

a) Which sampling method was used for this study? **[1]**

Language, Thought and Communication

b) Referring to the study above, how did they use eye contact to regulate the flow of the conversation? **[4]**

c) How could the people be randomly paired? **[2]**

d) What is a covert observation? **[2]**

e) Explain an ethical issue that would need to be addressed with a covert observation. **[2]**

f) With reference to one function of eye contact, what conclusions could be reached in this study (apart from the one stated)? **[3]**

17 What is postural echo? **[2]**

18 Outline **one** difference between closed posture and open posture. **[2]**

19 How could cultural norms affect touch as a form of body language? **[2]**

20 Using the table below, briefly describe how each of the factors affects personal space. **[6]**

Factor affecting personal space	Description
Culture	
Status	
Gender	

21 Describe Darwin's evolutionary theory of non-verbal communication. **[4]**

22 Explain what evidence there is to suggest that non-verbal behaviour is innate. **[4]**

23 Describe and evaluate Yuki's study of emoticons. **[6]**

Brain and Neuropsychology

Where space is not provided, write your answers on a separate piece of paper.

1 The human nervous system is divided into which main divisions? Shade **one** box only. **[2]**

   A Central and somatic ⃝

   B Peripheral and autonomic ⃝

   C Somatic and autonomic ⃝

   D Central and peripheral ⃝

2 The central nervous system consists of which of the following? Shade **one** box only. **[1]**

   A The brain and spinal cord ⃝

   B Nerves and ganglia ⃝

   C Sensory receptors and effectors ⃝

   D Sympathetic and parasympathetic systems ⃝

3 The peripheral nervous system is further divided into which of the following? Shade **one** box only. **[2]**

   A Sensory and motor divisions ⃝

   B Somatic and autonomic divisions ⃝

   C Sympathetic and parasympathetic divisions ⃝

   D Cerebral cortex and limbic system ⃝

4 What does the somatic division of the peripheral nervous system control? Shade **one** box only. **[1]**

   A Involuntary bodily functions ⃝

   B Conscious movements and sensory perception ⃝

   C Fight-or-flight responses ⃝

   D Internal organs and glands ⃝

5 The autonomic division of the peripheral nervous system regulates which of the following? Shade **one** box only. **[1]**

A Voluntary muscle movements ◯

B Somatic reflexes and reactions ◯

C Heart rate, digestion and glandular activity ◯

D Sensory processing and perception ◯

6 Outline **one** difference between the somatic nervous system and the autonomic nervous system. **[2]**

7 Describe the fight or flight response. **[5]**

8 What is adrenaline? **[1]**

9 Describe the James-Lange theory of emotion. **[4]**

10 What are sensory neurons responsible for? Shade **one** box only. **[1]**

A Transmitting signals from the brain to the body ◯

B Controlling voluntary muscle movements ◯

C Receiving and transmitting sensory information ◯

D Initiating and regulating immune responses ◯

11 What are motor neurons responsible for? Shade **one** box only. **[1]**

A Transmitting signals from the brain to the body ◯

B Controlling involuntary muscle contractions ◯

C Receiving and transmitting sensory information ◯

D Initiating and regulating immune responses ◯

12 Describe the process of synaptic transmission. **[5]**

13 What did Hebb suggest about learning and neuronal growth? **[4]**

14 Describe the **four** lobes of the brain and the function of each. **[6]**

Brain and Neuropsychology

15 Label the areas of the brain that are responsible for motor, somatosensory, visual, auditory and language skills. **[6]**

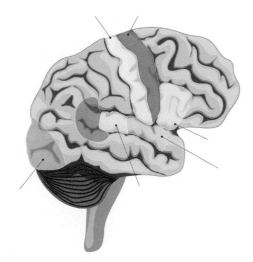

16 What is cognitive neuroscience? **[3]**

17 Complete **Table 1**. **[5]**

Table 1.

	fMRI	PET	CT
How it works	Measures changes in blood flow		Produces X-ray images
What it does		Measures brain activity	Provides detailed structural images
Resolution	High		High
Exposure to radiation	No		

18 Describe Tulving's 'gold' memory study. **[4]**

19 Describe how neurological damage such as stroke or injury can affect motor abilities and behaviour. **[4]**

Psychological Problems

Where space is not provided, write your answers on a separate piece of paper.

1 How has the incidence of mental health problems changed over time? [2]

2 Give **one** reason why this might be the case. [2]

3 How does culture affect the perception of mental health problems? [2]

4 Describe **two** characteristics of good mental health. [2]

5 Describe how the stigma of mental health problems has been reduced. [2]

6 A researcher wanted to find out if there was a relationship between people coping with stressful life events and their incidence of depression. Stressful life events were measured via a self-report questionnaire (the Social Readjustment Rating Scale (SRRS)) and the extent of someone's depression was also measured via self-report using Beck's Depression Inventory (BDI).

Scores of both were collected.

a) One factor that could influence life events is modern living. Identify a potential factor of modern living. [1]

b) The study above suggests that stressful life events and depression could be correlated. If both scores are high on the two questionnaires, what we could assume about depression? [2]

c) The researcher is collecting quantitative data. How could the researcher collect qualitative data in this study? [3]

Psychological Problems

The results for the study are shown in **Table 1**.

Table 1.

Participant	1	2	3	4	5
SRRS score	12	14	12	16	17
BDI score	9	10	18	11	12

d) Draw a scatter graph of the data. Include a title and label both axes. **[4]**

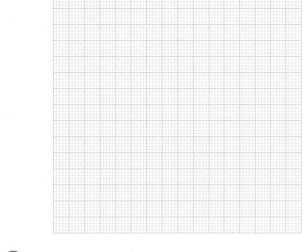

7 Describe **one** difference between unipolar and bipolar depression. **[2]**

_____

_____

8 Classification systems for mental health problems have been in place for over a
hundred years. Give **one** reason why they are frequently updated. **[2]**

_____

_____

9 Briefly discuss a strength of using the International Classification of Diseases (ICD)
in diagnosing unipolar depression. **[3]**

10 Unipolar depression is characterised by which of the following? Shade **one** box only. **[1]**

A Periods of extreme mood swings ⃝

B Fluctuating episodes of depression and mania ⃝

C Persistent feelings of sadness and loss of interest ⃝

D Symptoms of anxiety and panic attacks ⃝

Psychological Problems

11 Which **one** of the following are symptoms of bipolar depression? Shade **one** box only. **[1]**

   A Excessive happiness and euphoria ◯

   B Chronic fatigue and low energy levels ◯

   C Hallucinations and delusions ◯

   D Mania and depression ◯

12 According to the biological explanation of depression, which neurotransmitter is commonly implicated? Shade **one** box only. **[1]**

   A Serotonin ◯

   B Acetylcholine ◯

   C Endorphins ◯

   D Histamine ◯

13 Describe **one** strength and **one** weakness of the biological explanation of depression. **[4]**

14 According to the cognitive explanation of depression, individuals with depression tend to do which of the following? Shade **one** box only. **[1]**

   A Have overly positive thoughts and beliefs ◯

   B Focus on positive aspects of their lives ◯

   C Engage in negative thinking patterns ◯

   D Have accurate perceptions of reality ◯

15 Describe **one** strength and **one** weakness of the psychological explanation of depression. **[4]**

16 There are different interventions for the treatment of depression, one is regarded as reductionist and the other is regarded as more holistic. Describe and evaluate both the interventions using examples in your answer. **[9]**

17 Outline the difference between addiction and substance abuse. **[2]**

18 Cary has been prescribed painkillers for a bad back that she sustained in an accident. She started off with one tablet three time a day but now takes two tablets three times a day as she said she 'got used to the pills' and that 'they no longer numbed the pain'.

   Is Cary showing signs of substance dependence or misuse? Explain your answer. **[4]**

Psychological Problems

19 The ICD criteria for addiction include which of the following? Shade **one** box only. **[1]**

    A Withdrawal symptoms ◯

    B Priority given to substance ◯

    C Strong desire to use ◯

    D All of the above ◯

20 What is meant by genetic vulnerability to addiction? **[2]**

21 How have researchers investigated a genetic explanation of addiction? **[3]**

22 This method of investigation that is influenced by nature has its problems.
Identify **one** problem with the method of investigation. **[2]**

23 Describe how Kaij investigated alcohol abuse. **[4]**

24 What conclusions can be made from Kaij's findings? **[2]**

25 Ashley has been drinking alcohol on a regular basis since she started work. Her work colleagues who are of a similar age to Ashley, all go for drinks after work so she has been joining them. She has noticed that her wages don't last as long as they did and she has started to borrow money so she can continue to go out after work. Her friends who she went to school with have complained that she no longer prioritises them over her new friends.

What aspects of Ashley's behaviour suggest she may be developing a dependence on alcohol? **[3]**

26 Describe how a psychological explanation would explain Ashley's behaviour. **[4]**

Collins

GCSE Psychology

Paper 1: Cognition and Behaviour

Time allowed: 1 hour 45 minutes

The maximum mark for this paper is 100

Materials

For this paper you may have:

- a calculator.

Instructions

- Use black ink or black ball-point pen.
- Answer **all** questions. You must answer the questions in the spaces provided.
- Do all rough work in this book.

Information

- The marks for questions are shown in brackets.
- Questions should be answered in continuous prose. You will be assessed on your ability to:
  - use good English
  - organise information clearly
  - use specialist vocabulary where appropriate.

Name: ....

Practice Exam Paper 1

Section A
Memory

Answer **all** questions in the spaces provided.

---

0 1 James goes to the supermarket without writing a list. Once there, he gets mixed up with the fruit and vegetables that he needed to purchase. If James is accessing his long-term memory for the information, how has this been encoded? Shade **one** box only. **[1 mark]**

A Visually ◯

B Semantically ◯

C Acoustically ◯

D Olfactory ◯

0 2 Bartlett's War of the Ghosts study investigated reconstructive memory. What is meant by 'reconstructive memory'? **[2 marks]**

....

....

0 3 Bartlett's study asked participants to retell a story several times. The procedure was not well controlled. Identify **one** problem with having a lack of control over the procedures when carrying out research. **[2 marks]**

....

....

0 4 Stella is sporty and participates in various team sports for her college. However, sometimes her teammates get frustrated with her when she seems to ignore the court markings and the rules for netball after she has played basketball.

0 4 · 1 Name the factor that is affecting Stella's accuracy of memory. **[1 mark]**

....

0 4 · 2 Using your knowledge of this factor, explain why Stella's teammates get frustrated with her. **[4 marks]**

0 5 A group of year 10 students believe that if they sit their end-of-year mocks in their classrooms they will perform better. They lobby fellow pupils who agree. They then present a proposal to the school to be allowed to sit exams in their classroom rather than the hall.

0 5 · 1 Using your knowledge of the accuracy of memory, explain why the students are convinced that they will perform better in the exams if they are allowed to sit them in their classes.

Briefly evaluate this explanation. **[9 marks]**

0 5 · 2 Outline the differences between episodic, semantic and procedural memories. Use examples in your answer. **[6 marks]**

Section B
Perception
Answer **all** questions in the spaces provided.

---

0 6 Which **one** of the following is not an explanation of a misinterpreted depth cue? Shade **one** box only. **[1 mark]**

A The Ponzo illusion ◯

B The Muller-Lyer illusion ◯

C Rubin's vase ◯

D The Ames Room ◯

0 7 Identify **one** monocular depth cue. **[1 mark]**

0 8 · 1 Explain what is meant by size constancy. Include an example. **[3 marks]**

0 8 · 2 Identify **one** binocular depth cue and explain how it works. **[4 marks]**

Practice Exam Paper 1

0 9 Briefly evaluate Bruner and Minturn's study of perceptual set. **[4 marks]**

....

....

....

....

....

1 0 Explain how Gregory's constructivist theory of perception is influenced by nurture. **[4 marks]**

....

....

....

....

....

1 1 · 1 Describe Gibson's direct theory of visual perception. **[4 marks]**

....

....

....

....

....

1 1 · 2 Explain how Gibson's theory of perception is influenced by nature, using research evidence. **[4 marks]**

....

....

....

....

....

Section C
Development
Answer all questions in the spaces provided.

---

1 2 · 1 Which **one** of the following best describes the brain stem?
Shade **one** box only. **[1 mark]**

A Located deep inside the brain ◯

B Most highly developed part of the brain at birth ◯

C The last part of the brain to reach maturity ◯

D Where thinking takes place ◯

1 2 · 2 Which **one** of the following best describes the function of the cerebellum?
Shade **one** box only. **[1 mark]**

A Processes auditory information ◯

B Controls automatic functions ◯

C Processes visual information ◯

D Co-ordinates movement and balance ◯

1 3 · 1 Which **one** of the following best describes the role of nurture in
early brain development? Shade **one** box only. **[1 mark]**

A The way our brain forms is inherited ◯

B The way our brain forms depends on our environment ◯

C Our brain's development relies on our genes and environment ◯

1 3 · 2 Which **one** of the following best describes the role of nature in early brain development? Shade **one** box only. **[1 mark]**

    A The way our brain forms is inherited ○

    B The way our brain forms depends on our environment ○

    C Our brain's development relies on our genes and environment ○

1 3 · 3 What did Piaget mean by 'egocentricism'? **[2 marks]**

1 4 Byron's two children are Kane who is three and Tulula who is four. When playing hide and seek, Kane hides on the sofa under cushions so is clearly visible. Tulula hides in places where she is unseen. Kane gets upset as he cannot work out why he cannot find Tulula but she finds him easily.

1 4 · 1 Name the stage of cognitive development that Kane is in. **[1 mark]**

1 4 · 2 Explain how Tulula is showing a reduction in egocentrism. **[3 marks]**

1 5 · 1 You are interested in Piaget's theory of egocentrism. Using three-year-old children in their nursery playground, design an observation to see if they display egocentrism. You need to include:

- What type of observation and why

- At least **two** examples of behaviour you could observe

- One ethical issue that you would need to address and how you could deal with it. **[6 marks]**

_____

_____

_____

_____

_____

_____

_____

1 5 · 2 Briefly outline a fixed mindset. **[2 marks]**

_____

_____

Practice Exam Paper 1

Jamal, Mina and Carlos were revising. Carlos said he cannot revise for exams and would prefer to be completing his media work, making videos and designing magazine covers. Mina has lots of mind maps and diagrams to aid her revision. Jamal continuously writes notes and even rewrites them.

1 5 · 3 Describe and explain the learning styles each is displaying. **[6 marks]**

1 5 · 4 Which **one** of the following is a criticism of learning styles, according Willingham? Shade **one** box only. **[1 mark]**

A Learning styles are scientific ○

B Learning styles show how children learn ○

C Learning styles are unscientific ○

Section D
Research methods
Answer **all** questions in the spaces provided.

---

1 6 Serena is carrying out research on people's views of UFOs. She decided to interview each participant who responded to her advert in an air and space magazine. Serena used a structured interview.

1 6 · **1** Some of the participants may have felt embarrassed if they agreed with the existence of UFOs. This would be an ethical issue. Describe this ethical issue and suggest **one** way Serena could deal with it. **[4 marks]**

....

....

....

....

1 6 · **2** Explain **one** weakness of using a structured interview. **[2 marks]**

....

....

Participants who indicated that they believed in UFOs were asked back for a further interview. This time Serena used an unstructured interview.

1 7 · **1** Name the type of data that Serena would gather using an unstructured interview. **[1 mark]**

....

Practice Exam Paper 1

1 7 · 2 Explain the difference between an unstructured and a structured interview. **[4 marks]**

Another researcher analysed the data Serena collected. They had noticed in the interviews that people who held a strong belief in the existence of UFOs were very confident. The second researcher decided to carry out a correlation between the participant's confidence and their belief in UFOs. They predicted that the more confident they were, the stronger their belief would be.

1 7 · 3 Write a suitable hypothesis for this correlation. **[2 marks]**

1 7 · 4 Name the type of correlation that will be found if the researcher's prediction is true. **[1 mark]**

1 7 · 5 What is the strength of using a correlation for this research? **[3 marks]**

18·1 Using the graph paper, sketch a scatter diagram to show the results in **Table 1**.
Provide a suitable title and labels for your diagram. **[4 marks]**

Table 1.

Participant	Confidence/10	Beliefs/10
1	3	7
2	5	8
3	8	10
4	9	9
5	3	6
6	5	7
7	4	4
8	10	8
9	7	9
10	6	9

1 8 · 2 Identify the mode for the confidence ratings. **[1 mark]**

1 8 · 3 Identify the mode for the beliefs rating. **[1 mark]**

1 8 · 4 The median for the confidence was 5.5 and the mean was 6. What type of distribution is shown in the confidence ratings? Shade **one** box only. **[1 mark]**

A Normal ⭕

B Negative ⭕

C Positive ⭕

1 8 · 5 The correlation was carried out by another researcher using the original data collected by Serena. What would this data be called? Shade **one** box only. **[1 mark]**

A Secondary ⭕

B Primary ⭕

C Normal ⭕

Collins

GCSE Psychology
Paper 2: Social Context and Behaviour

Time allowed: 1 hour 45 minutes

The maximum mark for this paper is 100

Materials

For this paper you may have:

- a calculator.

Instructions

- Use black ink or black ball-point pen.
- Answer all questions. You must answer the questions in the spaces provided.
- Do all rough work in this book.

Information

- The marks for questions are shown in brackets.
- Questions should be answered in continuous prose. You will be assessed on your ability to:
  - use good English
  - organise information clearly
  - use specialist vocabulary where appropriate.

Name: ....

Practice Exam Paper 2

Section A
Social Influence

Answer **all** questions in the spaces provided.

---

0 1 In Asch's study of conformity the genuine participant would usually be one of the last because of which of the following? Shade **one** box only. **[1 mark]**

    A It would increase the chances of demand characteristics ◯

    B It was an unambiguous situation so participants did not need to see how to behave, which would show conformity ◯

    C They would hear a minority of answers ◯

    D It was an ambiguous situation so participants needed to see how to behave, which would show conformity. ◯

0 2 Tom and Lilah were having a conversation about their psychology lessons. Lilah told Tom that he only answers questions when at least three others have already answered, so he conforms to their answers. Tom disputes this and accuses Lilah of the same. Lilah says she only ever conforms to other people's answers for guidance when the question is challenging.

0 2 · 1 Explain using social factors why Lilah thinks that Tom conforms during their lessons. **[2 marks]**

_____

_____

0 2 · 2 Explain using task difficulty why Lilah claims to only conform if the question is difficult. Use research evidence in your answer. **[3 marks]**

_____

_____

_____

0 3 · 1 In Milgram's study, what percentage of participants went to 300 volts?   **[1 mark]**

0 3 · 2 Compare Milgram's explanation of obedience with Adorno's explanation of obedience.   **[4 marks]**

0 4 · 1 Describe the **two** independent variables in Piliavin's subway study and explain how they were clearly defined.   **[4 marks]**

0 4 · 2 How did the Piliavin study collect the data?   **[1 mark]**

0 4 · 3 Explain **one** weakness of collecting the data for this study in this way.   **[2 marks]**

Practice Exam Paper 2

0 5   Researchers carried out an observation looking at helping behaviour. They observed whether wearing a uniform influenced behaviour. Participants were told they were taking part in a study of helping others. They were given either a nurse's uniform or a football top and shorts or they remained in their own clothes. They then completed a computer simulation where different scenarios were shown where people needed help such as when falling over. They had to indicate whether they would help or not. For each scenario they were told if they helped it could come at personal cost to them, such as missing a job interview because they would be late.

Table 1.

Number of helping scenarios	People dressed as a nurse helping	People in football kit helping	Own clothes helping
12	8	3	5

0 5 · 1   Identify and describe the social factor that could explain the behaviour in **Table 1**. **[2 marks]**

0 5 · 2   Using research, evaluate how social factors affect collective behaviour. **[5 marks]**

Section B
Language, thought and communication

Answer **all** questions in the spaces provided.

---

0 6 Outline how language affects the recall of events and colour recognition in different cultures. **[4 marks]**

....

....

....

....

0 7 Describe **two** ethical issues that could arise when carrying out research into personal space. **[4 marks]**

....

....

....

....

0 8 Which behaviours are functions of animal behaviour and which behaviours are functions of human behaviour? Write **A** or **B** in the boxes.

A = Animal, B = Human **[4 marks]**

Planning ahead	
Leave pheromones	
Use communication for specific events	
Advertise fitness	

0 9 Which **one** of the following is an example that does not show innate non-verbal communication? Shade **one** box only. **[1 mark]**

A Neonates using non-verbal behaviours such as smiling ⃝

B Babies show a disgusted facial expression when given something sour ⃝

C Children born blind have been found to show facial expressions, such as surprise ⃝

D People from contact cultures prefer a small personal space whereas people from non-contact cultures prefer a larger one. ⃝

1 0 Piaget said children can only understand words when they are cognitively ready. Sapir & Whorf would suggest the opposite – that language comes before thought. Use your knowledge of both Piaget and Sapir & Whorf to discuss the way language develops. **[9 marks]**

1 1 Briefly describe Yuki's study of emoticons. **[3 marks]**

_____

_____

_____

_____

Section C
Brain and neuropsychology

Answer **all** questions in the spaces provided.

---

1 2 Complete boxes A, B, C and D.

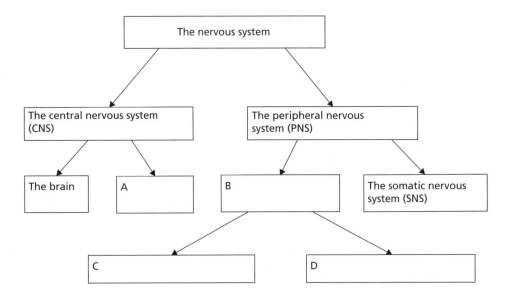

[4 marks]

1 3 Which **one** of the following is false regarding the fight or flight response?
Shade **one** box only.

[1 mark]

A The hormone adrenaline is released from the adrenal glands ◯

B The hypothalamus detects a stressor (a threat) ◯

C Adrenaline causes the heartrate to slow down ◯

D When the threat is over, saliva is produced again ◯

1 4 A patient who suffered a brain injury and then had some memory problems, attended the hospital. The doctor discussed an appropriate scan to find out the extent of the damage.

1 4 · 1 Identify three scans the doctor could discuss with the patient.   **[3 marks]**

1 4 · 2 Name the scan that would be able to detect the area of the brain being used whilst carrying out a memory task, without using radiation.   **[1 mark]**

1 4 · 3 Evaluate the scanning technique that does not use radiation.   **[4 marks]**

1 5 Evaluate Hebb's theory of learning and neuronal growth.   **[4 marks]**

Practice Exam Paper 2

1 6 Name the hemisphere of the brain where we usually find the language areas.   **[1 mark]**

_____

1 7 Name the area of the brain that contains the somatosensory area.   **[1 mark]**

_____

1 8 What is cognitive neuroscience? How has it helped us to understand neurological damage?   **[6 marks]**

_____

_____

_____

_____

_____

_____

_____

Section D
Psychological problems
Answer **all** questions in the spaces provided.

---

1 9 Which **two** of the following are often seen in people with unipolar depression?
Shade **two** boxes. **[2 marks]**

A Appetite changes (loss or increase) ◯

B Being happier in usual activities ◯

C Disruption of sleep pattern (sleeping more or less) ◯

D Greater self-confidence and esteem ◯

2 0 Explain how significant mental health problems can affect the individual. **[6 marks]**

....

....

....

....

....

....

Practice Exam Paper 2

2 1 Out-patients attending a clinic for treatment for their depression were asked to take part in research. The participants were the ones who happened to be there on that day and who agreed to take part. The study consisted of them giving a score of their symptoms on that day. They were then asked if they would repeat the questionnaire after six months. The first set of data received from the questionnaires (out of ten for severity of symptoms) gave the following scores:

5, 6, 7, 8, 8, 8, 9, 9, 10, 10

2 1 · 1 Which sampling method was used in this study? Justify your answer. **[2 marks]**

....

....

....

2 1 · 2 Calculate the median rating of severity of symptoms. Show your workings. **[2 marks]**

....

....

....

2 1 · 3 After six months the same participants filled in the same questionnaire giving the following scores: 3, 3, 3, 3, 6, 6, 6, 7, 7, 7

The median rating in the follow-up study was 6. Explain what the results suggest about the effectiveness of the treatment the patients were receiving, referring to the median scores. **[4 marks]**

....

....

....

....

....

....

2 1 · 4 Identify and evaluate **one** therapy the patients could have been given in
this study. **[5 marks]**

....

....

....

....

....

....

....

2 2 Outline peer influence as a psychological explanation of addiction. **[4 marks]**

....

....

....

....

....

....

Notes

Answers

1. Alina: semantic **[1]**; George: visual **[1]**
2. **Encoding:** the process of acquiring, processing and organising incoming information in a way that allows it to be stored and later retrieved from memory. **[2]**
Storage: the phase of memory where information that has been encoded is retained and maintained over time. **[2]**
Retrieval: the process of accessing and recalling stored information from memory. It involves locating and bringing back the stored information to conscious awareness. **[2]**
3. A and B should be shaded. **[2]**
4. Storage can be in short-term memory, held for a short time up to 30 seconds. Storage can be in long-term memory for up to a lifetime. **[2]**
5. Bobby uses cued recall to remember the names of the football teams, such as his friend giving him the first letter to help him. Anil uses recognition to help him remember the names of the teams – once he is shown a list of all the team names, he can recognise the ones in their league. Nick doesn't need help, he can free recall the names of the football teams without any aid. **[6]**
6. Research supporting semantic memory as a separate type of memory comes from the Clive Wearing case study. Clive had damage to his hippocampus but could still remember facts and retained the ability to speak and understand language (semantic memory). Clive Wearing's case also supports the notion that we have a separate memory of procedural information. For example, Clive retained the ability to play the piano, even after his brain damage (a type of procedural memory). However, he was unable to retain his episodic memory (the ability to recall episodes in your life). He could not remember much of his life prior to his illness and this demonstrates that episodic memory is in a different part of the brain to semantic and procedural memory. **[5]**
7. According to the MSM, memory is divided into three main stores:
Sensory Memory (SM): holds incoming sensory information from the environment for a very brief period. It codes information via the five senses. SM allows for a brief retention of sensory stimuli, giving us a continuous perception of the world. If information is paid attention to it will transfer to the STM. **Short-term Memory (STM):** has a limited capacity of 5-9 items and duration of up to 30 seconds without rehearsal. Without rehearsal or further processing, information in STM is likely to be forgotten. It codes information acoustically. Rehearsal will transfer information to LTM. **Long-term Memory (LTM):** has a vast capacity and stores information for a relatively longer duration, from minutes to a lifetime. LTM is believed to have an unlimited capacity, although retrieval of information from LTM can vary in terms of accessibility. It codes information semantically. **[6]**
8. One strength of the model is it shows us that we have separate stores for short-term and long-term memories. Evidence supports this idea. **[2]**
9. The duration of STM is up to 30 seconds.
10. a) Archie **[1]**
    b) primacy and recency effect. **[1]**
11. Short term memory only holds information for up to 30 seconds **[1]**, whereas long term memory can store information permanently, potentially a lifetime. **[1]**
12. Murdock's study supports the MSM as participants could recall the first words in the list, because they would have been rehearsed and transferred to LTM. The words at the end were recalled easily as they were the most recent and still in the short-term memory. **[4]**
13. D and E should be shaded. **[2]**
14. The focus on the meaning of events rather than the details. For example, describing the way people try to make sense of new information, by using past information to make sense of it, such as in the War of the Ghosts study. **[2]**
15. Reconstructive memory is when we fill in any gaps in our memories using our existing schemas so we can make sense of things. For example, in the Bartlett study, participants had no idea in places what the story was about so they reconstructed the story to retell it using their own schemas based on experience and culture. **[3]**
16. Participants tended to omit or simplify details of the story that were unfamiliar or culturally inconsistent with their own background. They unconsciously filled in gaps with information that was more familiar and coherent with their own schemas. The story became more familiar and aligned with their own cultural norms and expectations and lost its original cultural context, such as using 'boats' rather than 'canoes'. **[3]**
17. a) Lab experiment **[1]**
    b) A weakness of a lab experiment is that they can have low validity as the set-up doesn't really reflect a real-life situation. **[2]**
18. False memories are memories about an event that did not happen but the person feels that it did. For example, in a study by Loftus where participants were given four short stories about their childhood, three were true and one wasn't. The participants had to read each story and write down afterwards what they remembered. Six of the participants recalled the false story as being true. **[3]**
19. **The procedure:** Participants could be gathered using an opportunity sample – people who were there at the time for a lesson. You could give the participants a topic to revise for thirty minutes, followed by a test. Both revision and the test take place in the same classroom. On a different day, the same group could be given a different topic of equal difficulty to revise in the psychology room but sit the test in a different classroom. The test would get a score out of twenty.
Hypothesis: Participants who revise and sit the psychology test in the same room will get a higher score out of twenty compared to if they revise in one classroom and sit the test in a different room.
Expected results: In line with context affecting the accuracy of memory, the results should show that the students' scores are higher when they sat the test in the same room as they revised. Context acts as a cue for recall. This would be in line with research, such as Godden and Baddeley, who found when the context of learning either underwater or at a beach was different to recall, participants performed worse. **[6]**

1. Sensation refers to the process of detecting and receiving sensory information from the environment through our sensory organs such as eyes, ears, mouth, nose and skin. In order for us to make sense of the information, our brain needs to interpret these sensations and this is what perception is. Perception is the process of interpreting and making sense of the sensory information received through sensation. It involves the organisation, identification, and interpretation of sensory inputs by the brain. **[4]**
2. Monocular depth cues are visual cues that provide information about depth and distance using only one eye. These cues help us perceive depth and three-dimensional space, even when we view the world with just a single eye. **[2]**

3. B and D should be shaded. **[2]**
4. Binocular depth cues are visual cues that rely on the use of both eyes to perceive depth and three-dimensional space. These cues take advantage of the slight differences in the images received by each eye to create a sense of depth perception. **[2]**
5.

[1]
6. Psychologists would explain the Ponzo illusion based on our perception of depth and distance. Our brain uses various depth cues, such as linear perspective and size-distance relationship, to judge the relative size and distance of objects. In the Ponzo illusion, the converging lines create the impression of depth, so the depth cue is misinterpreted, with the top line appearing further away and the bottom line appearing closer. **[3]**
7. a)

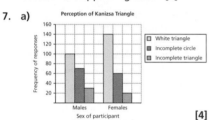

[4]
   b) 200 ÷ 20 = 10
   220 ÷ 20 = 11 so ratio is 10:11 **[2]**
   c) (140/220) × 100 = 0.6364 × 100 = 63.64% to three significant figures = 63.6 **[2]**
   d) D
8. Perceptual set refers to a predisposition or readiness to perceive certain stimuli or interpret sensory information in a particular way. It is influenced by our prior experiences, expectations, beliefs, and cultural factors. We 'see' what we want to see. **[2]**
9. Perceptual set can be affected by culture. Culture refers to the shared beliefs, values, norms and practices of a particular group or society. It influences the way individuals perceive and interpret the world around them. What we are familiar with influences our interpretation of things. **[2]**
10. Researchers would expect the vegetarians to take longer to complete the word search in condition two (the meat-related one). This is because emotion can affect perceptual set and, in this case, the vegetarians may have blocked out the words to do with meat as they may have found them threatening or anxiety-inducing. **[3]**

11. Findings may be unreliable because on some days people may be more likely to notice emotional stimuli and on other days less likely to notice. Therefore depending on the person's mood on a particular day could affect the findings. **[2]**
12. Gilchrist and Nesberg's study has support from other researchers, showing it has validity. Other studies found motivation influenced behaviour, such as being hungry influences our perception and interpretation of pictures. The Gilchrist and Nesberg study could have had ethical issues as preventing people from eating could be problematic. People went without food for twenty hours which could affect some participants. The study also is low in validity as they didn't use real food to show to participants, only pictures, so may not be generalisable to real-life situations. **[4]**
13. 24 participants were split into two groups where half were shown some letters with an ambiguous figure in the middle, a B that was broken that could read as 13 or B. The other half were shown some numbers with the same ambiguous figure in the middle. Bruner and Minturn found the participants in the number group mostly drew 13. The group who saw letters mainly drew a B. The researchers concluded that expectation affects perception. **[6]**
14. The name of the perceptual set is emotion. This is similar to research carried out where participants had to look at displayed words – some were taboo whilst others were neutral. They measured their skin conductance as a sign of anxiety. The taboo words took longer for the participants to say out loud and their skin conductance increased showing they were more anxious. **[4]**
15. Because it was collected solely for the purpose of this study. It wasn't collected by someone else. **[2]**

Pages 163–166 Development

1. C
2. Processes in the body that are outside of our conscious control, such as our heart beating. We do not have to think about it, it does it automatically. **[3]**
3. B
4. The influence on our behaviour that is external. Anything outside of the body, such as a person's environment, could play a role in the nurturing of a person and ultimately affect their behaviour. **[2]**
5. Infection can be considered nurture that could affect a growing brain. For example, pregnant women, in the first twenty weeks, need to keep away from others who have German measles

because they could put the baby at risk of brain damage. **[1]**
6. 87 – 69 = 18
   18/87 = 0.20689655 × 100 = 20.68 to two significant figures = 21 **[3]**
7. Opportunity sample as she asked people who were attending the clinic who were present and available at the time. **[2]**
8. Our internal processes that influence our behaviour, through our genes from our parents and ancestors. **[2]**
9. a) A-brain stem, B-cerebral cortex, C-cerebellum, D-Thalamus

   b)
Autonomic functions such as breathing and heartbeat	A
Precise physical movement/ coordinates actions	C
Cognition/thinking/ perception/memory processes	B
Some sensory processing/ relaying signals to the cerebral cortex	D

   [4]
10. Assimilation is the process by which individuals incorporate new information or experiences into their existing cognitive structures or schemas. According to Piaget, children actively engage with the world around them, seeking to make sense of new experiences by relating them to their existing knowledge. Accommodation is the process by which children modify their existing cognitive structures or schemas in response to new information or experiences that cannot be easily assimilated. When children encounter new information or experiences that do not fit into their existing schemas, they undergo accommodation. **[4]**
11. Seb is showing accommodation as his existing schema was that the teacher was nice and that Keshav must be wrong. However, when Seb encountered the same experience that did not fit into his schema of the teacher (and therefore this new experience does not fit his schema), he has undergone accommodation and now his schema has been modified. **[4]**
12. a) Maya is the youngest. **[1]**
    b) Around the age of 11 **[1]**
    c) Pre-operational **[1]**
13. C
14. Children develop at different rates at some of the stages. For example, in the naughty teddy study, some children at the pre-operational stage, could conserve. Therefore showing a weakness of Piaget's stages as being too rigid. Some children will do things at a different pace. A second weakness is that his research was on European children and could be culturally biased as the age at which the stages are reached can vary between cultures. **[5]**

15. When children can only see things from their own viewpoint and no-one else's. This applies to both physical objects and other's points of view. **[2]**

16. Piaget presented children with a model containing three small mountains with different characteristics, such as varying heights, shapes and details. Each mountain could be viewed from different angles. The child was seated on one side of the model and shown pictures depicting what each mountain would look like from the perspective of a doll positioned on the other side of the model. The task required the child to choose a picture that accurately represented what the doll would see when looking at the mountains from its position. Piaget found that young children, particularly those in the pre-operational stage (around 2 to 7 years old), consistently chose the picture that matched their own perspective rather than the doll's perspective. **[3]**

17. 30 children between the ages of three and a half and five years were shown a model comprising two intersecting walls, a "boy" doll and a "policeman" doll. The policeman doll was put in various positions and the children were asked to hide the boy doll from the policeman. A second policeman doll was then introduced, and both dolls were placed at the end of the walls. The child was asked to hide the boy from both policemen; the children now had to take account of two different points of view. 90% were able to put the boy doll where the two policemen could not see it. A more complex situation was introduced with more walls and a third policeman. 90% of four-year-olds were successful. The three-year-olds had more difficulty. This study showed that by age four children have lost their egocentrism because they are able to take the view of another. This study used a lab experiment and so validity was low. The task did not reflect what the children would do in real life. This means we cannot generalise findings to a real-life situation. **[9]**

18.

Stage	Age
Sensorimotor	0-2 years
Pre-operational	2-7 years
Concrete operational	8-11 years
Formal operational	11+

[4]

19. The sensorimotor stage is the first stage of cognitive development which occurs from birth to approximately two years of age. During this stage, infants and young children learn about the world primarily through their senses and actions. The main characteristics of the sensorimotor stage include object permanence / constancy – where infants gradually develop the understanding that objects continue to exist even when they are out of sight. Development of motor skills occurs where infants explore, learn to grasp objects, crawl, walk and develop other motor skills. The pre-operational stage is the second stage. It typically occurs between the ages of two and seven years. During this stage, children become more capable of symbolic thinking and representation and engage in pretend play and make-believe scenarios. They use objects symbolically and create imaginary situations. Children in this stage tend to have difficulty understanding or considering the perspectives of others. They view the world primarily from their own point of view. **[4]**

20. Piaget has played a role in education through suggesting there is a stage of cognitive development when children are biologically ready to learn certain things and not before. Activities need to be age-appropriate for learning to take place. Piaget also believed that children learn through discovery rather than by rote, so they play a part alongside the teacher who stimulates the children through activities. These should be suitably challenging. Piaget acknowledged children progress through the stages of development at different rates so activities need to reflect this. This introduced the idea of smaller group activities occurring in the same classroom. Finally, Piaget suggested that, for the different stages of development, there should be a suitable environment in which the stage would be reflected. For example, in the pre-operational stage opportunities for role play should be offered. **[4]**

21. One weakness of Piaget's theory is that children develop at different rates but according to Piaget there is a set time frame in which development occurs. A second weakness is that his research could be culturally bias as it was carried out on European children. Non-European children could develop at different rates and his research does not acknowledge this fact. **[4]**

22. A belief that innate abilities are responsible for any achievements. Extra work and trying harder to achieve something is pointless, you won't be able to achieve it, because of the fixed innate abilities you have. If people with a fixed mindset fail at something, they will give up as they think it's pointless. **[2]**

23. A growth mindset is the opposite of a fixed one. People believe that if they work harder at something, they will experience an improved outcome. They believe that ability can be developed and failure is not an option and they will work harder to achieve. **[2]**

24. Darragh has a fixed mindset – he believes missing school isn't a problem because he isn't very able and therefore school makes no difference to his abilities. Adam has a growth mindset – he doesn't like missing school as he knows he benefits from being there to improve his abilities. **[2]**

25. Praise could benefit Darragh as it could increase his motivation to try and work harder and this may improve his abilities. This could improve his self-efficacy: his belief in himself that maybe he could do better if he tried. It could be a motivating force that he needs. Adam already has a positive self-efficacy as he believes he could improve through hard work. This in turn increases his motivation to continue to try and improve. Praise could further Adam's self-efficacy as it would give him feelings of reward which again could motivate him. **[6]**

26.

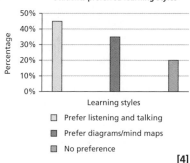

Students preferred learning styles

- Prefer listening and talking
- Prefer diagrams/mind maps
- No preference

[4]

Pages 167–170 **Research**

1. A random sample can be selected by putting the names of the target population into a hat or assigning each participant a number and putting the numbers into a computer random number generator. Set the parameters for how many participants you want and you then get your random sample. **[2]**

2. It is the least biased sampling method as every member of the target population has an equal chance of being chosen. It is also free from researcher bias. **[2]**

3. a) Stratified sampling should be more representative of the target population compared to a systematic sample because using systematic means taking every nth person from the register. This could result in every participant having one set of characteristics, such as being all men, so would not be representative. However, stratified sampling chooses a strata of the target population. For example, if your target population of people working in the college was 50% men and 50% women then your participants need to reflect this, making it more representative. **[4]**

    b) They could put all the participants' names into a hat and pick out the first ten for example and they could be condition one, then the second ten could be in condition two. **[2]**

c) The colleague could have mentioned participant variables being an issue with an independent groups design. Using either a matched pairs design, matching people on relevant characteristics, or switching to a repeated measures design would eliminate this issue. **[4]**

d) An ethical issue could be informed consent. This is an issue as participants may need to drink alcohol if they are in the alcohol condition. They will need to be informed of this so they can agree. It could be a problem if they are intolerant to alcohol or are on medication that could have consequences if mixed with drink. Or they may simply not drink so they need informed consent so they have the right to withdraw before starting the study. **[4]**

e) The IV is the (one bottle of 300ml beer) alcohol or no alcohol conditions. **[2]**

f) The dependent variable, effect on driving, could be operationalised by using a driving simulation like in a theory driving test, to see the number of errors made. **[2]**

4. A potential extraneous variable could be the clarity of the driving video used. If it is unclear or too small, participants may not be able to see the hazards clearly and this affects their driving, not whether they have had alcohol. Or it could be the environment in which they sit the video, if it's too bright and they cannot see the screen properly this could also affect their driving skills on the hazard test. **[3]**

5. There will be a difference in the number of errors made in a driving simulation hazard test between participants who drank alcohol (a bottle of 300ml beer), compared to those who had no alcohol OR participants who drank alcohol will record more errors on a hazard test compared to those who drank no alcohol. **[3]**

6. a) The range is higher in the alcohol condition compared to the non-alcohol telling us that results were more consistent in the non-alcohol condition and more spread in the alcohol group. **[2]**

b) A problem with the range is that it is affected by anomalies. If there are extreme scores this extends the highest or lowest number and doesn't really tell us much information about the actual number of errors the participants made, only the difference between the highest and lowest score. **[2]**

7. a) A consent form includes all details about the study including the aims, the procedures, ethical issues that

will be addressed and a place for the participant to sign to agree to take part. **[2]**

b) Opportunity **[1]**

8. a) A lab experiment **[1]**

b) A strength of a lab experiment is it is a highly controlled environment. This means any extraneous variables have been controlled and won't affect results. This allows researchers to establish cause and effect. A weakness is that because of the controlled environment the study may have low validity as it isn't showing people's behaviour in real life, only under strict lab conditions. **[4]**

9. a) Field experiment **[1]**

b) A strength of a field experiment is that it occurs in a real environment therefore increasing the validity as it shows people's behaviour in everyday life. However there is no control over extraneous variables and therefore these can affect the results of the study. **[4]**

c) The difference between the two studies were that the lab experiment took place under highly controlled conditions, meaning no extraneous variables could affect the results, whereas scenario two was a field experiment meaning extraneous variables could not be controlled and could have affected results. However the scenario two environment is true to real life as it takes place in the real world, whereas scenario one does not. This means scenario two has high validity whereas scenario one has low validity. **[4]**

10. C
11. B
12. A
13. Primary data is collected first-hand by a researcher for the purpose of the study. Secondary data is where a researcher uses data that somebody else had collected i.e. reading about what research has found in a textbook. **[2]**

14. a) Data reordered: 41, 52, 53, 59, 64, 67, 72, 75, 75, 82, 88, 90, 95 **[1]**
Median = 72 **[1]**

b) 95 – 41 **[1]**
Range = 54 **[1]**

c) 75 **[1]**

15. a) 25 + 28 + 24 + 26 + 23 + 27 + 26 = 179 **[1]**
179 ÷ 7 = 25.57 (2 d.p.) **[1]**

b) (23 ÷ 35) × 100 = 65.714… **[1]**
= 66% (2 s.f.) **[1]**

c)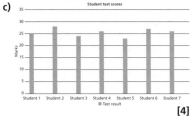

[4]

1. C
2. The number of people giving the wrong answer affects an individual's tendency to conform to the majority opinion. Asch's experiment involved a group of participants who were shown simple line comparison tasks. The participants were asked to indicate which of three comparison lines (labelled A, B, and C) matched a target line in length. The correct answer was always obvious. The participants were the last ones to give their answers after hearing the confederates' responses. Asch varied the number of confederates in each group. The presence of two confederates increased conformity to the wrong answer in 13.6% of the trails. Three confederates increased conformity to 31.8%. Once the group reached a certain size, around four, conformity did not continue to increase. **[3]**

3. Locus of control is a dispositional explanation of conformity as it refers to an individual's belief about the degree of control they have over their own life and the outcomes they experience. People with an internal locus of control believe that they have control over their own actions and the events that occur in their lives and are less likely to conform to the majority. They are more likely to resist conformity and maintain their independent judgements and behaviours. They do not need validation or approval from others. Whereas individuals with an external locus of control believe that external factors or forces, such as luck, fate, or powerful others, determine their outcomes. Having an external locus of control suggests a person is more likely to conform to the majority as they look to others to see how to act. As a result, they may be more likely to conform to group norms and conforming behaviours to fit in or avoid social disapproval. However, personality is only one factor that could play a part in conformity. There are other factors such as the situation a person is in. If the situation is a familiar one or the people are familiar, conformity could change depending on these social factors. When a situation is new or ambiguous, conformity may occur as the person is unsure how to act and therefore it is not due to their dispositional factors. **[6]**

4. Asch's line study aimed to investigate whether people would conform to the answers of a majority group, even when they are clearly incorrect. The procedure involved 123 participants, all men, tested with a group of 6-8 confederates. In any trial, there was only ever one real participant. The participants were shown a series of lines and asked to match a standard

line with one of the comparison lines. However, the majority of the confederates intentionally gave incorrect answers. 75% of the participants conformed to the incorrect majority opinion on at least one occasion during the study. 25% never conformed at all. Participants would often give incorrect answers to match the majority's responses, even when they were obviously wrong. The study showed the importance of social pressure on behaviour and the tendency for people to conform to judgements of a majority group, even when they knew those judgements were wrong. Asch's research demonstrated that people have a desire to fit in and avoid social disapproval. However, the Asch line study has limitations and has faced criticisms. Some argue that the study lacks validity as the task of comparing line lengths in a controlled laboratory setting may not fully represent real-world conformity situations. The pressure to conform in everyday life can be more complex. Additionally, cultural factors play a role in conformity levels, and the original study primarily focused on Western, individualistic cultures. Cultural differences may affect the extent to which individuals conform to group norms. It could be that the findings were a sign of the times in America in the 1950s, a period known as McCarthyism when people who acted outside of expected norms could be accused of being a spy with communist tendencies. Therefore people tried to fit in and not stand out. **[9]**

5. C
6. One strength of Milgram's agency theory is its ability to explain the high levels of obedience observed in Milgram's famous experiments. The theory offers insights into how individuals may willingly carry out harmful actions under the influence of perceived authority. It highlights the role of situational factors, such as the presence of an authority figure, in shaping behaviour. The theory provides an understanding of real-world instances of obedience to authority, such as in military settings and oppressive regimes. It helps explain why individuals may engage in morally questionable acts when they perceive themselves as acting on behalf of an authority figure. However, there are several limitations. Some argue that the theory may oversimplify the complexity of obedience. Human behaviour is influenced by a multitude of factors including personal values, moral principles, and social norms. Not all particpants obeyed in Milgram's study, which shows there must be other explanations of obedience. It does not

explain why some individuals choose to defy authority or engage in acts of disobedience, even in situations where they may be in an agentic state. **[5]**

7. According to Adorno, individuals with an authoritarian personality exhibit several traits. These traits include sticking to social norms and values, a tendency to be submissive to authority figures, a rigid and inflexible mindset, a belief in the inherent superiority of certain social groups, and a high level of aggression towards those who deviate from established norms. Adorno believed that the authoritarian personality develops as a result of certain childhood experiences, that a combination of harsh and strict parenting, a strict adherence to traditional values, and a lack of critical thinking and independent exploration can contribute to the development of an authoritarian mindset. Individuals with an authoritarian personality have a specific cognitive style characterised by a black-and-white, dichotomous thinking pattern. They tend to view the world in terms of absolutes, categorising people and situations into rigid and simplistic categories of good or bad, right or wrong. **[3]**

8. C
9. A weakness of using questionnaires to assess personality type could be people giving socially desirable responses. If people don't give honest answers then the results will lack validity. **[2]**
10. In an interview, if you don't understand a question, you can ask the interviewer to clarify. With a questionnaire, if a person has been left to fill it out by themselves, they cannot check any questions they are unsure of. **[2]**
11. B
12. C
13. The presence of other people when a situation occurs results in less help being offered. People assume that others will help so stand back and don't help themselves. Also, some people are wary of helping as it may put them at risk of harm if the situation is a dangerous one. If the cost of helping outweighs the benefits, people are less likely to help. **[4]**
14. If the characteristics of the victim are similar to the bystander then they may be more likely to help. For example, in Piliavin's study, if the race of the victim was similar to the bystander then help was more likely. Expertise is another dispositional factor that can influence bystander intervention whereby if the bystander has medical knowledge that could help they would be more likely to intervene. **[4]**
15. A psychological state in which an individual experiences a loss of personal identity and a decrease in self-awareness when they are part of

a group or in a situation where their individuality is diminished. People may feel a reduced sense of personal responsibility and a decreased concern for the consequences of their actions, leading to a potential increase in impulsive and uninhibited behaviours. Contexts, such as during large gatherings, riots, football matches, or in situations where individuals are wearing uniforms or masks that conceal their identity, are more likely to see behaviour consistent with deindividuation. **[3]**

16. Personality is one dispositional factor affecting collective behaviour. For example, people with internal locus of control are less likely to lose their self-identity as they do not feel the need to look to others and are more likely to follow their own personal norms of behaviour. Morality is another dispositional factor affecting collective behaviour as some people have their own strong sense of moral values which means they will be less likely to follow the crowd. Their moral values will override any social norms being created by a crowd if they go against the person's own values and moral judgement. **[4]**

Pages 173–175 **Language, Thought and Communication**

1. C
2. A
3. Piaget's theory emphasises cognitive development in shaping language, whereas the Sapir-Whorf hypothesis suggests that language influences thought and perception. Piaget's theory of language focuses on the development of thinking and reasoning abilities in children and states that cognitive development precedes and shapes language development. Piaget's theory focuses on universal stages of cognitive development, while the Sapir-Whorf hypothesis explores the potential variations in cognition and perception across different languages and believes that the structure, vocabulary and concepts embedded within a language shape the way individuals think and perceive their experiences. **[4]**
4. Different languages may have distinct colour terminology, including the number and categorisation of colours. For example, some languages have separate words for different shades of a colour, while others may use more general terms. This can affect how individuals perceive and categorise colours, potentially leading to differences in colour recognition and memory. Cultural factors play a significant role in colour perception. Language is often influenced by cultural norms and

practices related to colour symbolism and meaning. These cultural influences can shape an individual's perception and memory of colours. For example, the Himba tribe have the same word for green and blue (bura) but use different words to distinguish between shades of green. When shown 11 green squares and one blue square, they had difficulty indicating which square was the odd one out but when shown 12 green squares, one of which was a lighter green, they had no problem identifying the odd one out. The Zuni people have one word for yellow and orange and in testing, when compared to English-speaking people, they had more problems in recall of those colours. **[4]**

5. The groups in the table have limited groups of colour, in particular the Dani people. If carrying out a recall task involving colour, the Dani people would struggle to perform well because of their limited naming of colours compared to English speakers. The same would be true of the Zuni and Berinmo. Therefore showing them a colour chart and asking them to recall the colours would be problematic. **[3]**

6. Using a questionnaire could pose problems for the different groups as if the variation language is more limited, compared to the English language, this could impact on the understanding of a questionnaire. If the questionnaire had been developed by English-speaking people the words used may not have the same meaning for the different groups. For example, a group of people living in one of the South Pacific islands use one word to mean a range of emotions of love, compassion and sadness. English speakers would find it difficult to understand the variation of emotions using just one word. **[3]**

7. Von Frisch, an ethologist, studied the dances performed by bees and suggested this was their way of communication. He wanted to understand the meaning of this dance and to understand how bees communicate information about food sources to their hive. He suggested that when the honeybees returned to their hives after finding a food source, they performed a series of movements known as the 'waggle' dance. The 'waggle' dance involves a figure-eight pattern, with the bee waggling its abdomen and vibrating its wings. The direction and duration of the dance convey information about the distance and direction of the food source relative to the position of the sun. Von Frisch demonstrated that honeybees rely on visual cues, such as the angle of the dance relative to gravity and the position of the sun, to interpret the information conveyed in the 'waggle' dance. **[4]**

8. Von Frisch's research on bee communication contributed to our understanding of animal communication. The research took place over many years, adding scientific credibility to the findings. The work earned him the Nobel Prize, the highest commendation in academia. However, Von Frisch did not study the sound that the bees made and it was discovered later that if the dance was performed without noise then other bees would not go to the food sources. Therefore this may be another form of communication that Von Frisch overlooked. He also found that not all bees did go to the food regardless of the dance or sound and so there must be other signals that the bees give that have yet to be discovered. But his work did have an impact on human understanding of animal communication. **[4]**

9.

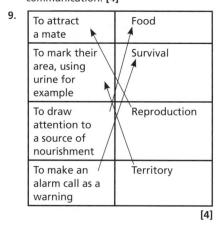

[4]

10. One thing that human communication has that animals do not is the ability to plan ahead. For example, we can make plans with each other and put important events in a diary but animals cannot do this. **[2]**

11. Gestures, for example, beating its chest. **[1]**

12. Inter-observer reliability could be a problem in the observation if only one researcher is observing. The observer could be biased in what they record and this could make findings unreliable. In order to improve the reliability, the observer would need another observer to carry out the same observation. They could each have a table of behavioural categories to look out for. This would have been devised by them already so they both know what they are looking for. Each time they see a behaviour in the table they would put a tally mark. At the end of the observation they can compare the tallies to see if they agree. **[4]**

13. A strength of an observation is that real behaviour is being observed by another person, in an objective way. It is not reliant on self-reporting which could give a biased view by the participant themselves. Therefore

observation has higher validity. A weakness of observations is that they can be affected by observer bias. The observer may record behaviour that they want to see that fits their hypothesis. In this way, the expectations of the researcher have an effect on the findings. **[4]**

14. Verbal communication is anything that is written or spoken in words. For example, having a conversation with someone or writing a text message is verbal communication. Non-verbal communication is communication without the use of words. For example, facial expressions to show happiness (smiling) or anger (scowling). **[4]**

15. Three functions of eye contact are: to regulate the flow of conversation, this shows the person who you are speaking with that you are interested in what they are saying. To signal attraction, for example, we may look at someone and catch their eye if we like a person. To express emotion, for example, when people are upset the eye contact can be quite intense. **[3]**

16. a) Opportunity **[1]**
   b) The participants appeared to use eye contact to regulate the conversation flow as when one person stopped speaking they would look at the other person. This would signal they had finished speaking and then they would expect the other person to speak. As in the study above, when the person was ready to speak they would break eye contact, giving signals they were about to talk. **[4]**
   c) The people could be randomly paired by putting all the names into a hat and pulling out the first name followed by the second name and they are the first pair. Then continue to do this until all the participants are paired. **[2]**
   d) A covert observation is hidden. This means the participants are unaware they are being observed. The researcher will be watching from a hidden place. **[2]**
   e) One ethical issue with covert observations is the lack of informed consent. As people are unaware they are being watched they cannot give their consent. This is a problem because if they were made aware they may not agree to be observed. People should have the right to refuse to participate. **[2]**
   f) It could be concluded that eye contact regulates the flow of conversation as the people in the cafe would use their eyes to give a prolonged look to show when they had finished speaking. They also used them to show when they were about to speak, by breaking eye contact. **[3]**

17. Postural echo, also known as mirroring or mimicry, refers to the subconscious imitation of another person's body posture, gestures or movements. It is a non-verbal behaviour where an individual unintentionally mimics the postures and movements of another person they are interacting with. [2]

18. Closed posture is when a person pulls themselves close to their own body when interacting with someone else. For example, crossing their arms or legs. It is thought to happen when a person doesn't feel very comfortable or as a way of rejecting the other person. Open posture is relaxed and shows the person is completely at ease. [2]

19. Cultural norms can affect personal space and touch. For example, in some cultures it is completely acceptable to stand up close and personal to another person, even if they are not very familiar with each other. In other cultures this would come across as an invasion of personal space and unacceptable as it may make the person feel uncomfortable. It has been found that English people prefer a personal space of about 1.5m whereas Arabs are comfortable a lot closer together. [2]

20.

Factor affecting personal space	Description
Culture	Differences for personal space between cultures. For example, English prefer 1.5m distance but Arabs are comfortable with less distance.
Status	People who are of similar status are comfortable standing close together, compared to those who are unequal in status.
Gender	Men appear to prefer a bigger social distance compared to women. With friends, men still prefer to sit opposite their friend whereas women will sit closer, side-by-side.

[6]

21. Darwin believed that non-verbal communication was an innate, evolutionary mechanism; it has evolved and is adaptive. All mammals show emotions through facial expression and the behaviour is universal and therefore evolutionary. Non-verbal behaviours persist in humans because they have been acquired for their value throughout evolutionary history. For example, showing anger, which could signal to others to stay away from potential harm. [4]

22. Non-verbal behaviour appears to be innate. For example, children who have been blind since birth show the same facial expressions as sighted children. A study of sighted and blind judo athletes found that both groups produced the same facial expressions in certain emotional situations, suggesting the behaviour is innate as the blind students would have been unable to learn the expressions. This supports the evolutionary theory of non-verbal behaviour. [4]

23. Yuki investigated cultural differences in the perception and interpretation of facial expressions, specifically focusing on the role of the eyes and mouth as cues for recognising emotions. The study compared participants from Japan and the United States. Over several trials, participants were shown photographs of facial expressions with varying combinations of eye and mouth expressions. They were then asked to identify the emotion being displayed. The results indicated that Japanese participants paid more attention to the eyes when interpreting emotions, whilst American participants focused more on the mouth region. The study examined the impact of culture on the recognition of emotions conveyed through emoticons. The study was criticised for not using real faces, so could lack in validity and applying findings to real life interpretations of facial expressions could be difficult. The findings revealed that Japanese participants were better at identifying emotions expressed through emoticons compared to American participants. This highlighted cultural differences in the interpretation of facial expressions and the role of different facial cues in emotion recognition. It also shed light on the cross-cultural understanding of emoticons and their usage as a form of non-verbal communication. [6]

Pages 176–178 Brain and Neuropsychology

1. D
2. A
3. B
4. B
5. C
6. The somatic nervous system is responsible for voluntary control of skeletal muscles. It allows individuals to consciously initiate and control movements, such as walking, talking, or writing. In contrast, the autonomic nervous system regulates involuntary functions, such as heartbeat, digestion, respiration, and glandular activity. These processes occur automatically and are not under conscious control. The autonomic nervous system is further divided into two branches, the sympathetic nervous system and the parasympathetic nervous system. The sympathetic branch prepares the body for "fight-or-flight" responses during times of stress or danger, while the parasympathetic branch promotes relaxation, rest and digestion. The somatic nervous system has no subdivisions. [2]

7. The fight-or-flight response is a physiological and psychological reaction triggered in response to a perceived threat or stressful situation. The response begins with the brain's recognition of a potential threat or danger. The hypothalamus detects the stressor and activates the sympathetic branch of the autonomic nervous system. This triggers the release of a stress hormone adrenaline, from the adrenal glands, into the bloodstream. The release of adrenaline produces several physiological changes in the body, preparing it for action. These changes include, amongst others, increased heart rate to pump more oxygenated blood to the muscles and vital organs, rapid breathing to increase oxygen and dilation of the pupils. The fight-or-flight response enhances mental alertness, attention, and sensory perception. Non-essential bodily functions, such as digestion and immune response, are temporarily suppressed to allocate resources to more immediate survival needs. The response mobilises energy resources in the body to support physical exertion. At the same time as the signal for the sympathetic branch is triggered, the hypothalamic-adrenal (HPA) axis is activated. This pathway is much slower so the effects are delayed. This pathway leads to the release of cortisol, a stress hormone that helps to sustain the body's stress response. This HPA returns the body to its resting state once the stressor has passed. [5]

8. A hormone

9. The James-Lange theory of emotion suggests that emotions are a result of our bodily reactions to external stimuli. According to the theory, an external event or stimulus triggers a physiological response in the body. This could be a visual, auditory or sensory input that we perceive through our senses. The physiological response comes before the experience of emotion. The body reacts to the stimulus by producing specific physiological changes, such as increased heart rate, sweaty palms or a racing pulse. Our conscious experience of emotion is a result of perceiving and interpreting the

physiological changes in our body. For example, if you encounter a spider in the bath and you don't like spiders, the heart rate will increase and the palms of your hands may get sweaty. This is interpreted as fear, leading to the experience of fear itself. [4]

10. C
11. A
12. Synaptic transmission is where information is transmitted from one neuron to another across a synapse. The electrical signals, known as action potentials, are converted into chemical signals and then transmitted to the post-synaptic neuron. When an electrical signal, known as an action potential, reaches the pre-synaptic terminal of a neuron, it causes synaptic vesicles, small sacs containing neurotransmitters, to fuse with the pre-synaptic membrane. This fusion releases the neurotransmitters into the synapse, the small gap between the pre-synaptic and post-synaptic neurons. The released neurotransmitter molecules diffuse across the synaptic cleft and bind to specific receptors located on the post-synaptic membrane. The binding of neurotransmitters to the receptors results in the generation of a post-synaptic potential, which can be excitatory or inhibitory depending on the type of neurotransmitter and receptor involved. Excitatory post-synaptic potentials (EPSPs) increase the likelihood of generating an action potential, while inhibitory post-synaptic potentials (IPSPs) decrease the likelihood of generating an action potential. [5]

13. Hebb's theory suggests that if one neuron consistently activates another, the synapse between them becomes stronger, facilitating communication between the two neurons. When we learn, neurons make new neural connections with other neurons and the more that information is visited the stronger the connections become. Hebb's theory suggests that we have synaptic plasticity, which refers to the ability of synapses to change their strength based on neural activity. When a pre-synaptic neuron repeatedly and consistently stimulates a post-synaptic neuron, the synapse between them undergoes long-term potentiation, leading to a strengthening of the connection between the two neurons which promotes learning and memory formation. [7]

14. The frontal lobe deals with thinking and planning. The motor cortex is in the frontal lobe of the brain, as is Broca's area. The motor cortex deals with voluntary movement. Broca's area, usually only in the left hemisphere, plays a role in the production of speech. The parietal lobe contains the somatosensory cortex which deals with incoming sensory information. The occipital lobe is at the back of the brain and contains the visual area dealing with visual information from the eyes. The temporal lobe contains the auditory cortex, which deals with sound-based information. The temporal lobe contains Wernicke's area which processes language comprehension. [6]

15.

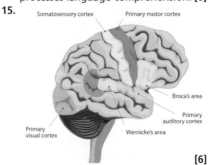

[6]

16. Cognitive neuroscience is the joining together of biological structures with mental processes and involves studying the influence of the brain's structure on cognitions and behaviour. Cognitive neuroscience uses brain scanning to map which areas of the brain are active when doing a particular activity, e.g. mapping activity in the motor cortex when voluntary movement is happening. This supports the idea that the brain is localised – that particular areas have a particular function. [3]

17.

	fMRI	PET	CT
How it works	Measures changes in blood flow	Measures metabolic activity	Produces X-ray images
What it does	Captures brain activity in real time	Measures brain function and activity	Provides detailed structural images
Resolution	High	Low	High
Exposure to radiation	No	Uses radioactive tracers	Uses X-ray radiation

18. Tulving's study wanted to find out whether episodic memories caused blood flow to different areas of the brain compared to when thinking about semantic memories. Volunteers were injected with radioactive gold which would get picked up on a PET scan. The participants took part in eight trials carrying out four each of both episodic (thinking about childhood holidays for example) and semantic tasks (recalling historical facts). Tulving found that blood flow was in different places depending on the task they were completing. Semantic information was taking place in the posterior cortex and the frontal lobe was more active when they were using episodic memories. [4]

19. Neurological damage such as a stroke can cause the area in which it occurred to die. This can result in disruption of function, which can be temporary or permanent. After trauma to the brain, some people can regain functions when another area picks up that particular function. For example, if the stroke or damage occurs in the motor area then walking could be a problem. If the damage occurs in the left hemisphere of the brain then Broca's area could be affected and speech may be affected (Broca's aphasia). If the damage is in the left temporal lobe then Wernicke's area could be affected and the person may struggle to understand language. [4]

Pages 179–182 Psychological Problems

1. It is predicted that by 2030 there will be two million more people in the world with mental health problems, compared to 2013. Women are more likely to be treated for mental health issues than men and this is becoming more of a significant gap. [2]

2. One reason could be the way lifestyles have changed over the years. There is a bigger gap in socio-economic status with the poorest people getting poorer which will affect mental health. Social isolation is also becoming more of a feature of modern living and that can play a part in mental health problems. [2]

3. Culture affects the way people think about poor mental health. For example, in some cultures hearing voices is seen as a way of communicating with spirits of the deceased whereas in the Western world it would be considered to be a disorder such a schizophrenia. [2]

4. One characteristic of good mental health is a positive self-attitude. This is where a person would be deemed to have good mental health if they have high self-esteem and view themselves in a positive light. Another characteristic is having an accurate perception of reality. People who find it difficult to face up to reality can suffer from disorders such as schizophrenia where they lose touch with reality. [2]

5. The language used to describe mental health issues has changed over the years which has helped to reduce the stigma. High-profile people have spoken openly about their mental health problems to help normalise various illnesses. [2]

6. a) Any factor such as work, school, loneliness, technology [1]
   b) We could assume that that there is a positive relationship between depression and life events but one does not cause the other. Only that when one is experienced the other is frequently present at the same time. [2]
   c) In this study, the researcher could collect qualitative data by asking the participants to keep a diary. This way they could record how

they are feeling on a daily basis and note down whether there were particular things that triggered their feelings. They could also say how they were feeling rather than just giving a score. **[3]**

d)

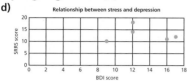

Relationship between stress and depression

[4]

7. Unipolar depression is when a person presents with the one emotional state of feeling depressed with low mood continuously. Bipolar depression is when the person can fluctuate between feelings of low mood and depression and heightened states of mania, feeling and behaving in a frenzied way. **[2]**

8. The classifications are updated frequently to keep up-to-date with new behaviours or symptoms to ensure that people are getting appropriate treatments. **[2]**

9. One strength of using the ICD to diagnose unipolar depression is to ensure a valid diagnosis is made. The classification system allows for a checklist of behaviours to be compared against the person's symptoms to ensure the correct diagnosis is made. This ensures that a diagnosis is as objective as it can be and should mean that, if a different doctor was to carry out an assessment, they would reach the same diagnosis. **[3]**

10. C

11. D

12. A

13. One strength of the biological explanation of depression is its emphasis on the role of neurotransmitters and brain chemistry. Research has shown that imbalances in neurotransmitters such as serotonin are associated with depression. This has led to the development of effective drug treatments, such as selective serotonin reuptake inhibitors (SSRIs) that target these imbalances and help alleviate symptoms in many individuals. However, the biological explanation simplifies the complex nature of depression by focusing on biological factors and neglecting the influence of other explanations, such as cognitive ones. Depression is a multifaceted illness that can be influenced by other factors; attributing depression to biological causes overlooks other vitally important reasons for the depression. **[4]**

14. C

15. One strength of the psychological explanation of depression is its focus on individual experiences, thoughts and emotions. It recognises the significance of psychological processes, such as negative cognitive patterns, in the development and maintenance of depression. By addressing these psychological factors, therapeutic approaches like cognitive-behavioural therapy (CBT) can be effective in helping individuals manage and overcome depressive symptoms. A weakness of the psychological explanation is that it may overlook the role of biological factors in depression. Psychological factors may be important, but there is also evidence suggesting that biological factors, such as neurotransmitter imbalances and genetic predispositions, contribute to the development of depression. This may limit the effectiveness of psychological interventions for individuals whose depression has a strong biological component. **[4]**

16. Biological interventions such as antidepressant medications, SSRIs, are commonly prescribed to help regulate neurotransmitter levels in the brain and alleviate depressive symptoms. Serotonin is released by one neuron and binds to receptors on the post-synaptic neuron, transmitting signals. After the transmission, serotonin is taken back up by the releasing neuron through a process called reuptake. SSRIs work by blocking the reuptake process. By doing so, it allows serotonin to remain in the synaptic gap between neurons for a longer time, giving it more to bind. SSRIs can be effective in reducing symptoms of depression but may have side effects and require careful monitoring. They quickly block the reuptake but the symptoms do not start to lessen for at least three months which is puzzling if this is the only reason for the depression. There is no commitment for drug treatment so it is relatively easy to engage with. This treatment could be considered to take a reductionist approach as it is only targeting the neurotransmitter serotonin and not looking at anything else as the cause. This may explain why the treatment doesn't work for everyone, if the cause is something other than serotonin. CBT is a psychological therapy for depression that targets the way someone with depression thinks. The belief is that if the negative thinking is changed, the behaviour will change. The treatment gets the patient involved by encouraging them to take part in an activity that they used to enjoy for example. They try and deal with the negative patterns of thinking during the therapy sessions by disputing the negative and sometimes irrational thoughts. Patients are also asked to keep a diary so any triggers can be identified. One strength of CBT is that the patient has control over their treatment unlike drugs where it is not within the patient's hands as to how they respond. The treatment also takes a holistic approach, examining different factors that might be the underlying cause of the depression such as work or family life. The person is encouraged to assess any changes they could implement which could improve their life and subsequently their depression. Once a person has been through CBT they can use the strategies again by themselves in future if needed. **[9]**

17. Addiction refers to a behaviour that leads to dependency. For example, an addiction to alcohol results in a dependency where individuals feel that they are unable to survive without it. However, substance misuse results in the substance being taken to excess but does not necessarily lead to addiction, they don't feel unable to survive if they don't have it. **[2]**

18. It could be argued that Cary is showing signs of substance misuse as she is not following the rules for her medication because she is taking double the prescribed dosage. It could be that she is also showing a dependence as she is relying on the tablets to manage her pain. She could build up a tolerance to the pills that could result in side effects and eventually addiction. **[4]**

19. D

20. A genetic vulnerability is where a person inherits a particular gene that increases the risk of a certain behaviour or characteristic. However having a vulnerability does not determine that an addiction will occur, only that it predisposes the person to that behaviour. **[2]**

21. To investigate genetic explanations of addiction researchers will use twin or family studies. Identical twins are 100% the same and therefore it is easier to identify a particular gene playing a part in addictions. By comparing twins, both monozygotic (MZ) identical and dizygotic (DZ) non-identical, natural experiments can be used to see if addictions are genetically inherited. **[3]**

22. Looking at twin studies is problematic as the twins have usually been brought up together in the same environment. This means it is difficult to separate the influence of nature or nurture. Also families can often treat twins exactly the same which makes it less clear regarding the influence of nature or nurture. **[2]**

23. Kaij studied male twins from Sweden and conducted interviews to find out about their alcohol use. Kaij found that from 48 MZ twins and 126 DZ twins, who were registered with a society to reduce their consumption of alcohol, 61% of the MZ twins were concordant in being registered with the group, compared to 39% of the DZ twins. **[4]**

24. Kaij's study supports the theory that alcohol consumption is linked

to genetics because there were significantly more MZ twins seeking support than DZ. **[2]**

25. Ashley is showing a dependence on alcohol because she is beginning to prioritise alcohol over other things such as being with her old friends. She is also showing signs that it is becoming the most important thing to her as she is spending too much money and having to borrow more so she can go out drinking. **[3]**

26. A psychological explanation would suggest that through social learning theory, Ashley is vicariously learning that drinking with her friends is fun. She sees the fun they have and is learning vicariously that she can enjoy the same feelings of pleasure when out socialising and drinking. This gives her the rewards of being sociable and potentially popular with her work colleagues. She has imitated their drinking culture and, as they are of a similar age to Ashley, she is imitating their behaviour. The social norms in her new work place are such that socialising out of work and drinking is the behaviour that people engage in. Ashley may also have gained a new social identity in that she now feels she belongs to this new group of friends, whereas she no longer feels so close to her old friends. **[4]**

Practice Exam Papers

Pages 183–196 **Practice Exam Paper 1 Cognition and Behaviour**

A Memory

01 B
02 When we store information, we don't remember everything **[1]** so when we go to recall it, we fill in any gaps so it makes sense (using schemas, beliefs etc.) **[1]**
03 A lack of standardisation of procedures can lead to a lack of validity in research **[1]**. In Bartlett's research, participants having no clear idea of what they had to do in the series of studies could have affected the results therefore reducing the validity of his findings on reconstructive memory. **[1]**
04.1 Interference is affecting Stella
04.2 If Stella plays basketball first, the rules of this could interfere with her playing netball afterwards as they are similar sports but the rules are different such as running with the ball). **[1]** She may then run with the ball in netball (which isn't allowed) and could get penalised **[1]**; this could cause her friends to get frustrated with her **[1]** and they could lose matches because of the interference of the two similar sports. **[1]**
05.1 Students are convinced they will do well because of context acting as a prompt **[1]**. They feel that doing exams in their learning classroom

will act as a cue and this will increase the accuracy of their memory. **[1]** The classroom may help to prompt a memory of something they learned in the room and this will enhance their memory. **[1]** Other factors, such as emotional states, can also act as a cue to affect recall. **[1]**
Research to support context was carried out showing that divers learning word lists and recalling them either in the same or different environment affected accuracy. **[1]** When the recall environment mirrored the learning environment, e.g. learning words on the beach and recalling them on the beach, recall was superior compared to when they learned the words on the beach but recalled them under water. **[1]** This evidence supports context as a cue for memory. However, the recall was carried out immediately and in real life we don't usually have to recall immediately after learning things. **[1]** In school there is significant time lapse between learning and recall in exams, so this supporting evidence has its weaknesses. **[1]** However, we do know that when we struggle to recall information, cues such as the first letter of someone's name do prompt recall so the theory does have validity in real life. **[1]**
05.2 Episodic memories are memories of events in a person's life **[1]** e.g. the first day at secondary school. These are time-stamped so more details are recalled such as the time of year or who else was there. **[1]** Semantic memories are memories of all the facts and knowledge a person has learned over their life e.g. knowing London is the capital city of England. **[1]** These memories are not time-stamped so you won't remember when you learned the information. **[1]** Procedural memories are skills that we learn, how to do something e.g. riding a bike. **[1]** These memories are implicit as we know how to do the skill but cannot explain afterwards how we do it. **[1]**

B Perception

06 C
07 **One** mark for **any one** of the following:
Height in plane
Relative size
Occlusion
Linear perspective
08.1 Size constancy is the ability to perceive objects as being the same size, even if we are viewing them at a distance. **[1]** It helps maintain a stable and accurate perception of the world because objects at a distance will produce a retinal image that will be smaller, but the brain will perceive the object's size as constant **[1]** e.g. when looking out of a window of a

tall building, the cars below will look small but our brain will retain the size of them. **[1]**
08.2 **One** mark for either:
Retinal disparity **[1]** or Convergence **[1]**
Retinal disparity occurs because the view we see from each eye is different due to the distance between our eyes (about 6cm); **[1]** the closer the object is, the bigger the retinal disparity; **[1]** the further away the object is, the smaller the retinal disparity. **[1]**
Convergence is when we view an object close up and our eyes converge (turn inwards); **[1]** the muscles work harder when the object is closer and it's this information that gives the brain the information regarding distance and depth. **[1]** The further away the object is, our muscles can relax and we look straight ahead. **[1]**
09 Bruner and Minturn's findings have real-life application as they help to explain why we sometimes make mistakes even when the stimulus is right in front of us; **[1]** e.g. if you're reading something about rabbits and there's an error and the word rabbi is written instead, you may continue to read it as rabbit as this is what you expect to be written. **[1]** However, the study does not account for individual differences as it used an independent group design that may affect the study's validity as people in one group may have had key differences to people in the other group. **[1]** In real life we wouldn't usually look at ambiguous figures and therefore these findings may not be applied to a real-life setting so are low in validity. **[1]**
10 Gregory believed that we construct the world around us by making an interpretation of what we are seeing, based on information from our past experiences. **[1]** This suggests that perception develops more from nurture than nature. **[1]** Sometimes when we lack some details or information, our brain fills in the gaps (using inferences). **[1]** This allows us to construct an idea of what we are seeing based on previous sensory experiences. **[1]**
11.1 Gibson's theory suggests that perception is innate and has evolved and that no learning is required. **[1]** We don't need to perceive anything as everything we sense is detailed enough and allows us to judge distance and depth without any interpretation being needed. **[1]** When we move, our brain receives this information, via optic flow patterns, so movement and direction can be judged. **[1]** e.g. when we are travelling in a car, the visual image we receive changes, objects that are closer appear to move faster as we

go past them while things that are further away appear to move slowly (motion parallax). [1]

11.2 Gibson's theory can support the nature side of the nature-nurture debate through an experiment that was carried out on young babies. [1] The visual cliff was devised and tested six-month-old babies on the edge of what looked like a drop off a cliff, but the drop was covered in a see-through Perspex screen. [1] Even though the infants were encouraged to crawl across by their mothers, most wouldn't, showing this behaviour to be innate, not learned. [1] Gibson suggested this supported his theory as no learning was necessary for the babies to perceive depth. [1]

C Development

12.1 C
12.2 D
13.1 B
13.2 A
13.3 **One** mark for **any one** of the following:
Egocentrism is a feature of children's cognition; [1] they are unable to put themselves in the position of another mentally, physically or emotionally; [1] they are selfish. [1]
Plus one mark for: Children only see things from their own perspective, they are unable to take on anyone else's view. [1]
14.1 Kane is in the pre-operational stage [1]
14.2 Tulula is showing a reduction in egocentrism as she is able to take on another perspective. [1] She understands hide and seek involves the other person not being able to see her at all. [1] Unlike Kane who can be seen, Tulula hides fully. [1]
15.1 Covert observation [1]
The children will behave naturally and not differently as they would if they were in front of an observer. [1] Choose **any two** behaviours e.g. child cannot share a ball; [1] cannot take turns in a game [1]
Informed consent [1]
As they are children under the age of 16, informed consent must be gained from the parent or guardian prior to the study being carried out. [1]
15.2 **Any two** points from the following:
A fixed mindset is someone who will give up. [1] They will see no point in trying to do well as failure is evidence they cannot do it. [1] No amount of effort will make any difference, [1] intelligence is fixed, [1] ability is passed down through a person's genes. [1]
15.3 Carlos is a kinaesthetic learner [1]. He prefers to physically do work, such as making videos, rather than reading his notes. [1] Mina is a visual learner. [1] She prefers to use images and diagrams for her revision. [1] Jamal is a verbaliser. [1] He demonstrates this

as he prefers to write his notes more than once as he prefers words. [1]
15.4 C

D Research Methods

16.1 The ethical issue is protection from harm. [1] Serena could protect the participants from feeling embarrassed by ensuring their details are kept confidential. [1] She could use their initials or a number [1] as this would ensure no-one knew about their beliefs about UFOs. [1]
16.2 A weakness is that responses may lack detail because they use closed questions [1] which means no in-depth information will be gathered. [1]
17.1 Qualitative
17.2 A structured interview contains pre-set closed questions [1] that will be asked in order to follow a script that has been prepared [1] whereas an unstructured interview may have one or two prepared questions that are open [1] but the interview develops in response to the answers. [1]
17.3 There will be a correlation [1] between the confidence score /10 and the score /10 in the belief of UFOs. [1]
17.4 Positive correlation
17.5 A strength is that it allows a starting point for more research [1] because it could tell us that these two variables are related (that the more confident people are, the more likely they believe in UFOs). [1] This could lead to understanding how these variables are related (people who are confident might feel they are more able to admit to their beliefs). [1]
18.1 **One** mark for title e.g. scattergraph of a correlation between confidence levels and beliefs of UFO. [1] **One** mark for labelled axis e.g. belief in UFOs /10. [1] **One** mark for labelled axis e.g confidence score /10. [1] Appropriate plots not joined up. [1]

Scattergraph of correlation between confidence and belief in UFO

18.2 The mode for confidence is 3 + 5
18.3 The mode for belief is 9
18.4 C
18.5 A

A Social Influence

01 B
2.1 Lilah thinks Tom conforms due to group size. [1] This is because she says

he waits for at least three people to answer and this is the number Asch suggested is optimum for conformity to occur. [1]
2.2 Lilah claims to only conform when she finds questions too difficult which is more likely in an ambiguous situation. [1] This is because people often lack confidence in their own ability. [1] Asch found when the stimulus line was made more similar to the comparison line, conformity increased. [1]
3.1 100%
3.2 Milgram suggested a social explanation of obedience, such as the role of authority having an influence. [1] He suggested that if someone is perceived as having the right to tell you what to do, by wearing a uniform for example, then obedience is more likely. [1] Adorno on the other hand suggested a person's disposition or personality influenced obedience. [1] Adorno suggested this was due to their upbringing that made them more likely to obey someone who is superior to them. [1]
4.1 The IV in Piliavin's study was the victim being drunk; [1] drunk was described as smelling of alcohol and carrying a brown bag with a bottle of alcohol. [1] The second independent variable was being disabled; [1] this was defined as walking with a cane. [1]
4.2 Through observation
4.3 The observer could have been biased (to support a diffusion of responsibility hypothesis) e.g. by noting down that a passenger did not help when they may have tried to but could not get to where the victim was; [1] this could make findings low in validity. [1] **Or** If the carriage was crowded/view obstructed, the observers may not have seen properly what was happening [1] so relevant data could have been missed giving low validity of findings. [1] **Or** the observers had a lot of data to record and they may have missed something [1], so data was unreliable. [1]
5.1 Deindividuation. [1] This is when people lose their sense of self-identity through things e.g. wearing a uniform/being part of a big crowd. [1]
5.2 Deindividuation affects collective behaviour through individuals becoming anonymous. [1] When people go into a deindividuated state they lose their sense of self, behaving in ways they may not normally behave. [1] This often occurs when part of a crowd, such as being at a demonstration. [1] Zimbardo found in his studies that when participants were given a uniform such as hoods to hide their faces, they were more likely to deliver an electric shock to another person. [1] This was in comparison to participants who wore their own clothing and were less likely to do this. [1]

B Language, Thought and Communication

06 Language can influence the way in which people remember events. Nonsense pictures, paired with a label, were shown to two groups. The label was different for each group. [1] When asked to draw the picture from memory, it was found that the label had influenced the participants' memory of it. [1] Recognition of colour is influenced by language as seen by The Zuni who only use one term for the yellow-orange region of the colour spectrum. [1] When Zuni participants were shown a coloured chip and asked to locate it amongst other chips, they performed better if there was a simple colour name (e.g. red) rather than a mixture of red and blue showing language can affect recall in different cultures. [1]

07 Research into personal space is often carried out without the informed consent from the participant. [1] For example, this is an ethical issue because if they knew what they were participating in and how they would react when people get close to them, they may not want to take part [1] as it may not portray them in a positive light if they move away. Another ethical issue is the right to withdraw. [1] If the participant doesn't know they are taking part, they can't withdraw their data even if they felt uncomfortable if people were too close to them. [1]

08

Planning ahead	B
Leave pheromones	A
Use communication for specific events	A
Advertise fitness	A

09 D

10 Piaget said children need to be at the right stage of their cognitive development in order to understand words otherwise they will just say words they don't understand. [1] He suggested they develop language in the sensorimotor stage, at the end of their first year. Before this they develop schema, which is a mental representation about the world e.g. a child develops a schema for a cat that begins as something that is furry, purrs and has four legs before learning the name, cat. Children develop language by matching words to their existing knowledge/schema as they understand the concept first and then learn the words. [1] In the pre-operational stage, children learn language rapidly and they can talk in sentences. In the concrete operational stage, their language matures and becomes more logical. [1] It is difficult to prove Piaget's theory as we have no way of knowing if someone has a schema or not. [1] However, language appears not to be random e.g. a child might say "Teddy shoe" to show the shoe is owned by them. This shows schemas are being used to build language. [1] However, Sapir and Whorf said it was impossible to think about things if we have no words for it, we only think about things that we have the words for. [1] There is supporting evidence for the Sapir-Whorf hypothesis, such as the variation in recognition of colours and recall of events. [1] For example, the Berinmo have problems recognising different colours because they only have five words for them [1] limiting their ability to recognise a range of colours. This supports the Sapir and Whorf hypothesis as Berinmo cannot recognise the colours they have no words for. [1]

11 Yuki wanted to see if emoticons are understood differently by people in Japan compared to America. [1] 95 Japanese and 118 American students took part and were shown six sad, happy or neutral emoticons. [1] Using a 9-point happiness scale, Japanese participants gave higher ratings to faces with happy eyes, even when the mouth was sad. The opposite was found with the American participants (higher ratings when mouths were happy even when the eyes were sad). [1]

C Brain and Neuropsychology

12 A Spinal cord [1], B Autonomic nervous system [1], C Sympathetic or parasympathetic [1], D Parasympathetic or sympathetic [1]

13 C

14.1 fMRI [1], CT [1] and PET scans [1]

14.2 fMRI [1]

14.3 fMRI does not use radiation which is a strength of this scanning technique. [1] It also shows almost live activity as it occurs. [1] However, it is expensive to use [1] so there may be cheaper alternatives that might be more cost effective. [1]

15 Hebb's theory has scientific support from recent research and advances in cognitive neuroscience. [1] His theory has provided useful application to real life such as in education where some of the principles are utilised, such as practising information (rehearsal) to strengthen neural pathways which form memories. [1] However, Hebb's theory only looks at structural changes in the brain during learning, whilst ignoring cognitive processes. [1] This reductionism is seen as a weakness of his theory because it attempts to explain the complexity of learning by mainly focusing on brain activity. [1]

16 Left hemisphere

17 Parietal lobe

18 Cognitive neuroscience is the combination of biology (brain activity/ biological structures) and mental processes (such as perception, learning and memory) used to explain the neurobiological basis of thought processes and disorders. [1] With the introduction and improvements in technology such as fMRI, CT and PET scans, science has been able to investigate live brains, unlike previously where it was reliant on post-mortems. [1] Research, such as Tulving's study using PET scans, has shown the neurological basis of mental processes where different types of memories are located in different areas of the brain. [1] This has helped us to understand how neurological damage in a particular area of the brain can affect different abilities. [1] So if a person has a brain injury to their frontal lobe, their episodic memories could be affected. [1] Strokes that occur in the left hemisphere could result in loss of speech (Broca's aphasia) or loss of language comprehension (Wernicke's aphasia). Cognitive neuroscience has helped science to understand neurological damage and its impact on behaviour. [1]

D Psychological Problems

19 A [1] and C [1]

20 One individual effect could be damage to relationships. [1] Partner, family and friend relationships can often be damaged or even break down because the individual wants to isolate themselves, unable to cope with social interaction. [1] Or An individual effect could be not being able to cope with everyday tasks and living. [1] Things that people take for granted, such as getting out of bed in the morning and taking a shower can become a problem for an individual with mental health problems. [1] Or Physical well-being can also be affected by mental health problems. [1] For example, when people are mentally unwell this usually makes them suffer with stress. When we suffer long-term stress, it impacts our immune system and leaves us more vulnerable to physical illnesses such as colds. [1]

21.1 Opportunity [1] as they happened to be there at the clinic, were available at the time and agreed to take part. [1]

21.2 8 [1] 5, 6, 7, 8, **8, 8**, 9, 9, 10, 10 [1]

21.3 The results suggest that the treatment the patients were undergoing was effective [1] as all patients gave a lower score out of ten after six months. [1] However, the median score after six months is only two lower than the original median score [1] which could suggest we cannot draw conclusions about how effective the treatment was. [1]

21.4 The patients could have been given antidepressants. [1] These could have side-effects such as weight gain or sleeping problems, which can make them undesirable to take. [1] However, they are thought to be effective in over 50% of patients, although about 25-30% of people taking placebos also report improvements. [1] This makes it difficult to assess how effective they really are. [1] They are not suitable for everyone, e.g. children, and they only treat the symptoms not the cause. [1] Or The patients could have been given CBT. [1] This has no side-effects, which can make it seem a more desirable treatment. [1] However, it is not suitable for severe cases of depression and usually the best treatment is a combination of drugs and CBT. [1] CBT requires commitment from the patient, attending regular sessions, so may not be suitable for everyone [1] but it is seen as a more holistic therapy that aims to treat the symptoms and the cause of the depression. [1]

22 Based on social learning theory, DeBlasio and Benda (1993) found, in adolescents, the influence of peers play a big part in taking alcohol and drugs. [1] For example, observing other teenagers who smoke, influences them to smoke. [1] They are more likely to associate with other adolescents who smoke, with adolescent risk taking more likely to occur in a group situation. [1] This shows that social learning can explain the influence of others and imitation of behaviour to occur. [1]

Acknowledgements

The authors and publisher are grateful to the copyright
holders for permission to use quoted materials and images.

p.23 © ANIMATED HEALTHCARE LTD/SCIENCE PHOTO LIBRARY
p.23 © SCIENCE SOURCE/SCIENCE PHOTO LIBRARY
p.36 © Granger Historical Picture Archive/Alamy Stock Photo;
© Marmaduke St. John/Alamy Stock Photo
All other images © Shutterstock.com

Every effort has been made to trace copyright holders and obtain their
permission for the use of copyright material. The authors and publisher will
gladly receive information enabling them to rectify any error or omission in
subsequent editions. All facts are correct at time of going to press.

Published by Collins
An imprint of HarperCollins*Publishers* Ltd
1 London Bridge Street
London SE1 9GF

HarperCollins*Publishers*
Macken House, 39/40 Mayor Street Upper,
Dublin 1, D01 C9W8, Ireland

© HarperCollins*Publishers* Limited 2024

ISBN 9780008646431

First published 2017

This edition published 2024

10 9 8 7 6 5 4 3 2

British Library Cataloguing in Publication Data.

A CIP record of this book is available from the British Library.

Authors: Jonathan Firth, Marc Smith and Sally White
Publisher: Sara Bennett
Commissioning Editors: Katherine Wilkinson and Charlotte Christensen
Editors: Shelley Teasdale and Charlotte Christensen
Project Managers: Shelley Teasdale and Tracey Cowell
Cover Design: Sarah Duxbury and Kevin Robbins
Inside Concept Design: Sarah Duxbury and Paul Oates
Text Design and Layout: Jouve India Private Limited
Production: Bethany Brohm
Printed in India by Multivista Global Pvt.Ltd.